Current Directions
Directions
in
ABNORMAL
PSYCHOLOGY

READINGS FROM THE
ASSOCIATION FOR
PSYCHOLOGICAL SCIENCE

Current
Directions
in
ABNORMAL
PSYCHOLOGY

Second Edition

EDITED BY

C. Emily Durbin

Northwestern University

Boston • New York • San Francisco
Mexico City • Montreal • Toronto • London • Madrid • Munich • Paris
Hong Kong • Singapore • Tokyo • Cape Town • Sydney

Acquisitions Editor: Michelle Limoges
Series Editorial Assistant: Christina Manfroni
Marketing Manager: Kate Mitchell
Production Editor: Patty Bergin
Editorial Production Service: TexTech International
Composition Buyer: Linda Cox
Manufacturing Buyer: JoAnne Sweeney
Electronic Composition: TexTech International
Cover Administrator: Linda Knowles

For related titles and support materials, visit our online catalog at www.ablongman.com.

Between the time website information is gathered and then published, it is not unusual for some sites to have closed. Also, the transcription of URLs can result in typographical errors. The publisher would appreciate notification where these errors occur so that they may be corrected in subsequent editions.

Library of Congress Cataloging-in-Publication Data

Current directions in abnormal psychology / edited by Emily Durbin—2nd edition
    p. ; cm.—(Readings from the Association for Psychological Science)
"Reprinted as [they] originally appeared in Current directions in psychological science."
Includes bibliographical references.
ISBN-13: 978-0-205-59741-3
ISBN-10:   0-205-59741-6
1. Psychology, Pathological.   I. Durbin, Emily   II. Association for Psychological Science.   III. Current directions in psychological science.   IV. Series.
[DNLM: 1. Psychopathology—Collected Works   2. Mental Disorders—Collected Works. WM 100 C976r 2008]
RC467.C867   2008
616.89—dc22   2007051147

Printed in the United States of America

10 9 8 7 6 5 4 3 2   11 10 09 08

Contents

Introduction

The aim of this reader is to provide students of abnormal psychology with a sophisticated but accessible introduction to cutting edge scholarship in clinical science, as well as the related fields of personality, emotion, and developmental psychology. These primary materials are meant to serve as a supplement to traditional textbooks in Abnormal Psychology, presenting theories and findings regarding current hot topics in the field via focused reviews that summarize bodies of work or lines of inquiry. The articles selected for this reader cover a range of topics in psychopathology, but all share theoretical clarity, straightforward descriptions of the crucial issues characterizing recent research in an area, and a succinct style. These attributes combine to make high level work in scientific psychology approachable and engaging to undergraduate students. The particular topics addressed by the selected readings are intended to reinforce the overarching concepts presented in the textbook, as well as to (1) provide students with introductions to specific lines of research in more detail than is typically possible in textbooks; (2) give shape to broad theoretical models guiding research in psychopathology; (3) help students see connections between traditional domains of abnormal psychology and other fields of study; and (4) present the latest in research findings and most exciting new avenues of study, many of which may not yet be represented in the textbook.

The reader is divided into five sections, with readings in each section addressing a particular framework, methodological approach, or set of related topics. The section foci were selected to represent broad organizing themes in clinical science and to specifically address forms of psychopathlogy and/or conceptual frameworks represented in the textbook. Within each section, readings were chosen to stimulate students' integration of material across papers either by contrasting different viewpoints or approaches to a problem, or by highlighting common themes or questions raised by multiple papers. Instructors may wish to approach the material in this manner, assigning multiple readings within a section in order to provide a comprehensive discussion of a particular issue or set of related issues. However, individual papers within each section may also be approached individually as providing an opportunity to think deeply about a specific line of research and the questions and implications raised by that review. Critical thinking questions are provided for each section, some of which integrate across multiple papers and others focused on ideas generated by a single paper. These questions should be considered a jumping off point for discussion and student reflection, and hopefully, should encourage students to approach the readings with curiosity and critical analysis skills. Hopefully, the content of these papers will both impress students with the considerable progress made by psychological science on difficult and important questions, as well as impress upon them the general concept that psychological science is constantly evolving, such that our current knowledge will be refined or overthrown as a result of rigorous research.

The first section of the reader, similar to early chapters in the textbook, deals with conceptual issues in the study of psychopathology. This section provides an excellent introduction to important topics in abnormal psychology, doing so in a way that brings into focus the fundamental importance of theoretical and methodological issues, applied to particular problems. This section provides perspective for the other sections that follow. The second section addresses approaches to understanding the role of stress, stressful events, and environmental influences on psychopathology. It provides a compelling picture of the range of contextual factors that we now know are relevant to understanding risk for and manifestation of mental health problems. The papers in this section derive from a variety of perspectives, including family psychology, social context, and comparative psychology, and illustrate the principal that the environment can be explored at both macro and micro levels of analysis. Taken together, these reviews should challenge students to see both the areas of convergence and divergence across these levels. The third section broadly focuses on the intersection between biological and psychological central to understanding psychopathology. Included in this section are papers dealing with the biology of psychosocial stressors, health psychology, and gene-environment correlations and interactions. These sophisticated reviews present interdisciplinary research in an accessible and engaging way, and should be particularly useful for helping students break down the perceived boundary differences between psychological science and the natural sciences.

The final two sections of the reader concern the group of disorders characterized by internalizing problems and those defined by externalizing patterns of behavior. Section four includes papers on anxiety disorders (phobias, PTSD), depression, and eating disorders. Although disparate in their particular research focus, each of these papers describes new work on the etiology and underpinnings of these psychopathologies. Several of the studies detailed in this section provide excellent examples of laboratory paradigms for testing hypotheses about psychopathology. Finally, the fifth section of the reader is composed of papers dealing with externalizing forms of psychopathology. Several of these reviews concern topics of interest in substance use disorders. These readings should provide students with a broad overview of the multidisciplinary nature of current research on these disorders.

The reviews included in this reader can be used to supplement primary course materials in abnormal psychology courses either individually, in groups of related papers, or as entire units. Hopefully, exposure to some of the most rapidly evolving, methodologically innovative, and theoretically compelling avenues of modern psychological science will engage students around questions they find particularly compelling, and motivate them to pursue these questions even further into the clinical science literature.

Section 1: General Issues in Understanding, Modeling, and Measuring Psychopathology

A strong grasp of methodological and theoretical approaches to the study of psychopathology, while typically viewed by instructors as central to understanding research on any particular disorder, are often difficult frameworks for new students of psychopathology to connect with. Students are often more engaged by descriptions of disorders than they are by explanations of how scientists model and study the origins, correlates, and treatment of those disorders. Students can often find these sections of textbooks dry or decontextualized. The papers in this section are particularly useful for helping students to gain intellectual traction on these issues in that they provide an excellent introduction to the challenges and excitement of wrapping one's mind around the hows of studying psychopathology, and a window into how logical and methodological rigor can reveal exciting new findings about psychological disorders. Each paper also serves as a jumping off point for raising deeper questions about the science of psychology, how our theoretical models of disorders drive our conceptualization of their etiology and treatment, and how to reconcile the requirements of the various stakeholders in the science of mental health.

Miller and Keller's paper provides a thoughtful introduction to current tensions in modern psychological research concerning the intersection of psychological and biological explanations for behavioral phenomena. They provide a trenchant analysis of some of the tendencies in the literature to view behavioral and biological data as being reducible to one another. The authors stimulate readers to challenge the assumption that biological mechanisms "underlie" psychological phenomena, pointing out that while these biological and psychological phenomena are not physically distinct from one another, they are logically separable. This paper should challenge students to think in a more sophisticated way about models of psychopathology that consider both biological and psychological factors, as well as stimulate a critical analysis about other papers in the reader.

The other selections in this section illuminate a number of issues in the study of psychopathology. Lenzenweger's review of Meehl's seminal model of latent risk factors for schizophrenia and the decades of research it inspired provides an introduction to important methods in the study of psychopathology, including high risk designs. This paper provides an excellent example of the variety of approaches that can be utilized to study the etiology of complex disorders and their association with normal variations in more basic biopsychological processes.

Krueger and Markon review a number of issues central to problems in the classification and conceptualization of mental disorders, providing students an excellent introduction to both psychometric methods of exploring psychiatric disorders as well as to modern conceptions of underlying organizing constructs in psychopathology. Their paper reviews evidence indicating that common mental disorders can be understood as varying expressions of two correlated dimensional spectra — internalizing and externalizing problems — that together explain a large proportion of the variation in and covariation among disorders. This paper provides an important link to relevant literature in other fields, notably personality psychology, and encourages students to question whether the reified disorder constructs with which they are familiar reflect the true nature of pathological phenomena.

Similar to Krueger and Markon, Moses and Barlow describe an approach to mental disorders that refers to core underlying dimensions that cut across traditional categories. They view such a model as providing a potentially more efficacious approach to the development and implementation of treatments for internalizing disorders, and this paper is a compelling argument for the integration of basic and intervention science.

Finally, Achenbach reviews the literature examining convergence between self- and informant reports of psychopathology. While long recognized in the child literature, existing data on adult samples indicates that agreement between self and others for psychopathology and functioning is generally modest to moderate. These data point to the importance of considering the means by which psychopathology is assessed, and the possibility that individuals' psychological functioning may appear quite different when viewed through distinct lenses.

Psychology and Neuroscience: Making Peace

Gregory A. Miller[1] and Jennifer Keller

*Department of Psychology, University of Illinois
at Urbana-Champaign, Champaign, Illinois*

Abstract

There has been no historically stable consensus about the relationship between psychological and biological concepts and data. A naively reductionist view of this relationship is prevalent in psychology, medicine, and basic and clinical neuroscience. This view undermines the ability of psychology and related sciences to achieve their individual and combined potential. A nondualistic, nonreductionist, noninteractive perspective is recommended, with psychological and biological concepts both having central, distinct roles.

Keywords

psychology; biology; neuroscience; psychopathology

With the Decade of the Brain just ended, it is useful to consider the impact that it has had on psychological research and what should come next. Impressive progress occurred on many fronts, including methodologies used to understand the brain events associated with psychological functions. However, much controversy remains about where biological phenomena fit into psychological science and vice versa. This controversy is especially pronounced in research on psychopathology, a field in which ambitious claims on behalf of narrowly conceived psychological or biological factors often arise, but this fundamental issue applies to the full range of psychological research. Unfortunately, the Decade of the Brain has fostered a naively reductionist view that sets biology and psychology at odds and often casts psychological events as unimportant epiphenomena. We and other researchers have been developing a proposal that rejects this view and provides a different perspective on the relationship between biology and psychology.

A FAILURE OF REDUCTIONISM

A term defined in one domain is characterized as *reduced* to terms in another domain (called the reduction science) when all meaning in the former is captured in the latter. The reduced term thus becomes unnecessary. If, for example, the meaning of the (traditionally psychological) term "fear" is entirely representable in language about a brain region called the amygdala, one does not need the (psychological) term "fear," or one can redefine "fear" to refer merely to a particular biological phenomenon.

Impressive progress in the characterization of neural circuits typically active in (psychologically defined) fear does not justify dismissing the concept or altering the meaning of the term. The phenomena that "fear" typically refers to include a functional state (a way of being or being prepared to act), a cognitive processing bias, and a variety of judgments and associations all of which are conceived

5

psychologically (Miller & Kozak, 1993). Because "fear" means more than a given type of neural activity, the concept of fear is not reducible to neural activity. Researchers are learning a great deal about the biology of fear—and the psychology of fear—from studies of the amygdala (e.g., Lang, Davis, & Öhman, in press), but this does not mean that fear *is* activity in the amygdala. That is simply not the meaning of the term. "Fear" is not reducible to biology.

This logical fact is widely misunderstood, as evidenced in phrases such as "underlying brain dysfunction" or "neurochemical basis of psychopathology." Most remarkably, major portions of the federal research establishment have recently adopted a distinctly nonmental notion of mental health, referring to "the biobehavioral factors which may underly [sic] mood states" (National Institute of Mental Health, 1999). Similarly, a plan to reorganize grant review committees reflects "the context of the biological question that is being investigated" (National Institutes of Health, 1999, p. 2). Mental health researchers motivated by psychological or sociological questions apparently should take their applications elsewhere.

More subtly problematic than such naive reductionism are terms, such as "biobehavioral marker" or "neurocognitive measure," that appear to cross the boundary between psychological and biological domains. It is not at all apparent what meaning the "bio" or "neuro" prefix adds in these terms, as typically the data referred to are behavioral. Under the political pressures of the Decade of the Brain, psychologists were tempted to repackage their phenomena to sound biological, but the relationship of psychology and biology cannot be addressed by confusing them.

WHOSE WORK IS MORE FUNDAMENTAL?

Such phrases often appear in contexts that assume that biological phenomena are somehow more fundamental than psychological phenomena. Statements that psychological events are nothing more than brain events are clearly logical errors (see the extensive analysis by Marr, 1982). More cautious statements, such as that psychological events "reflect" or "arise from" brain events, are at best incomplete in what they convey about the relationship between psychology and biology. It is not a property of biological data that they "underlie" psychological data. A given theory may explicitly propose such a relationship, but it must be treated as a proposal, not as a fact about the data. Biological data provide valuable information that may not be obtainable with self-report or overt behavioral measures, but biological information is not inherently more fundamental, more accurate, more representative, or even more objective.

The converse problem also arises—psychology allegedly "underlying" or being more fundamental than biology. There is a long tradition of ignoring biological phenomena in clinical psychology. As Zuckerman (1999) noted, "One thing that both behavioral and post-Freudian psychoanalytic theories had in common was the conviction that learning and life experiences alone could account for all disorders" (p. 413). In those traditions, it is psychology that "underlies" biology, not the converse. Biology is seen as merely the implementation of psychology, and psychology is where the intellectually interesting action is. Cognitive theory can thus evolve without the discipline of biological plausibility. As suggested at the midpoint of the Decade of the Brain (Miller, 1995), such a view would justify a Decade of Cognition.

Such a one-sided emphasis would once again be misguided. Anderson and Scott (1999) expressed concern that "the majority of research in the health sciences occurs within a single level of analysis, closely tied to specific disciplines" (p. 5), with most psychologists studying phenomena only in terms of behavior. We advocate not that every study employ both psychological and biological methods, but that researchers not ignore or dismiss relevant literatures, particularly in the conceptualization of their research.

Psychological and biological approaches offer distinct types of data of potentially equal relevance for understanding psychological phenomena. For example, we use magnetoencephalography (MEG) recordings of the magnetic fields generated by neural activity to identify multiple areas of brain tissue that are generating what is typically measured electrically at the scalp (via electroencephalography, or EEG) as the response of the brain associated with cognitive tasks (Cañive, Edgar, Miller, & Weisend, 1999). One of the most firmly established biological findings in schizophrenia is a smaller than normal brain response called the P300 component (Ford, 1999), and there is considerable consensus on the functional significance of P300 in the psychological domain. There is, however, no consensus on what neural generators produce the electrical activity or on what distinct functions those generators serve. Neural sources are often difficult to identify with confidence from EEG alone, whereas for biophysical reasons MEG (which shows brain function) coupled with structural magnetic resonance data (which show brain anatomy) promises localization as good as any other available noninvasive method. If researchers understand the distinct functional significance of various neural generators of P300, and if only some generators are compromised in schizophrenia, this will be informative about the nature of cognitive deficits in schizophrenia. Conversely, what researchers know about cognitive deficits will be informative about the function of the different generators.

MEG and EEG do not "underlie" and are not the "basis" of (the psychological phenomena that define) the functions or mental operations invoked in tasks associated with the P300 response. Neural generators implement functions, but functions do not have locations (Fodor, 1968). For example, a working memory deficit in schizophrenia could not be located in a specific brain region. The psychological and the neuromagnetic are not simply different "levels" of analysis, except in a very loose (and unhelpful) metaphorical sense. Neither underlies the other, neither is more fundamental, and neither explains away the other. There are simply two domains of data, and each can help to explicate the other because of the relationships theories propose.

Psychophysiological research provides many other examples in which the notion of "underlying" is unhelpful. Rather than attributing mood changes to activity in specific brain regions, why not attribute changes in brain activity to changes in mood? In light of EEG (Deldin, Keller, Gergen, & Miller, 2000) or behavioral (Keller et al., 2000) data on regional brain activity in depression, are people depressed because of low activity in left frontal areas of the brain, or do they have low activity in these areas because they are depressed? Under the present view, such a question, trying to establish causal relations *between* psychology and biology, is misguided. These are not empirical issues but logical and theoretical issues. They turn on the kind of relationship that psychological and biological concepts are proposed to have.

CLINICAL IMPLICATIONS

In psychopathology, one of the most unfortunate consequences of the naive competition between psychology and biology is the assumption that dysfunctions conceptualized biologically require biological interventions and that those con-ceptualized psychologically require psychological interventions. The best way to alter one system may be a direct intervention in another system. Even, for example, if the chemistry of catecholamines (chemicals used for communication to nerve, muscle, and other cells) were the best place to intervene in schizophrenia, it does not follow that a direct biological intervention in that system would be opti-mal. A variety of experiences that people construe as psychosocial prompt their adrenal glands to flood them with catecholamines. There are psychological inter-ventions associated with this chemistry that can work more effectively or with fewer side effects than medications aimed directly at the chemistry.

Unfortunately, the assumption that disorders construed biologically warrant exclusively biological interventions influences not only theories of psychopathol-ogy but also available treatments. For example, major depression is increasingly viewed as a "chemical imbalance." If such (psychological) disorders are assumed to "be" biological, then medical insurers are more likely to fund only biological treatments. Yet Thase et al. (1997) found that medication and psychotherapy were equally effective in treating moderately depressed patients and that the combination of these treatments was more effective than either alone in treating more severely depressed patients. Hollon (1995) discussed how negative life events may alter biological factors that increase risk for depression. Meany (1998) explained how the psychological environment can affect gene activity. The indefensible conceptualization of depression solely as a biological disorder prompts inappropriately narrow (biological) interventions. Thus, treatment as well as theory is hampered by naive reductionism.

WHAT TO DO?

"Underlying" (implying one is more fundamental than the other) is not a satisfac-tory way to characterize the relationship between biological and psychological concepts. We recommend characterizing the biological as "implementing" the psychology—that is, we see cognition and emotion as implemented in neural sys-tems. Fodor (1968) distinguished between *contingent* and *necessary* identity in the relationship between psychological and biological phenomena. A person in any given psychological state is momentarily in some biological state as well: There is a *contingent* identity between the psychological and the biological at that moment. The psychological phenomenon implemented in a given neural circuit is not the same as, is not accounted for by, and is not reducible to that cir-cuit. There is an indefinite set of potential neural implementations of a given psychological phenomenon. Conversely, a given neural circuit might implement different psychological functions at different times or in different individuals. Thus, there is no *necessary* identity between psychological states and brain states. Distinct psychological and biological theories are needed to explain their respective domains, and additional theoretical work is needed to relate them.

Nor is it viable (though it is common) to say that psychological and biological phenomena "interact." Such a claim begs the question of how they interact and even what it means to interact. The concept of the experience of "red" does not "interact" with the concept of photon-driven chemical changes in the retina and their neural sequelae. One may propose that those neural sequelae implement the perceptual experience of "red," but "red" *means* not the neural sequelae, but something psychological—a perception.

Biology and psychology often are set up as competitors for public mindshare, research funding, and scientific legitimacy. We are not arguing for a psychological explanation of cognition and emotion *instead of* a biological explanation. Rather, we are arguing against framing biology and psychology in a way that forces a choice between those kinds of explanations. The hyperbiological bias ascendant at the end of the 20th century was no wiser and no more fruitful than the hyperpsychological bias of the behaviorist movement earlier in the 20th century. Scientists can avoid turf battles by approaching the relationship between the psychological and the biological as fundamentally theoretical, not empirical. Working out the biology will not make psychology obsolete, any more than behaviorism rendered biology obsolete. Scientists can avoid dualism by avoiding interactionism (having two distinct domains in a position to interact implies separate realities, hence dualism). Psychological and biological domains can be viewed as logically distinct but not physically distinct, and hence neither dualistic nor interacting. Psychological and biological concepts are not merely different terms for the same phenomena (and thus not reducible in either direction), and psychological and biological explanations are not explanations of the same things. If one views brain tissue as implementing psychological functions, the expertise of cognitive science is needed to characterize those functions, and the expertise of neuroscience is needed to study their implementation. Each of those disciplines will benefit greatly from the other, but neither encompasses, reduces, or underlies the other.

Fundamentally psychological concepts require fundamentally psychological explanations. Stories about biological phenomena can richly inform, but not supplant, those explanations. Yet when psychological events unfold, they are implemented in biology, and those implementations are extremely important to study as well. For example, rather than merely pursuing, in quite separate literatures, anomalies in either expressed emotion or biochemistry, research on schizophrenia should investigate biological mechanisms involved in expressed-emotion phenomena. Similarly, the largely separate literatures on biological and psychosocial mechanisms in emotion should give way to conceptual and methodological collaboration. Research in the next few decades will need not only the improving spatial resolution of newer brain-imaging technologies and the high temporal resolution of established brain-imaging technologies, but also the advancing cognitive resolution of the best psychological science.

Recommended Reading

Anderson, N.B., & Scott, P.A. (1999). (See References)

Cacioppo, J.T., & Berntson, G.G. (1992). Social psychological contributions to the Decade of the Brain. *American Psychologist, 47*, 1019–1028.

Kosslyn, S.M., & Koenig, O. (1992). *Wet mind: The new cognitive neuroscience.* New York: Free Press.

Miller, G.A. (1996). Presidential address: How we think about cognition, emotion, and biology in psychopathology. *Psychophysiology, 33*, 615–628.

Ross, C.A., & Pam, A. (1995). *Pseudoscience in biological psychiatry: Blaming the body.* New York: Wiley.

Acknowledgments—The authors' work has been supported in part by National Institute of Mental Health Grants R01 MH39628, F31 MH11758, and T32 MH19554; by the Department of Psychiatry of Provena Covenant Medical Center; and by the Research Board, the Beckman Institute, and the Departments of Psychology and Psychiatry of the University of Illinois at Urbana-Champaign. The authors appreciate the comments of Howard Berenbaum, Patricia Deldin, Wendy Heller, Karen Rudolph, Judith Ford, Michael Kozak, Sumie Okazaki, and Robert Simons on an earlier draft.

Note

1. Address correspondence to Gregory A. Miller, Departments of Psychology and Psychiatry, University of Illinois, 603 E. Daniel St., Champaign, IL 61820; e-mail: gamiller@uiuc.edu.

References

Anderson, N.B., & Scott, P.A. (1999). Making the case for psychophysiology during the era of molecular biology. *Psychophysiology, 36*, 1–14.

Cañive, J.M., Edgar, J.C., Miller, G.A., & Weisend, M.P. (1999, April). *MEG recordings of M300 in controls and schizophrenics.* Paper presented at the biennial meeting of the International Congress on Schizophrenia Research, Santa Fe, NM.

Deldin, P.J., Keller, J., Gergen, J.A., & Miller, G.A. (2000). Right-posterior N200 anomaly in depression. *Journal of Abnormal Psychology, 109*, 116–121.

Fodor, J.A. (1968). *Psychological explanation.* New York: Random House.

Ford, J.M. (1999). Schizophrenia: The broken P300 and beyond. *Psychophysiology, 36*, 667–682.

Hollon, S.D. (1995). Depression and the behavioral high-risk paradigm. In G.A. Miller (Ed.), *The behavioral high-risk paradigm in psychopathology* (pp. 289–302). New York: Springer-Verlag.

Keller, J., Nitschke, J.B., Bhargava, T., Deldin, P.J., Gergen, J.A., Miller, G.A., & Heller, W. (2000). Neuropsychological differentiation of depression and anxiety. *Journal of Abnormal Psychology, 109*, 3–10.

Lang, P.J., Davis, M., & Öhman, A. (in press). Fear and anxiety: Animal models and human cognitive psychophysiology. *Journal of Affective Disorders.*

Marr, D. (1982). *Vision: A computational investigation into the human representation and processing of visual information.* New York: Freeman.

Meany, M.J. (1998, September). *Variations in maternal care and the development of individual differences in neural systems mediating behavioral and endocrine responses to stress.* Address presented at the annual meeting of the Society for Psychophysiological Research, Denver, CO.

Miller, G.A. (1995, October). *How we think about cognition, emotion, and biology in psychopathology.* Presidential address presented at the annual meeting of the Society for Psychophysiological Research, Toronto, Ontario, Canada.

Miller, G.A., & Kozak, M.J. (1993). A philosophy for the study of emotion: Three-systems theory. In N. Birbaumer & A. Öhman (Eds.), *The structure of emotion: Physiological, cognitive and clinical aspects* (pp. 31–47). Seattle, WA: Hogrefe & Huber.

National Institute of Mental Health. (1999, February 12). [Announcement of NIMH workshop, "Emotion and mood"]. Unpublished e-mail.

National Institutes of Health. (1999, February). *Peer review notes*. Washington, DC: Author.

Thase, M.E., Greenhouse, J.B., Frank, E., Reynold, C.F., Pilkonis, P.A., Hurley, K., Grochocinski, V., & Kupfer, D.J. (1997). Treatment of major depression with psychotherapy or psychotherapy-pharmacotherapy combinations. *Archives of General Psychiatry, 54*, 1009–1015.

Zuckerman, M. (1999). *Vulnerability to psychopathology: A biosocial model*. Washington, DC: American Psychological Association.

This article has been reprinted as it originally appeared in *Current Directions in Psychological Science*. Citation information for this article as originally published appears above.

Schizotypy: An Organizing Framework for Schizophrenia Research

Mark F. Lenzenweger

Department of Psychology, State University of New York at Binghamton, and Department of Psychiatry, Weill College of Medicine of Cornell University

Abstract

Schizophrenia is the most devastating form of psychopathology known to humankind, and it has been slow to yield clues to its origins. Meehl's (1962, 1990) model detailed the nature of the latent liability for schizophrenia known as schizotypy and provided a major organizing function for research on schizophrenia. The schizotypy model integrates genetic and environmental contributions to liability as well as accounting for a range of clinical outcomes, all deriving from a genuine liability for the illness. Schizotypy, as a latent personality organization that harbors the liability for schizophrenia, provides a framework for detecting fundamental features of liability to schizophrenia prior to the onset of clinical illness. The schizotypy model is reviewed, the strategic benefits of it are discussed, and methods for detecting schizotypy are presented. A focus on perceptual aberrations—a schizotypic feature—in individuals unaffected by schizophrenia has yielded valuable clues to preclinical disturbances in neurocognitive processes, risk for schizophrenia among biological relatives, and genomic substrates, all of which are of interest to schizophrenia researchers.

Keywords

schizotypy; schizophrenia; endophenotype; perceptual aberrations; psychometric high-risk strategy

Understanding the origins and development of schizophrenia looms large as a research and clinical goal for psychopathologists. Because of the considerable heterogeneity in its manifestations and in its likely determinants, the illness remains a frustrating enigma at many levels of inquiry, including genetics, neuroimaging, and neurocognition. Affecting 1 in every 100 persons, the illness is massively debilitating and the economic cost and societal burden of schizophrenia are consistently estimated as exceeding those of most other physical and mental illnesses. Efforts to gain leverage on the pathological processes in schizophrenia have focused increasingly on persons carrying the liability for schizophrenia but who have not expressed the illness per se. Such individuals are referred to as *schizotypes* due to the fact that they possess (or carry) *schizotypy*, or a latent personality organization that harbors the genetic liability for schizophrenia.

P.E. MEEHL'S MODEL OF SCHIZOTAXIA, SCHIZOTYPY, AND SCHIZOPHRENIA

The central model in schizophrenia research that defined schizotypy and placed it within a developmental-psychopathology context was proposed by Paul Meehl

(1962, 1990). His model encompassed not only genetic factors, social-learning influences, and clinical symptomatology, but also set forth hypotheses about the precise nature of the fundamental defect underlying schizotypic functioning. Proposed in the 1960s, when many psychologists and psychiatrists thought schizophrenia was caused by unhealthy childrearing practices (e.g., the "schizophrenogenic mother"), Meehl emphasized the role of genetics in the etiology of the illness. Today, his model of schizotypy is so firmly implanted in schizophrenia research that it is often assumed to be the organizing framework (and, on occasion, is not even cited), or it is presented from time to time as a "new" model.

Meehl's (1962, 1990) model holds that a single major gene (which he called the "schizogene") exerts its influence during brain development by coding for a specific "aberration of the synaptic control system" in the central nervous system (CNS; Meehl, 1990, pp. 14–15). He suggested that this neuronal-level aberration, which he termed *hypokrisia*, is characterized by an "insufficiency of separation, differentiation, or discrimination" in neural transmission. It amounts to slippage of neural transmission at the CNS synapse, which manifests itself behaviorally in the glaring symptomatology of clinically expressed schizophrenia. Hypokrisia was hypothesized to characterize neuronal-functioning difficulty throughout the brain, thus producing a ubiquitous CNS anomaly (Meehl, 1990; p. 14), which Meehl termed *schizotaxia*. Schizotaxia, therefore, is the "genetically determined integrative defect, predisposing to schizophrenia and a *sine qua non* for that disorder" (Meehl, 1990; p. 35) and is conjectured to occur in 10% of the general population (see Lenzenweger & Korfine, 1992).

Schizotaxia denotes an aberration in brain functioning—it is not itself a behavior or observable personality pattern. The schizotaxic brain, however, becomes the foundation that other factors will build upon and interact adversely with to possibly produce clinically diagnosable schizophrenia. In particular, those factors may include (a) the individual's social-learning history (i.e., environmental influences) and (b) other genetic factors, termed *polygenic potentiators* (i.e., personality dimensions independent of schizotaxia, such as social introversion, anxiety proneness, aggressivity, and diminished pleasure capacity; Fig. 1). Such potentiators interact with the established schizotypic personality organization and the social environment to facilitate (or, in some cases, hinder) the development of schizophrenia. According to the model, all (or nearly all) schizotaxic individuals would develop schizotypy in most social environments. Schizotypy, therefore, refers to the latent psychological and personality organization resulting from the schizotaxic individual interacting with and developing within the world of social-learning influences. An individual who displays schizotypy is considered a *schizotype* according to the model (schizotype does not connote a diagnosable entity according to the *Diagnostic and Statistical Manual of Mental Disorders, DSM,* or the *International Classification of Diseases*).

Meehl theorized a "mixed" model of genetic influence—namely, a single major gene with two alleles (alternate forms) operating against an additive polygenic (i.e., sum of individual genetic effects) and environmental background. Although modern genetic research does not support a simple single-major-locus model, empirical and simulation studies have long suggested that a mixed model is clearly plausible for schizophrenia (as are several other models).

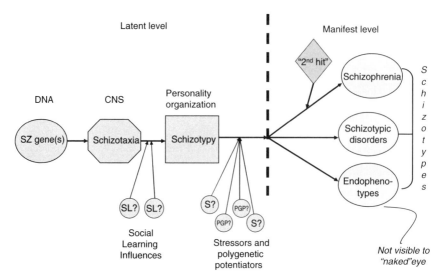

Fig. 1. Developmental model relating the genetic diathesis for schizophrenia, schizo-taxia, and schizotypy and implied levels of analysis (following Meehl 1962, 1990). A DNA-based liability (SZ = schizophrenia) creates impaired neural circuitry (schizotaxia) in the central nervous system (CNS) that eventuates in a personality organization (schizotypy) that harbors the liability for schizophrenia. Social-learning (SL) schedules interact with schizotaxia to yield schizotypy. Psychosocial stressors (S) and polygenic potentiators (PGP) interact with schizotypy to yield manifest outcomes across a range of clinical expression (from essentially asymptomatic to full-blown clinical illness). Various possible manifest developmental outcomes are schizophrenia (assuming a "second hit," e.g., in utero exposure to maternal influenza); schizotypic psychopathology (e.g., schizotypal and/or paranoid personality disorders); or endophenotypes (e.g., sustained attention deficits, eye-tracking dysfunction, working-memory impairments, and/or psychometric deviance; see Gottesman & Gould, 2003), which are invisible to the naked eye (but detectable with appropriate technologies). All individuals represented across this range of manifest outcomes are considered "schizotypes," which does not necessarily imply an *International Classification of Diseases* or *Diagnostic and Statistical Manual of Mental Disorders* diagnosis.

Contemporary Research Strategies That Are Derivative of the Schizotypy Model

The schizotypy model has been a potent intellectual engine in the development of a number of derivative research strategies. These strategies depart from traditional psychopathology studies that focus solely on clinically expressed schizophrenia as the unit of analysis. Simply stated, reliance on the study of expressed cases—i.e., ones that have already developed—can never illuminate how schizophrenia emerges and develops in the first place. Such strategies include studies of those who are at high genetic risk, psychometric-high-risk research (i.e., studies of persons who are found to be deviant on psychometric measures of schizophrenia liability), and the recently reinvigorated focus on prodromal schizophrenia (the prospective study of early emerging signs of clinical schizophrenia in nonpsychotic individuals that are likely in transition, or "converting," to psychosis). All of these strategies fundamentally derive from Meehl's schizotypy model as they all posit a genetically influenced latent liability for schizophrenia that interacts with environmental stressors as well as other genetically determined assets or liabilities.

Strategic Value of the Approach

Mapping the Liability Construct   Schizophrenia liability does not manifest itself only in the form of clinical psychotic illness, and a comprehensive mapping of liability manifestations is required for a valid survey of the liability construct. This mapping derives in large part from the study of schizotypes, who are not so-called "analogs" of schizophrenia but are, rather, carriers of genuine schizophrenia liability. There is also considerable interest in determining the likelihood of schizophrenia outcomes given the presence of deviance on one or another schizotypy indicators or measures.

Eluding Third-Variable Confounds   The study of nonpsychotic and prepsychotic variants of schizophrenia liability allows for a cleaner window on underlying pathological processes—one that is free of the contaminatory effects of medication, cognitive and personality deterioration, and institutionalization.

Illumination of Premorbid Indicators   The study of schizotypy allows for illumination of truly premorbid indicators of schizophrenia rather than epiphenomena (i.e., secondary phenomena accompanying the clinical illness but not of causal importance for it), as such study is undertaken in persons who have never been psychotic.

Enhanced Statistical Power of Genetic Investigations   The use of reliable and valid schizotypy indicators can enhance the statistical power of genomic investigations of schizophrenia, even if such indicators are only modestly correlated with schizophrenia liability.

Endophenotype Approach   The schizotypy model clearly suggests that all who possess schizotypy will show some, even if very subtle, manifestation of that latent liability; therefore it implicitly embraces the endophenotype approach (Gottesman & Gould, 2003). Endophenotypes are those processes or markers invisible to the naked eye—but detectable with appropriate technologies—that, in principle, provide simpler clues to genetic underpinnings of schizophrenia than complex symptom patterns do (see Fig. 1).

HOW TO IDENTIFY THE SCHIZOTYPE

Schizotypes can be identified in one of three ways (Lenzenweger, 1998) that are best viewed as complementary and somewhat overlapping. The familial/biologic approach focuses on the biological first-degree relatives of persons affected by schizophrenia. Such persons represent, as a group, an enriched sample for schizophrenia liability, though not all such relatives necessarily carry schizophrenia liability. The clinical approach relies on psychiatrically defined schizotypic psychopathology such as schizotypal personality disorder (e.g., *DSM-IV*). Finally, the laboratory approach makes use of reliable and valid quantitative measures (e.g., sustained attention, eye tracking, psychometric inventories) that are indicators of schizophrenia liability. The benefit of the laboratory approach is that, in many cases, it makes use of phenomena that can be counted rather than rated, offering enhanced precision in measurement.

PERCEPTUAL ABERRATIONS, SCHIZOTYPY, AND SCHIZOPHRENIA: FROM PHENOMENOLOGY TO GENOMICS

The research utility of the schizotypy model is illustrated by following the development of one particular schizotypic feature—body-image and perceptual aberrations—from early clinical descriptions (Rado, 1960) and theoretical conjectures (Meehl, 1964), through empirical validation work, to current genomic investigations. There are other schizotypic features that are the focus of research efforts (e.g., magical ideation, social anhedonia). Rado (1960) described two key components of the diathesis (constitutional weakness or predisposition) for schizophrenia carried by the schizotype, one being a proposed proprioceptive (kinesthetic or body-sense) diathesis that results in an aberrant awareness of the body (a feature giving rise to schizotypic body-image distortions). Meehl (1964) richly described schizotypic signs and symptoms, one of which concerned body-image aberrations. These clinical observations were operationalized by a well-known psychometric measure, the Perceptual Aberration Scale (PAS; Chapman, Chapman, & Raulin, 1978). The PAS has been used as a tool for identifying subjects who may be at enhanced risk for schizophrenia (or, more generally, nonaffective psychosis).

A large research corpus has established links between deviance on the PAS and numerous valid indicators of schizophrenia liability. In my lab, we initially demonstrated that PAS deviance predicted an increased risk for schizophrenia in biological first-degree relatives, elevated and clinically significant schizotypal personality features, and numerous deficits in neurocognitive processes that are central to our understanding of schizophrenia (see Lenzenweger, 1998 for review). For example, PAS-identified schizotypes and persons with clinically diagnosed schizophrenia show deficits in sustained attention, executive functioning, working memory, attentional inhibition, smooth-pursuit eye tracking (smooth visual tracking of a target), and antisaccade (intentional movement of the eye away from a target that one would normally want to look at) performance, as well as increased thought disorder and schizophrenia-related deviance on the Minnesota Multiphasic Personality Inventory. This pattern of data demonstrated that psychometrically identified schizotypy is similar to schizophrenia in terms of associations with various psychological, cognitive, and other factors known to be validly related to schizophrenia, and is likely to reflect schizophrenia liability.

CURRENT FRUITFUL DIRECTIONS OF INQUIRY
INTO SCHIZOTYPY

Reduction of Heterogeneity: How to Refine Signal and Reduce Noise

No schizophrenia patient or schizotype will reveal deviant performance on all measures that tap liability, thus heterogeneity in performance data across measures is the norm. Heterogeneity poses a massive methodological and statistical challenge in efforts to detect the signal of schizophrenia liability. Any measure of schizotypy that is used to assemble a group of schizotypes for study will necessarily generate an admixture of "genuine" schizotypes as well as what might be termed false-positive cases. My colleagues and I developed a statistical model that parses a group of putative schizotypes into genuine versus false-positive cases (Lenzenweger, Jensen, & Rubin, 2003). This model makes use of the performance characteristics of both normal and schizotypic subjects in seeking to identify the true status of those subjects initially identified as being part of a putative schizotypic group. Our statistical model approaches the heterogeneity issue as a missing-data problem and provides a statistical framework for determining which of the putative schizotypes might be better classified as nonschizotypic. We applied our method to neuropsychological and eye-tracking performance data, conditioned on initial psychometric schizotypy status (i.e., presence or absence of deviance on the PAS), and we were able to parse out genuine from false-positive schizotypes. The genuine schizotypes were found to be significantly more impaired on measures of sustained attention, thought disorder, and working memory relative to both controls and false-positive cases (Lenzenweger et al., 2003).

Simpler May Be Better: Probing Basic Motor and Somatosensory Processes

Research in schizophrenia has long focused heavily on relatively complex cognitive processes, but the early observations of schizophrenia by Kraepelin and Bleuler pointed to deficits in very basic perception and motor processes. We have pursued some of these seminal clinical insights and used experimental methods to probe somatosensation and motor performance in schizotypic subjects. Initial work revealed deficits in exteroceptive sensitivity (perception of fine touch) in relation to psychometric schizotypy indicators, including the PAS. I (Lenzenweger, 2000) showed that elevations on the PAS were found among those subjects who had the most deviant two-point discrimination thresholds (i.e., threshold at which two points touching the skin can be differentiated from one point). Subsequent work (Chang & Lenzenweger, 2001) revealed that deficits in two-point discrimination among the first-degree relatives of schizophrenia patients was due to poor sensitivity rather than response bias, a finding subsequently replicated (Chang & Lenzenweger, 2005). We studied another aspect of somatosensation, namely proprioception (i.e., perception of movement and spatial orientation), in those at elevated risk for schizophrenia (i.e., first-degree relatives of schizophrenia patients) and, as predicted by Rado and Meehl, deficits on a proprioceptive task suggested genuine sensitivity impairments (rather than response-bias differences). The psychometric schizotypy reality-distortion factor, which includes perceptual aberrations, was significantly inversely correlated with sensitivity on both the exteroceptive and proprioceptive task-performance indices. Finally, probing fine psychomotor functioning, using a simple, low-demand line-drawing task, we have been able to demonstrate that motor deficits, assessed in persons with no history of psychosis, are also associated with increased levels of perceptual aberration (Lenzenweger & Maher, 2002). This association, moreover, maintained even in the face of numerous statistical controls for factors such as anxiety, depression, attention, and others. We emphasize the benefits of a focus on simpler psychological processes in schizotypy research, as such processes are not subserved by numerous neurocognitive systems, which often blur the meaning of findings from the study of complex constructs. Moreover, simpler processes may be more easily related to underlying biological and genomic substrates.

Long-Term Follow-up

It is known that deviance on the PAS, in part, helps to predict later psychosis and schizotypic features in previously nonpsychotic individuals. We are currently conducting a 17-year follow-up study to assess the extent to which initial deviance on the PAS and deviance on a measure of sustained attention jointly predict schizophrenia and nonaffective psychosis in subjects who were nonpsychotic upon initial evaluation—thus, joining two promising endophenotypes. This study is examining a wide range of psychosocial and psychological factors to illuminate the impact of schizotypy across the life course beyond simply psychopathological outcomes.

Latent Structure and the Link to Genomic Influences

An implication of Meehl's model is that individuals who carry schizotypy should constitute a qualitatively distinct class of persons, differing from others by kind, not by degree. Taxometric analysis (a statistical procedure designed to detect whether a construct is quantitative or qualitative in nature) of the PAS has consistently yielded evidence that supports this hypothesis: Large samples of individuals assessed on the PAS appear to represent a mixture of two latent classes; importantly, the smaller of these two classes (5–10% of the samples) demarcates a highly schizotypic group (Korfine & Lenzenweger, 1995; Lenzenweger & Korfine, 1992). Finally, although it is well known that taxometric analysis does not test genetic conjectures directly and only tests one aspect of Meehl's conjectures regarding the nature of schizotypy (see Lenzenweger, 2003), taxometric results can be suggestive regarding the possible structure of a genetic influence for schizotypy. Indeed, recent research (Lin et al., 2005) demonstrated one genomic association (the single nucleotide polymorphism rs3924999 for the neuregulin 1 [NRG1] gene at chromosome 8p22–p12, which is a locus of interest to schizophrenia researchers) with quantitative deviance on the PAS. Finally, in our most recent work we have been applying the statistical tool known as finite mixture modeling (an advanced statistical procedure for resolving latent components) to performance on objective laboratory measures known to be associated with schizophrenia liability (e.g., sustained attention and eye tracking) in order to examine latent structure (i.e., the underlying nature of the variables of interest).

This work, consistent with the early taxometric work, suggests the presence of discontinuities underlying performance on these tasks, and thus a real distinction between groups; moreover, this method allows us to identify with considerable precision, via statistical probabilities, those persons thought to be members of the schizotypy-positive class.

CONCLUSION

Use of laboratory measures to tap constructs of central importance within a schizotypy framework, in conjunction with statistical methods directed at the resolution of heterogeneity as well as latent structure, will provide a more precise and, hopefully, more fruitful direction in the discovery of genetic factors of causal importance for schizophrenia.

Recommended Reading

Gottesman, I.I., & Gould, T.D. (2003) (See References)

Meehl, P.E. (1990). (See References)

Lenzenweger, M.F. (2006). Schizotaxia, schizotypy and schizophrenia: Paul E. Meehl's blueprint for experimental psychopathology and the genetics of schizophrenia. *Journal of Abnormal Psychology, 115*, 195–200.

Lenzenweger, M.F., & Hooley, J.M., (Eds.). (2003). *Principles of experimental psychopathology: Essays in honor of Brendan A. Maher.* Washington, DC: American Psychological Association.

Waller, N.G., Yonce, L.J., Grove, W.M., Faust, D.A., & Lenzenweger, M.F. (2006). *A Paul Meehl Reader: Essays on the Practice of Scientific Psychology.* Mahwah, NJ: Erlbaum.

Acknowledgments—I thank Irving I. Gottesman for helpful comments on an earlier version of this article.

This work was supported in part by a National Alliance for Research in Schizophrenia and Depression Distinguished Investigator Award to the author.

Note

1. Address correspondence to Mark F. Lenzenweger, Department of Psychology, State University of New York at Binghamton, Science IV - Room G-08, Binghamton, New York 13902; e-mail: mlenzen@binghamton.edu.

References

Chang, B.P., & Lenzenweger, M.F. (2001). Somatosensory processing in the biological relatives of schizophrenia patients: A signal detection analysis of two-point discrimination thresholds. *Journal of Abnormal Psychology, 110*, 433–442.

Chang, B.P., & Lenzenweger, M.F. (2005). Somatosensory processing and schizophrenia liability: Proprioception, exteroceptive sensitivity, and graphesthesia performance in the biological relatives of schizophrenia patients. *Journal of Abnormal Psychology, 114*, 85–95.

Chapman, L.J., Chapman, J.P., & Raulin, M.L. (1978). Body-image aberration in schizophrenia. *Journal of Abnormal Psychology, 87*, 399–407.

Gottesman, I.I., & Gould, T.D. (2003). The endophenotype concept in psychiatry: Etymology and strategic intentions. *American Journal of Psychiatry, 160*, 636–645.

Korfine, L., & Lenzenweger, M.F. (1995). The taxonicity of schizotypy: A replication. *Journal of Abnormal Psychology, 104*, 26–31.

Lenzenweger, M.F. (1998). Schizotypy and schizotypic psychopathology: Mapping an alternative expression of schizophrenia liability. In M.F. Lenzenweger & R.H. Dworkin (Eds.), *Origins and development of schizophrenia: Advances in experimental psychopathology* (pp. 93–121). Washington, DC: American Psychological Association.

Lenzenweger, M.F. (2000). Two-point discrimination thresholds and schizotypy: Illuminating a somatosensory dysfunction. *Schizophrenia Research, 42*, 111–124.

Lenzenweger, M.F. (2003). On thinking clearly about taxometrics, schizotypy, and genetic influences: Correction to Widiger (2001). *Clinical Psychology: Science & Practice, 10*, 367–369.

Lenzenweger, M.F., Jensen, S., & Rubin, D.B. (2003). Finding the "genuine" schizotype: A model and method for resolving heterogeneity in performance on laboratory measures in experimental psychopathology research. *Journal of Abnormal Psychology, 112*, 457–468.

Lenzenweger, M.F., & Korfine, L. (1992). Confirming the latent structure and base rate of schizotypy: A taxometric analysis. *Journal of Abnormal Psychology, 101*, 567–571.

Lenzenweger, M.F., & Maher, B.A. (2002). Psychometric schizotypy and motor performance. *Journal of Abnormal Psychology, 111*, 546–555.

Lin, H-S., Liu, Y-L., Liu, C-M., Hung, S-I., Hwu, H-G., & Chen, W.J. (2005). Neuregulin 1 gene and variations in perceptual aberration of schizotypal personality in adolescents. *Psychological Medicine, 35*, 1589–1598.

Meehl, P.E. (1962). Schizotaxia, schizotypy, schizophrenia. *American Psychologist, 17*, 827–838.

Meehl, P.E. (1964). *Manual for use with checklist of schizotypic signs.* Minneapolis, MN: University of Minnesota. [Available as a PDF format reprint at: http://www.tc.umn.edu/~pemeehl/pubs.htm]

Meehl, P.E. (1990). Toward an integrated theory of schizotaxia, schizotypy, and schizophrenia. *Journal of Personality Disorders, 4*, 1–99.

Rado, S. (1960). Theory and therapy: The theory of schizotypal organization and its application to the treatment of decompensated schizotypal behavior. In S.C. Scher & H.R. Davis (Eds.), *The outpatient treatment of schizophrenia* (pp. 87–101). New York: Grune and Stratton.

This article has been reprinted as it originally appeared in *Current Directions in Psychological Science*. Citation information for this article as originally published appears above.

Understanding Psychopathology:
Melding Behavior Genetics, Personality, and Quantitative Psychology to Develop an Empirically Based Model

Robert F. Krueger and Kristian E. Markon
University of Minnesota

Abstract

Research on psychopathology is at a historical crossroads. New technologies offer the promise of lasting advances in our understanding of the causes of human psychological suffering. Making the best use of these technologies, however, requires an empirically accurate model of psychopathology. Much current research is framed by the model of psychopathology portrayed in current versions of the Diagnostic and Statistical Manual of Mental Disorders (DSM; American Psychiatric Association. 2000). Although the modern DSMs have been fundamental in advancing psychopathology research, recent research also challenges some assumptions made in the DSM—for example, the assumption that all forms of psychopathology are well conceived of as discrete categories. Psychological science has a critical role to play in working through the implications of this research and the challenges it presents. In particular, behavior-genetic, personality, and quantitative-psychological research perspectives can be melded to inform the development of an empirically based model of psychopathology that would constitute an evolution of the DSM.

Keywords

classification; DSM; statistics; comorbidity; dimensions; categories

Psychopathology research is at a historical crossroads. Powerful technologies, such as molecular genetics and sophisticated statistical models, now exist to aid us in our attempts to understand the origins of psychological suffering. To fully exploit these technologies, however, we need to know how to best conceptualize psychopathology. We need an empirically based model of psychopathology that can guide our inquiries into its origins.

Most psychopathology research is currently framed by the system provided in the fourth edition (text revision) of the *Diagnostic and Statistical Manual of Mental Disorders* (*DSM-IV-TR*; American Psychiatric Association. 2000). A number of specific assumptions underlie the classification of all disorders described in the *DSM-IV-TR*. A cardinal assumption is that mental disorders are categorical: The manual lists a large number of categories of mental disorder, and for each category, a series of criteria for category membership are listed. People are assumed to be either members of these categories or nonmembers; graded degrees of category membership are not permitted. Importantly, the *DSM-IV-TR* itself acknowledges potential limitations of this categorical approach to conceptualizing psychopathology, noting that "a categorical approach to classification works best when all members of a diagnostic class are homogenous, when there are clear boundaries between classes, and when the different classes are mutually exclusive" (p. xxxi).

Each of these areas has proven problematic for *DSM* categories. Members of specific diagnostic classes tend to be heterogeneous, boundaries between classes are often unclear, and classes are rarely mutually exclusive. This is the sense in which psychopathology research is at a historical crossroads. *DSM*-defined categories are the most frequent targets of psychopathological inquiry, yet reliance on *DSM*-defined categories often results in significant problems in research design and interpretation. To pick a specific example for illustrative purposes, if one wants to understand depression, what should be done about the fact that the boundary between depression and other *DSM* categories is often unclear (e.g., depression overlaps with dysthymia; Klein & Santiago, 2003) and many people who meet criteria for depression meet criteria for other disorders as well (e.g., anxiety disorders; Kessler, DuPont, Berglund, & Wittchen, 1999)? Is it possible to develop an empirically based approach to psychopathology that could overcome these limitations?

The development of such a system is a tractable goal, and the pursuit of this goal involves integrating a number of areas of inquiry that represent quintessential strengths of psychological science. Some broad outlines of such a system can be seen by tying together recent research findings from these areas: Specifically, research strategies, concepts, and findings from quantitative psychology, behavior genetics, and personality psychology provide the tools needed to develop an empirically based model of psychopathology.

CONTRIBUTIONS OF QUANTITATIVE PSYCHOLOGY TO UNDERSTANDING PSYCHOPATHOLOGY

One prominent movement in psychology during recent decades has been the use of explicit quantitative models to describe and predict psychological phenomena. Quantitative models are sets of mathematical and statistical equations describing and predicting psychological phenomena. Structural-equation models, item-response models, growth-curve models, and other latent-variable models have allowed tremendous increases in the sophistication of theories that can be tested and in the confidence of our conclusions about those theories. These methods also hold promise for understanding psychopathology, because they allow empirical comparison of different classification paradigms. Such paradigms can be represented by different quantitative models, and can be rigorously compared by comparing the fit of those models to psychological data.

Empirical comparisons between different factor models, for example, have indicated that common forms of psychopathology in adults can be understood in terms of a hierarchical factor model (Krueger & Markon, 2006; see Fig. 1) that bears a strong resemblance to influential factor models in child-psychopathology research (Achenbach & Edelbrock, 1984). At a high level of the hierarchy, psychopathological variation and covariation are organized by two broad, correlated dimensions, Internalizing and Externalizing. Internalizing psychopathology represents a spectrum of conditions characterized by negative emotion and includes phenomena such as depression, anxiety, and phobias. At a lower level of the hierarchy, the Internalizing spectrum splits into a Distress subspectrum and

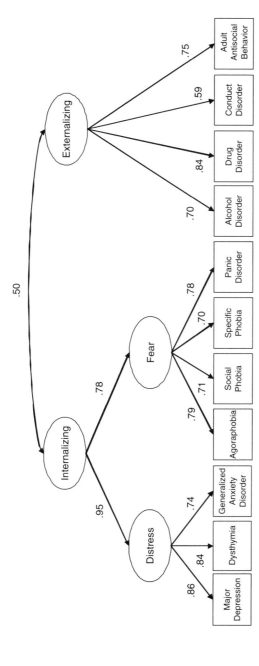

Fig. 1. A model of common forms of psychopathology. The numerical values are path coefficients, representing the strength of associations between constructs; stronger relationships are associated with larger values. The data on which the figure is based come from a meta-analysis presented in Krueger and Markon (2006). Reprinted from "Reinterpreting comorbidity: A model-based approach to understanding and classifying psychopathology," by Robert F. Krueger and Kristian E. Markon, 2006, *Annual Review of Clinical Psychology*, 2, page 126. Copyright 2006 by Annual Reviews (www.annualreviews.org). Reprinted with permission.

a Fear subspectrum; the former is characterized by ruminative disorders such as depression and generalized anxiety, the latter by paroxysmal disorders such as phobia and panic disorder. Externalizing psychopathology, in contrast, is characterized by disinhibition; this spectrum includes phenomena such as antisocial behavior and substance-use disorder. This hierarchical model provides a better account of patterns of psychopathology than do many competing factor models, including ones that contain fewer or more factors.

Recent latent-variable-modeling studies have suggested that, indeed, these common forms of psychopathology are best thought of as continuous, rather than categorical, in nature. Generally speaking, continuous models classify people by locating them along graded dimensions, whereas categorical models classify people into distinct groups. Explicit comparisons of continuous and categorical models of the occurrence and co-occurrence of externalizing disorders indicate that this broad domain of psychopathology is continuous in nature, reflecting a liability or underlying level of risk for disorder that is graded in severity rather than discrete and categorical (Krueger, Markon, Patrick, & Iacono, 2005; Markon & Krueger, 2005). Although, to our knowledge, continuous and categorical models of the overarching internalizing domain have not been compared directly, relevant research does exist for specific internalizing syndromes. For example, continuous models of depression have increased validity over categorical models (Aggen, Neale, and Kendler, 2005), and depressive symptoms appear to be continuously distributed (Hankin, Fraley, Lahey, & Waldman, 2005). Finding that common forms of psychopathology are best conceptualized as continuous in nature calls into question the current assumption of the *DSM* that psychopathology is always categorical.

Continuous models of psychopathology help delineate informativeness (how much a disorder or symptom is indicative of a dimension underlying multiple symptoms or disorders, akin to a factor loading in traditional factor analysis) and severity (where a disorder or symptom is located along a dimension underlying multiple symptoms or disorders). For example, such models delineate these characteristics of different disorders within the Internalizing and Externalizing spectra, as well as the informativeness and severity of specific symptoms with regard to individual disorders. Aggen et al. (2005), for example, evaluated the informativeness and severity of different symptoms of depression. They demonstrated that the most informative symptoms were depressed mood, lack of interest, and duration greater than 2 weeks. The most severe symptoms, however, were suicidal ideation, inability to concentrate, and feelings of worthlessness. This picture of the differential informativeness and severity of depression symptoms is in contrast to the classification approach taken in the current *DSM*, in which different symptoms are mostly equal in their usefulness as indicators of disorder categories.

CONTRIBUTIONS OF BEHAVIOR GENETICS TO UNDERSTANDING PSYCHOPATHOLOGY

Models that have proven useful in understanding psychopathology can be extended to include information on genetic and environmental influences. By including data on the relatedness of different individuals in families, similarities in patterns of psychopathology across individuals can be modeled as a function of how related the individuals are. For example, to the extent that distinct patterns of psychopathology are manifested more frequently among genetically related individuals than among unrelated individuals, taking into account potential environmental reasons for resemblance, those patterns reflect genetic influences. Such research thereby helps inform the understanding of psychopathology by incorporating information on the origins, or etiology, of disorders.

Evidence suggests that patterns of etiologic influence on common forms of psychopathology generally mimic observed, or phenotypic, patterns. Kendler, Prescott, Myers, and Neale (2003) modeled patterns of psychopathology among twins and concluded that genetic influences have the same hierarchical internalizing–externalizing factor structure seen phenotypically. Their results indicate, for example, that if one identical twin has one internalizing disorder, his or her twin is more likely to have another internalizing disorder than to have an externalizing disorder, and vice versa. These findings are important because they suggest that etiologic influences on common forms of psychopathology share the same organization as psychopathology itself—psychopathology appears to derive its observed structure from the structure of its underlying etiology. That is, the internalizing and externalizing spectra are observable not only in the phenotypic patterning of mental disorders, but also in the patterning of underlying genetic risk factors for these disorders.

As our understanding of molecular neurobiology and genetics improves, it will also become possible to delineate the physical nature of the biological structures underlying psychopathology and its etiology. A greater understanding of the molecular-genetic substrates of psychopathology will help refine psycho-pathology models by providing details about the structures underlying the phenotypic organization of psychopathology. In this regard, molecular genetics not only helps explain why psychopathology occurs but also what psychopathology is—how it is best thought about and best organized conceptually. Along these lines, recent research indicates that genes are organized in functional systems of variation—that is, genes are inherited together in sets that parallel the functions of the proteins they encode (Petkov et al., 2005). In the future, it may be possible to link gene-expression variation in these systems to dimensions of psychopathology.

Research on psychopathology framed by dimensions such as those described in this article can help delineate the links between phenotypes and functional genetic systems. For example, Stallings et al. (2005) reported that a composite externalizing index provided stronger evidence for linkage to specific areas of the genome, when compared with separate antisocial and substance-dependence indices used alone. This composite index provided the strongest evidence of genetic linkage in a sample of adolescents and young adults, suggesting that a locus on chromosome 9 increases risk for externalizing psychopathology in general, as opposed to risk for only specific externalizing syndromes.

CONTRIBUTIONS OF PERSONALITY PSYCHOLOGY TO UNDERSTANDING PSYCHOPATHOLOGY

Constructs such as the Internalizing and Externalizing spectrums bear a notable resemblance to personality constructs. Like personality constructs, psychopathology-spectrum constructs organize broad domains of human individual differences and provide theoretical coherence for those domains. In addition to these conceptual parallels, data also link personality constructs per se to the model in Figure 1 in a way that is psychologically meaningful. Internalizing-spectrum disorders are associated with the broad personality domain of negative emotionality or neuroticism, whereas externalizing-spectrum disorders are associated both with constructs in that domain and with constructs in the broad domain of disinhibition—a domain that intersects unconscientiousness and disagreeableness (for a meta-analytic perspective on the structure of these personality constructs, see Markon, Krueger, & Watson, 2005; for a recent review of these personality–psychopathology connections, see Krueger, 2005). Psychologically speaking, negative emotionality confers risk for disorders in the internalizing spectrum, whereas a combination of negative emotionality and disinhibition confers risk for disorders in the externalizing spectrum. Moreover, these connections extend beyond phenotypic associations. Behavior-genetic research supports a genetic basis for these connections, indicating that personality and psychopathology are linked at an etiological level (Krueger, 2005).

CONCLUSIONS

The modern *DSMs* have been fundamentally helpful in psychopathology research. They have provided explicit definitions of categories of psychopathology. The research we reviewed would not have been possible without the foundation provided by these definitions. Nevertheless, the research reviewed here also underlines the value of some evolutionary steps in the field's conceptualization of psychopathology to further psychological research on the subject.

One evolutionary focus is the *DSM* itself. Psychological scientists have important roles to play in pushing for changes to the *DSM*. The processes that will eventuate in the publication of the next edition of the *DSM* (*DSM-V*) are just getting underway (see http://www.dsm5.org/), and there are reasons for optimism regarding the scientific bases for *DSM-V*. For example, a number of conferences have been organized to discuss research agendas to help place *DSM-V* on solid scientific footing (see, e.g., Widiger, Simonsen, Krueger, Livesley, & Verheul, 2005, for discussion of a research agenda for personality disorders articulated at one of these conferences).

Yet the *DSM* is a complex document, shaped in understandable and legitimate ways by considerations that extend beyond psychopathology research per se. To pick a single illustrative example, categories of psychopathology provide labels that are used routinely in facilitating third-party payment for professional services. This record-keeping function of the *DSM* is conceptually separate from the utility of the *DSM* as a framework for psychopathology research, but it is no less legitimate. As a result of this understandable multiplicity of influences and purposes, the *DSM* represents a compromise among diverse considerations.

Such compromises may not optimally serve the needs of the psychopathology research community. As a result, an empirically based model of psychopathology may develop separately from the *DSM*, to help frame and propel novel research.

Some specific steps in developing this kind of model can be gleaned from the current review, and constitute expansions of the conceptual framework represented in Figure 1. Specifically, it is necessary to better understand the substructure of psychopathology-spectrum concepts such as internalizing and externalizing, and it is also necessary to expand the model beyond these two spectra. This will require developing detailed databases at the symptom level, unconstrained by the a priori assumption that these symptoms are optimally sorted into current *DSM* categories or sorted by current *DSM* conventions. For example, close links between personality and psychopathology mean that both sorts of constructs should be covered in such databases. With such data in hand, distinct statistical models corresponding to distinct classification paradigms (e.g., categorical vs. continuous paradigms) can be fit, providing an empirical means of sorting symptoms into syndrome-level constructs and sorting syndromes into broader psychopathology spectra.

In developing such databases, it is also necessary to greatly expand the scope of the model in Figure 1. The model developed out of attempts to understand the comorbidity (co-occurrence) of the limited subset of *DSM* disorders that have been the primary focus of epidemiological inquiry; many psychopathology constructs were not included simply because the relevant data do not exist. Expanding the scope of the model requires coverage of a greater diversity of psychopathological symptoms and personality constructs, most likely using samples in which the prevalence of diverse forms of maladaptive behavior is higher than in the community-dwelling population (e.g., treatment-seeking samples).

Such an expanded and more detailed model would logically lead to novel questions in both treatment-oriented and etiologically oriented psychopathology research. With regard to studies of treatment, one could ask if interventions are impacting specific symptoms, specific syndromes, or broad spectra. Parallel questions would emerge in attempting to understand the etiology of psychopathology. For example, do specific genetic polymorphisms (distinct forms of genes) influence details of symptom presentation or overall risk for a broad spectrum of psychopathologies?

The development of this kind of empirically based model of psychopathology—separate from the *DSM*—might be viewed as unfortunate, in the sense that it might further separate science and practice. Yet it may also be a necessary step in realizing the promise of psychological science as a foundation for developing effective means to alleviate human suffering.

Recommended Reading

Kendler, K.S., Prescott, C.A., Myers, J., & Neale, M.C. (2003). (See References)
Krueger, R.F., & Markon, K. (2006). (See References)
Widiger, T.A., & Samuel, D.B. (2005). Diagnostic categories or dimensions? A question for the Diagnostic and Statistical Manual of Mental Disorders – Fifth Edition. *Journal of Abnormal Psychology, 114*, 494–504.

Acknowledgments—Preparation of this paper was supported in part by U.S. Public Health Service Grant MH65137.

Note

1. Address correspondence to Robert F. Krueger, Department of Psychology, University of Minnesota, Elliott Hall, 75 E. River Rd., Minneapolis, MN 55455; e-mail: krueg038@umn.edu.

References

Achenbach, T.M., & Edelbrock, C.S. (1984). Psychopathology of childhood. *Annual Review of Psychology, 35*, 227–256.

Aggen, S.H., Neale, M.C., & Kendler, K.S. (2005). DSM criteria for major depression: Evaluating symptom patterns using latent-trait item response models. *Psychological Medicine, 35*, 475–487.

American Psychiatric Association. (2000). *Diagnostic and statistical manual of mental disorders* (4th ed., Text Revision). Washington, DC: Author.

Hankin, B.L., Fraley, R.C., Lahey, B.B., & Waldman, I.D. (2005). Is depression best viewed as a continuum or discrete category? A taxometric analysis of childhood and adolescent depression in a population-based sample. *Journal of Abnormal Psychology, 114*, 96–110.

Kendler, K.S., Prescott, C.A., Myers, J., & Neale, M.C. (2003). The structure of genetic and environmental risk factors for common psychiatric and substance use disorders in men and women. *Archives of General Psychiatry, 60*, 929–937.

Kessler, R.C., DuPont, R.L., Berglund, P., & Wittchen, H.-U. (1999). Generalized anxiety disorder and major depression at 12 months in two national surveys. *American Journal of Psychiatry, 156*, 1915–1923.

Klein, D.N., & Santiago, N.J. (2003). Dysthymia and chronic depression: Introduction, classification, risk factors, and course. *Journal of Clinical Psychology, 59*, 807–816.

Krueger, R.F. (2005). Continuity of Axes I and II: Toward a unified model of personality, personality disorders, and clinical disorders. *Journal of Personality Disorders, 19*, 233–261.

Krueger, R.F., & Markon, K.E. (2006). Reinterpreting comorbidity: A model-based approach to understanding and classifying psychopathology. *Annual Review of Clinical Psychology, 2*, 111–133.

Krueger, R.F., Markon, K.E., Patrick, C.J., & Iacono, W.G. (2005). Externalizing psychopathology in adulthood: A dimensional-spectrum conceptualization and its implications for DSM-V. *Journal of Abnormal Psychology, 114*, 537–550.

Markon, K.E., & Krueger, R.F. (2005). Categorical and continuous models of liability to externalizing disorders: A direct comparison in NESARC. *Archives of General Psychiatry, 62*, 1352–1359.

Markon, K., Krueger, R.F., & Watson, D. (2005). Delineating the structure of normal and abnormal personality: An integrative hierarchical approach. *Journal of Personality and Social Psychology, 88*, 139–157.

Petkov, P.M., Graber, J.H., Churchill, G.A., DiPetrillo, K., King, B.L., & Paigen, K. (2005). Evidence of a large-scale functional organization of mammalian chromosomes. *Public Library of Science Genetics, 1*, 312–322.

Stallings, M.C., Corley, R.P., Dennehey, B., Hewitt, J.K., Krauter, K.S., Lessem, J.M., Mikulich, S.K., Rhee, S.H., Smolen, A., Young, S.E., & Crowley, T.J. (2005). A genome-wide search for quantitative trait loci that influence antisocial drug dependence in adolescence. *Archives of General Psychiatry, 62*, 1042–1051.

Widiger, T.A., Simonsen, E., Krueger, R., Livesley, J.W., & Verheul, R. (2005). Personality disorder research agenda for the DSM-V. *Journal of Personality Disorders, 19*, 315–338.

This article has been reprinted as it originally appeared in *Current Directions in Psychological Science*. Citation information for this article as originally published appears above.

A New Unified Treatment Approach for Emotional Disorders Based on Emotion Science

Erica B. Moses[1]

Department of Psychology, University at Albany, SUNY

David H. Barlow

Center for Anxiety and Related Disorders at Boston University

Abstract

Research on the nature of emotional disorders points toward a common set of diatheses (underlying psychological vulnerabilities) and functionally (but not superficially) similar expression of pathological emotional responding (e.g., Barlow, 2002). Successful drug treatments for different emotional disorders are very similar, with selective serotonin reuptake inhibitors or related compounds in wide use. Successful psychological treatments, on the other hand, are currently specifically targeted to each individual disorder. Distilling common principles among existing empirically supported psychological treatments, and giving attention to new findings on emotion regulation and dysregulation from emotion science, we propose and describe a new unified psychological treatment for emotional disorders.

Keywords

emotion; regulation; treatment; unified; avoidance

Psychological treatments emerging mostly from cognitive-behavioral traditions have been developed to accommodate the range of emotional disorders, defined here as the anxiety and unipolar mood disorders. A number of specific psychological treatments have gained empirical support in the treatment of these disorders, surpassing in most instances the efficacy of pharmacological treatments over the longer term (see Barlow, 2004). Despite this evidence, there are a number of limitations to current psychological treatments. Although approximately 50 to 80% of patients undergoing cognitive-behavioral psychological treatments for one or more of the emotional disorders achieve "responder" status (attainment of clinically significant treatment gains)—a higher figure than those typically achieved through alternative or "placebo" psychological treatments in anxiety and related disorders—this leaves a significant number of people who achieve less than optimal response or do not respond (see Barlow, 2002). In addition, successful psychological treatments are often complex and target individual disorders, making them numerous but narrowly construed (e.g., separate treatments for panic disorder, generalized anxiety disorder, major depressive disorder, etc.). These factors raise barriers to dissemination, as the separate protocols and materials for each disorder can require a significant amount of training, thus limiting clinician access to empirically supported treatments for the emotional disorders.

A solution may lie in the development of a common treatment approach applicable to a range of emotional disorders, one that distills hypothetically active procedures shared by current disparate treatments. Newly discovered commonalities within and between the anxiety and mood disorders, as well as the current emotion science literature, provide additional rationale for such a unified approach.

COMMONALITIES AMONG THE EMOTIONAL DISORDERS

Emerging evidence suggests considerable overlap among the anxiety and mood disorders. This is perhaps best seen in the high rates of current and lifetime comorbidity (presence of more than one disorder; e.g., Kessler, Chiu, Demler, Merikangas, & Walters, 2005). A large-scale study of 1,126 patients found that 55% of patients diagnosed with a principal anxiety disorder had at least one additional anxiety or depressive disorder at assessment (Brown, Campbell, Lehman, Grisham, & Mancill, 2001). This number increases to 76% if one considers lifetime diagnoses.

Possible explanations for these high levels of comorbidity have been reviewed extensively (Barlow, 2002) and include overlapping definitional criteria, varying base rates of occurrence in different study settings, and a possible sequential relationship among the disorders such that features of one disorder serve as risk factors for another. Another possible explanation for this comorbidity is the presence of a "negative affect syndrome" (NAS). The collective symptoms of emotional disorders have been theorized as merely variable responses emerging from a more fundamental disorder (Barlow, 2002). Among evidence for the existence of NAS is the common observation of generalizable effects in treatment: Psychological treatments targeting a specific anxiety disorder result in significant improvement in comorbid anxiety or mood disorders not specifically targeted by the treatments (reviewed in Barlow, Allen, & Choate, 2004). For example, successful treatment of panic disorder with or without agoraphobia (PDA) also impacts positively on comorbid diagnoses of generalized anxiety disorder (GAD) and depression, and these changes are largely maintained at follow-up. Although it cannot be determined from treatment outcomes if the treatment elements addressed the individual features of both disorders or if the disorders themselves contained similar underlying features that responded to treatment, the fact that a treatment for one disorder generalizes its effects to other comorbid disorders suggests the utility of a unified treatment approach.

In addition, research using confirmatory factor analysis to examine the factor structure (classification of variables into factors by the relationships between them) of the anxiety and mood disorders finds negative affect and positive affect to be higher-order factors to the symptom-specific disorder factors in the *Diagnostic and Statistical Manual of Mental Disorders* (*DSM-IV*; American Psychiatric Association, 1994), with significant pathways from negative affect to all of the disorder factors and autonomic arousal emerging as a lower-order factor (Brown, Chorpita, & Barlow, 1998). In other words, the model shows that negative affect influences all of the emotional disorders, which suggests a common diathesis (underlying psychological vulnerability). This study also found that certain mood disorders, such as major depressive disorder, overlap more strongly with some anxiety disorders (such as GAD) than with other mood disorders. These results again illustrate overlap both within and between the diagnostic categories of the anxiety and mood disorders. Much as our systems of classification appear to be moving away from "splitting" similar slices of symptoms into different disorders and toward a more dimensional approach (Krueger, Watson, & Barlow, 2005), it may be time to consider common principles of treatment.

EMOTION REGULATION AND EMOTIONAL DISORDERS

Although the scientific study of emotion has not, thus far, substantially influenced research on the nature and treatment of emotional disorders, attention is now turning to the process of emotion regulation (and dysregulation) as one facet in the development and treatment of anxiety and mood disorders. Reflecting Gross's definition (Gross & Thompson, in press), Barlow and colleagues have defined emotion regulation as strategies used by an individual to manipulate an emotion's occurrence, experience, duration, intensity, and expression (Campbell-Sills & Barlow, in press). Emotion regulation can be performed internally (e.g., trying not to think about an unpleasant feeling) or externally (e.g., smiling although feeling sad).

Goals of emotion regulation change depending on the context in which they are occurring. Emotion regulation is typically employed to decrease negative emotions and increase positive emotions. However, it may also be used to increase negative emotions and decrease positive emotions if doing so is situationally beneficial, such as masking joy at times when that emotion would be inappropriate to express, such as at a funeral or while empathizing with a sad friend (Gross & Thompson, in press).

Of course, emotion regulation serves an important purpose. Unregulated strong emotions might keep us from focusing on daily tasks or might result in socially undesirable behaviors such as emotional outbursts. However, maladaptive strategies for regulating emotion—particularly attempts to avoid emotion or to downregulate emotion during or after emotional provocation—can have unintended and negative consequences. For example, numerous studies have shown that use of emotional suppression, although intended to reduce emotional response, has little effect on emotional experience but can produce deleterious biological and cognitive effects such as increased sympathetic nervous system activation and impaired memory (Campbell-Sills, Barlow, Brown, & Hofmann, in press; see Gross & Thompson, in press).

Maladaptive emotion regulation seems to be a component of emotional disorders. In one study, individuals who tended to naturally suppress were more likely to be obsessional, anxious, and depressed (Marcks & Woods, 2004). From our own laboratory, a comparison of participants with anxiety and mood disorders to control participants found that the clinical participants were more likely to utilize maladaptive emotional-regulation strategies such as avoidant or suppressive behavior when viewing an emotion-provoking film (Campbell-Sills & Barlow, in press). Also, individuals with panic disorder fall back on emotional suppression or avoidant strategies in response to CO_2 challenge, a procedure that uses CO_2-enriched air inhalation to induce the physiological sensations associated with panic (Levitt, Brown, Orsillo, & Barlow, 2005).

A UNIFIED TREATMENT PROTOCOL

We have now developed a treatment protocol to target what we hypothesize to be the three main components of the major emotional disorders (Barlow et al., 2004). This approach distills and incorporates the most salient components of the currently empirically supported individualized treatments for various specific anxiety and mood disorders—namely, restructuring faulty cognitive appraisals, changing action tendencies associated with the disordered emotion, and preventing emotional avoidance and facilitating emotional exposure. The result is a conceptually sharper and (potentially) more widely applicable approach that incorporates advancing knowledge of modern learning theory, cognitive neuroscience, and emotion regulation (as reviewed above). We refer to this protocol as "unified" because it is designed to be applicable to all anxiety and unipolar mood disorders.

The protocol begins with a psychoeducation phase that describes emotions, their functions, and how they become disordered. The treatment then focuses on (a) altering antecedent cognitive appraisals, (b) modifying emotion-driven behaviors, and (c) preventing emotional avoidance.

Altering Antecedent Cognitive Appraisals

One adaptive antecedent-focused emotion-regulation strategy emerging from emotion science and cognitive-behavioral practice involves providing the patient with new attributions and appraisals to bring with them to their emotional experiences. In our view, there are two misappraisals common to the emotional disorders: Overestimating the probability of a negative event occurring and catastrophizing the consequences of a negative event should it occur. This strategy then utilizes standard cognitive restructuring techniques to help patients reappraise situations in a more adaptive manner. Importantly, these skills are practiced prior to emotion provocation and are not to be used to suppress or distract from emotional experience.

The positive benefits of antecedent reappraisal have been demonstrated in a study using CO_2 challenge for patients with PDA who typically panic in response to the procedure (e.g., Sanderson, Rapee, & Barlow, 1989). In this study, all patients were told that they would be able to adjust the mixture of CO_2 by turning a dial when a light was illuminated, thereby creating a sense of control over the biological challenge for this group of individuals. For the first 5 minutes, all patients received compressed air, followed by 15 minutes of 5.5% CO_2-enriched air. For 10 of the patients, the light was illuminated throughout the 15-minute CO_2 procedure, while for the other 10 patients, the light was never illuminated. The dial did not, in fact, control the flow of CO_2, and patients never actually resorted to using it, but patients in the perceived-control condition reported fewer panic attacks and less negative emotions than the patients in the no-control group did. Antecedent appraisals of control and familiarity prior to emotion-inducing stimuli have also been shown to reduce biobehavioral stress responses in the hypothalamic-pituitary-adrenal axis, a component of the neuroendocrine system that controls stress reactions (Abelson, Liberzon, Young, & Khan, 2005), and lead to attenuation of responding in the amygdala to anxiety-provoking stimuli (Hariri, Mattay, Tessitore, Fera, & Weinberger, 2003).

Modifying Emotion-Driven Behaviors

Emotion-driven behaviors (EDBs), often referred to as "action tendencies" in the literature of emotion science (Barlow, 2002), are motivated behaviors that naturally occur in response to emotional states. EDBs ordinarily serve an adaptive purpose in specific situational demands (e.g., running away in response to fear triggered by actual danger) but can contribute to emotional disorders when emotions occur at inappropriate times (e.g., running away from a social gathering in response to fears of rejection). EDBs are initially reinforcing as they reduce emotional intensity, but they can be ultimately maladaptive. For example, withdrawal in response to fear of rejection produces further social exclusion and prevents new positive associations (e.g., learning that social situations are not often associated with rejection and embarrassment). A century of tradition in emotion science suggests that one of the most powerful methods for modifying emotions is to change EDBs and thereby change feelings (see Barlow, 2002).

This portion of the protocol teaches patients to recognize their usual EDBs and the resultant (ineffective) consequences. This often involves taking the patient through emotion-induction exercises that elicit cognitive, physiological, and emotional responses. The patients are then instructed to practice responses that are incompatible with their EDBs. Some examples of EDBs are presented in Table 1.

Preventing Emotional Avoidance

Whereas EDBs are initiated to reduce (escape) emotion intensity once it has occurred, emotional avoidance is used to prevent the full experience of emotion in the first place. There are several forms of emotional avoidance. Subtle behavioral avoidance typically occurs when a person encounters a situation he or she

Table 1. *Emotion-driven behaviors, their associated disorders, and incompatible behaviors*

Emotion-driven behavior	Disorder most usually associated	Incompatible behaviors
Calling relatives to check on safety	Generalized anxiety disorder (GAD)	Restricting contact/calling relatives
Perfectionistic behavior at work or home	GAD	Leaving things untidy or unfinished
Checking locks, stove, or other appliances	Obsessive-compulsive disorder	Repeatedly locking/unlocking and turning on/off until memory is unclear
Leaving (escaping from) a theater, religious service, or other crowded area	Panic disorder with agoraphobia	Move to the center of the crowd; smile or produce nonfearful facial expressions
Social withdrawal	Depression	Behavioral activation
Leaving (escaping) a social situation	Social phobia	Staying in situation and approaching people
Verbally/physically attacking someone when in an argument	Posttraumatic stress disorder	Remove self from situation and/or practice relaxation techniques
Hypervigilance	All disorders	Focus attention on specific task at hand; meditation; relaxation

associates with strong emotions, such as the interoceptive avoidance (avoidance of somatic sensations) sometimes seen in individuals with panic disorder. Such individuals begin to avoid activities that may cause them to experience the physiological sensations associated with panic attacks, such as breathlessness caused by walking up a flight of stairs. Another form of emotional avoidance is cognitive avoidance. One example is distraction, in which the individual shifts attention to an alternative focus to avoid engaging in the emotional experience. The third form of emotional avoidance is use of safety signals. Individuals may carry objects that serve as talismans, such as a cell phone, toy animal, or empty pill bottle, because these objects convey superstitious feelings of security in the event of a strong emotional experience such as a panic attack. Some examples of emotional avoidance are presented in Table 2.

Table 2. *Emotional-avoidance strategies and their associated disorders*

Emotional-avoidance strategy	Disorder most usually associated
Subtle behavioral avoidance	
Avoiding eye contact	Social phobia
Avoiding drinking caffeine	Panic disorder with or without agoraphobia (PDA)
Attempting to control breathing	PDA
Avoiding exercise and other forms of physiological arousal (interoceptive avoidance)	PDA/depression
Avoiding touching sink/toilet	Obsessive-compulsive disorder (OCD)
Procrastination (avoiding emotionally salient tasks)	Generalized anxiety disorder (GAD)
Cognitive avoidance	
Distraction (reading a book, watching television)	Depression/PDA
"Tuning out" during a conversation	Social phobia
Reassuring self that everything is okay	GAD
Trying to prevent thoughts from coming into mind	OCD
Distraction from reminders of trauma	Posttraumatic stress disorder
Forcing self to "think positive"	Depression
Worrying	GAD
Rumination	Depression
Thought suppression	All disorders
Safety signals	
Carrying a cell phone	PDA/GAD
Carrying empty medication bottles	PDA
Holding onto "good luck" charms	OCD
Carrying items that are associated with positive experiences (e.g., teddy bears, pictures)	GAD/depression
Having mace at all times	PTSD
Carrying a water bottle	PDA
Having reading material/prayer books on hand	GAD
Carrying sunglasses or items to hide face/eyes	Social phobia

The patient must be made aware of the relationship between emotion avoidance and EDBs, for even a patient successful at modifying their EDBs may still be preventing full emotional arousal during exposure through emotional avoidance, creating difficulties in identifying and replacing faulty emotion regulation strategies with more adaptive techniques.

DIRECTIONS FOR FUTURE RESEARCH

All treatments utilized in health care systems around the world must now be based on evidence, but interventions for emotional disorders will evolve as our understanding of the connection between emotion development, emotion regulation, and the emotional disorders continues to grow. Thus, researchers must try to clarify how and why disordered emotion develops and why it leads to maladaptive emotion regulation. Increased knowledge in this area would lead to further treatment development and, perhaps, to strategies for primary prevention. More fundamentally, deeper knowledge of emotion development and regulation could result in a reorganization of our system of classification for emotional disorders that would be more functional and dimensional. For example, the *DSM-V* or DSM-VI might eliminate separate anxiety, mood, and related (e.g., dissociative) disorders and instead specify presence of negative affect with notational references to presence and severity of associated features such as (low) positive affect, intrusive thoughts, rumination or worry processes, panic attacks, and emotional and situational avoidance (or dissociative) behavior—possibly organized like a Minnesota Multiphasic Personality Inventory profile. This characterization could lead to more individually tailored treatments.

Recommended Reading

Barlow, D.H., Allen, L.B., & Choate, M.L. (2004). (See References)
Barlow, D.H. (2000). Unraveling the mysteries of anxiety and its disorders from the perspective of emotion theory. *American Psychologist, 55,* 1245–1263.
Campbell-Sills, L., & Barlow, D.H. (in press). (See References)
Krueger, R.F., Watson, D., & Barlow, D. (Eds.). (2005). Toward a dimensionally-based taxonomy of psychopathology [Special section]. *Journal of Abnormal Psychology, 114,* 491–569.

Note

1. Address correspondence to David H. Barlow, Center for Anxiety and Related Disorders at Boston University, 648 Beacon Street, 6th Floor, Boston, MA 02215; e-mail: dhbarlow@bu.edu.

References

Abelson, J.L., Liberzon, I., Young, E.A., & Khan, S. (2005). Cognitive modulation of the endocrine stress response to a pharmacological challenge in normal and panic disorder subjects. *Archives of General Psychiatry, 62,* 668–675.
American Psychiatric Association (1994). *Diagnostic and statistical manual of mental disorders* (Vol. 4). Washington, DC: Author.
Barlow, D.H. (2002). *Anxiety and its disorders: The nature and treatment of anxiety and panic* (2nd ed.). New York: The Guilford Press.

Barlow, D.H. (2004). Psychological treatments. *American Psychologist, 59*, 869–878.

Barlow, D.H., Allen, L.B., & Choate, M.L. (2004). Toward a unified treatment for emotional disorders. *Behavior Therapy, 35*, 205–230.

Brown, T.A., Campbell, L.A., Lehman, C.L., Grisham, J.R., & Mancill, R.B. (2001). Current and lifetime comorbidity of the DSM-IV anxiety and mood disorders in a large clinical sample. *Journal of Abnormal Psychology, 110*, 49–58.

Brown, T.A., Chorpita, B.F., & Barlow, D.H. (1998). Structural relationships among dimensions of the DSM-IV anxiety and mood disorders and dimensions of negative affect, positive affect, and autonomic arousal. *Journal of Abnormal Psychology, 107*, 179–192.

Campbell-Sills, L., & Barlow, D.H. (in press). Incorporating emotion regulation into conceptualizations and treatments of anxiety and mood disorders. In J.J. Gross (Ed.), *Handbook of emotion regulation*. New York: Guilford Press.

Campbell-Sills, L., Barlow, D.H., Brown, T.A., & Hofmann, S.G. (in press). Effects of emotional suppression and acceptance in anxiety and mood disorders. *Behavior Research and Therapy*.

Gross, J.J., & Thompson, R.A. (in press). Emotion Regulation: Conceptual Foundations. In J.J. Gross (Ed.), *Handbook of emotion regulation*. New York: Guilford Press.

Hariri, A.R., Mattay, V.S., Tessitore, A., Fera, F., & Weinberger, D.R. (2003). Neocortical modulation of the amygdala response to fearful stimuli. *Biological Psychiatry, 53*, 494–501.

Kessler, R.C., Chiu, W.T., Demler, O., Merikangas, K.R., & Walters, E.E. (2005). Prevalence, severity, and comorbidity of 12-month DSM-IV disorders in the National Comorbidity Survey Replication. *Archives of General Psychiatry, 62*, 617–627.

Krueger, R.F., Watson, D., & Barlow, D.H. (2005). Introduction to the special section: Toward a dimensionally-based taxonomy of psychopathology. *Journal of Abnormal Psychology, 114*, 491–493.

Levitt, J.T., Brown, T.A., Orsillo, S.M., & Barlow, D.H. (2005). The effects of acceptance versus suppression of emotion on subjective and psychophysiological response to carbon dioxide challenge in patients with panic disorder. *Behavior Therapy, 35*, 747–766.

Marcks, B.A., & Woods, D.W. (2004). A comparison of thought suppression to an acceptance-based technique in the management of personal intrusive thoughts: A controlled evaluation. *Behaviour Research and Therapy, 43*, 433–445.

Sanderson, W.C., Rapee, R.M., & Barlow, D.H. (1989). The influence of an illusion of control on panic attacks induced via inhalation of 5.5% carbon dioxide-enriched air. *Archives of General Psychiatry, 46*, 157–164.

This article has been reprinted as it originally appeared in *Current Directions in Psychological Science*. Citation information for this article as originally published appears above.

As Others See Us: Clinical and Research Implications of Cross-Informant Correlations for Psychopathology

Thomas M. Achenbach

University of Vermont

Abstract

Discrepancies are often found between self-reports and reports by others regarding psychopathology. Both the person being assessed and various informants may contribute crucial data concerning a person's functioning. Comprehensive assessment requires data from multiple informants. Such data can be easily obtained with parallel self-report and collateral-report forms. The multi-informant data can be compared, aggregated, and used in many ways. Optimal use of multi-source data is essential for clinical assessment and for discovering causes and cures of psychopathology.

Keywords

cross-informant correlations; psychopathology; assessment; interviews; multi-informant data

When evaluating physical symptoms of unknown cause, physicians use multiple assessment procedures. Examples include interviews, physical examinations, measurement of blood pressure and body temperature, laboratory tests, and imaging. Different procedures provide different and often discrepant results. When discrepancies occur, physicians may consider multiple diagnoses, seek additional information, reassess the problems later, and/or offer provisional palliative care.

For adults' mental health problems, interviews have long been the main assessment procedures. Interviews enable adult clients and clinicians to get acquainted and to reach mutual understandings of a client's needs and how the clinician might help. Interviews are thus essential for building therapeutic alliances and for making clinical decisions.

Since the third edition of the *Diagnostic and Statistical Manual of Mental Disorders* (*DSM-III*; American Psychiatric Association, APA, 1980) introduced explicit criteria for psychiatric diagnoses, interviews have been tailored to make *DSM* diagnoses. One type of interview uses highly structured questions to obtain yes/no answers regarding *DSM* criteria. Such interviews are called *respondent-based interviews*, because respondents' yes/no answers determine which diagnostic criteria are met.

The first respondent-based interviews for *DSM* diagnoses were designed to assess adults. When similar interviews were developed for children, it was found that children's answers were an inadequate basis for making diagnoses. Parallel interviews were therefore developed for the children's parents, whose answers often disagreed with their children's answers. Studies of other assessment procedures have also revealed low agreement between parents' reports and children's self-reports.

CORRELATIONS BETWEEN DIFFERENT INFORMANTS' REPORTS OF CHILDREN'S PROBLEMS

Low agreement between parents and children might be blamed on children's inability or reluctance to report their own problems. However, meta-analyses (which aggregate data across multiple studies) revealed that correlations between reports of children's problems by various adults are also only low to moderate. (As measures of agreement between two sets of scores, correlations can range from -1.00, indicating complete disagreement, to $+1.00$, indicating complete agreement; a correlation of 0.00 indicates that two sets of scores are unrelated to each other.)

Correlations among reports by parents, teachers, mental health workers, and trained observers were low, averaging only .28 (Achenbach, McConaughy, & Howell, 1987). Better agreement was found between reports by pairs of adults who play similar roles vis-à-vis the children (such as pairs of parents and pairs of teachers), as indicated by correlations averaging .60. However, even a correlation of .60 is too low to ensure that the same picture of a child would be obtained from the child's mother and father or from different teachers. Since the 1987 meta-analyses, low to moderate cross-informant correlations regarding children's problems continue to be found so consistently that they are cited as being among "the most robust findings in child clinical research" (De Los Reyes & Kazdin, 2005). Note that cross-informant correlations reflect agreement between reports by people who have different information and perspectives, in contrast to *interrater reliability*, which reflects agreement between people who have similar information and perspectives.

Most mental health clinicians now recognize that assessment of children requires reports from more informants than just the child or one parent. Whenever feasible, information is obtained from both parent figures and from multiple teachers, as well as from the child. Observations in environments such as classrooms are also sought. Many characteristics of the informants, the children, the contexts, and the assessment goals affect the kinds and sizes of discrepancies between informants' reports about children's problems. Consequently, when discrepancies are found between informants' reports of a child's problems, most mental health clinicians realize that each report may provide useful but different information about the child's functioning in different contexts, as viewed from different informants' perspectives. The use of often discrepant reports from multiple informants to evaluate children's mental health parallels physicians' use of often discrepant results from multiple procedures to evaluate physical health.

Discrepancies between reports of psychopathology can be affected by differences in how well informants remember relevant information and in how candid they are. Discrepancies can also be affected by whether problems are observed directly or are inferred, whether they occur in limited contexts or diverse ones, and whether they are mild or severe. Because many factors may differentially affect reports of different kinds of problems, complex models are needed to optimize the use of multi-informant data. Development of such models involves testing different informants' reports of different kinds of problems for large samples of people (Dumenci, 2006).

WHAT ABOUT ADULTS?

Do adults accurately report their own functioning? If they do, then self-report interviews, questionnaires, rating forms, and tests may be sufficient for assessing adult psychopathology. To determine how well adults' reports of their own psychopathology agree with reports by others, my colleagues and I examined some 51,000 articles published in 52 research journals (Achenbach, Krukowski, Dumenci, & Ivanova, 2005). We searched for correlations between self-reports of adult psychopathology and reports by "collaterals" (e.g., friends, family), and between self-reports and reports by clinicians who worked with the adults. We also searched for cross-informant correlations between pairs of people who knew the adults, including both collaterals and clinicians.

Our literature search revealed surprisingly few cross-informant correlations for adult psychopathology. Out of 51,000 articles, only 108 (0.2%) reported correlations that met our methodological criteria. This suggests that cross-informant issues may be neglected in research on adult psychopathology.

We found that correlations between self- and clinician reports differed little from correlations between self- and collateral reports. We also found that cross-informant correlations between self- and collateral reports obtained with interviews differed little from correlations between self- and collateral reports obtained with questionnaires.

When we analyzed correlations between self-reports and collateral reports for different kinds of problems, we found that the correlations averaged .44 for externalizing problems (aggression, rule-breaking) and .43 for internalizing problems (anxiety, depression, withdrawal). For reports obtained with instruments whose items differed (but were scored for similar kinds of psychopathology), the cross-informant correlations averaged .30. The cross-informant correlations between pairs of collaterals averaged .27.

Surprisingly, we found that correlations between self-reports and collateral reports of substance use averaged .68. This larger correlation may reflect the less inferential nature of reports of substance use than of those of other problems. Despite this relatively large correlation, informants' reports of substance use are valuable additions to self-reports, as clinicians who work with substance abusers know. The modest correlations between self- and other reports of problems other than substance use show that adults' reports of their problems often fail to agree with reports by their collaterals and clinicians.

WHAT IS TO BE DONE?

There is no doubt that self-reports are needed for mental health assessment. Reliance on *DSM* diagnoses for clinical decisions and for reimbursement, plus the cachet of *DSM*-based diagnostic interviews, foster expectations that self-report interviews should yield *DSM* diagnoses. Equally important, the widespread use of *DSM*-based interviews to make diagnoses for research implies that such interviews provide "gold standard" diagnoses. However, meta-analyses have yielded an average agreement of only 29% (after correction for chance via a statistic called *kappa*) between diagnoses made from *DSM*-based interviews of adults and diagnoses made from clinical evaluations (Rettew, Doyle, Achenbach, Dumenci, & Ivanova, 2006). For children, the average chance-corrected agreement was 15%. Furthermore, a review by Meyer et al. (2001) found chance-corrected agreement averaging only 12% between *DSM* diagnoses of adults made from self-versus collateral-reports.

The low agreement between *DSM* diagnoses based on gold-standard interviews versus clinical evaluations and the even lower agreement between diagnoses based on self-versus collateral reports raise questions about the adequacy of self-reports for making *DSM* diagnoses. The low agreement also raises questions about self-reports as the sole basis for other aspects of assessment. Because collateral reports might seem impractical, let's consider some possible alternatives to using them. We then consider whether collateral reports are practical.

Validity Scales for Self-Reports

One approach to overcoming the limitations of self-reports is to include validity scales (or "lie" scales) in self-report instruments. The validity scales are intended to detect lying and other distortions. However, in evaluating measures of psychopathology and personality, Piedmont, McCrae, Riemann, and Angleitner (2000) found that use of validity scales may actually reduce the validity of self-reports. They concluded that, "The best evidence on protocol validity, and the best alternative to the use of validity scales, comes from the comparison of self-report scores with independent assessments" (p. 590).

Biological and Observational Measures

Can other assessment procedures avoid the limitations of self- and collateral reports? Biological measures may offer alternatives for problems such as substance use. In our literature search, we found four studies that reported correlations of biological measures of substance use with self- and collateral reports. No correlations of biological measures with self-reports exceeded the correlations between self- and collateral reports of substance use, and some were smaller than the correlations between self- and collateral reports. Furthermore, a meta-analysis of 24 studies yielded only 42% agreement (corrected for chance) between self-reports and biological measures of substance use (Magura & Kang, 1996).

Observational measures offer additional alternatives, but no observational studies of adult psychopathology qualified for our meta-analyses. This is not surprising, because observations of adult psychopathology are seldom practical under real-world conditions. However, observations of children's problems may be instructive. Our meta-analyses of cross-informant agreement for child psychopathology yielded correlations averaging .27 for observational reports with parents' reports and .42 with teachers' reports (Achenbach et al., 1987). Between pairs of observers, the correlations averaged .57, which approximates the correlations averaging .59 between pairs of parents, .64 between pairs of teachers, and .54 between pairs of mental health workers. Thus, neither observational nor biological measures appear to be superior to collateral reports.

Is It Practical to Obtain Collateral Reports?

Collateral reports for assessing adult psychopathology raise the following questions: How many adults would identify appropriate collaterals? How many would consent to having collaterals provide data? How could the data be conveniently obtained? How many collaterals would actually provide data?

Answers are suggested by findings from the National Survey of Children, Youths, and Adults (Achenbach, Newhouse, & Rescorla, 2004; Achenbach & Rescorla, 2003). Interviewers visited randomly selected homes to administer self-report questionnaires assessing adaptive functioning, substance use, and mental health problems. The Adult Self-Report (ASR) was completed by 2,020 (94%) of the 2,146 eligible 18- to 59-year-olds. The Older Adult Self-Report was completed by 608 (90%) of the 678 eligible 60- to 96-year-olds.

Interviewees were asked to nominate collaterals to complete a parallel questionnaire describing the interviewee. For 81% of the 18- to 59-year-olds and 80% of the 60- to 96-year-olds, informed consents were obtained from the interviewees and their collaterals, and the collaterals completed the parallel questionnaires. This suggests that it is practical to obtain collateral reports for many people who are assessed for either clinical or research purposes. Although National Survey participants and collaterals received $10, this was probably no more persuasive than a request from a family member or friend to complete a collateral questionnaire for clinical or research purposes.

How Can We Use Multi-Informant Data?

Computers make it easy to compare and aggregate data from multiple informants. As an example, Figure 1 displays scores obtained on three of the syndromes from the ASR completed by 28-year-old Maria West (not her real name) and from Adult Behavior Checklists (ABCLs) completed by Maria's partner, mother, and friend. The syndromes were statistically derived from 4,628 ASRs and ABCLs. Each syndrome is scored by summing the ratings of items making up the syndrome.

The boxes in Figure 1 display standard scores (known as T scores) for syndromes scored from self- and collateral reports. For example, in the top box, the leftmost bar shows that Maria obtained a T score of 70 (97th percentile for national norms) on the Anxious/Depressed syndrome from her partner's ABCL ratings (designated as ABC1). Scores above the top broken line ($T > 69$) are in the *clinical* range, as indicated by "70-C" printed beneath the bar. The second bar shows Maria's T score of 68 from her mother's ABCL ratings (designated as ABC2). Scores between the two broken lines are in the *borderline* clinical range (T 65–69; 93rd–97th percentile), as indicated by the "68-B" printed beneath the bar. The third bar shows Maria's T score of 75 from her friend's ratings. And the fourth bar shows that Maria's own ratings yielded a T score of 74. It can be seen that all four respondents reported more problems on the Anxious/Depressed syndrome than are typical for women of Maria's age.

In contrast, there is a large discrepancy between the bar for Maria's self-ratings on the Attention Problems syndrome versus the bars for all three collaterals' ratings. Maria reported that she had trouble paying attention and that she

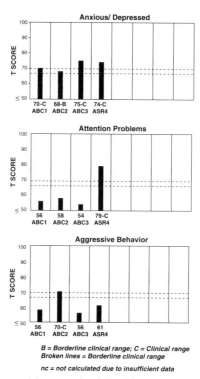

Anxious/ Depressed

Attention Problems

Aggressive Behavior

B = Borderline clinical range; C = Clinical range
Broken lines = Borderline clinical range

nc = not calculated due to insufficient data

Fig. 1. Bar graphs comparing Maria West's Adult Self-Report (ASR) scores with Adult Behavior Checklist (ABC) scores completed by Maria's partner, mother, and friend, for three of eight syndromes. The other syndromes (not shown) are *Withdrawn, Somatic Complaints, Thought Problems, Rule-Breaking Behavior*, and *Intrusive*. (From Achenbach & Rescorla, 2003.)

might have an attention deficit disorder. Yet, ratings by Maria's partner, mother, and friend did not indicate many attention problems.

The bottom box shows that ratings by Maria's partner, friend, and Maria herself were in the normal range on the Aggressive Behavior syndrome. However, her mother's ratings were much higher. Interviews subsequently revealed that this discrepancy reflected Maria's conflicts with her mother, which were unlike her behavior with others.

The software for scoring the ASR and ABCL also displays bar graphs comparing scores on *DSM*-oriented scales (Achenbach and Rescorla, 2003). These scales consist of ASR and ABCL items judged by an international panel of psychiatrists and psychologists as very consistent with *DSM-IV* (APA, 1994) diagnostic categories. ASR and ABCL ratings that yield scores such as those shown in Figure 1 also yield scores for DSM-oriented scales.

Visual comparisons of multi-informant data help users quickly spot agreements and disagreements between self- and other reports. For both clinical and research purposes, computerized multi-informant data can also be aggregated in various ways. For example, self- and other ratings can be averaged to identify scales on which individuals are most and least deviant. More complex algorithms can highlight similarities and differences between profiles of scores obtained from different informants.

Patterns of partial agreement may also be important. Some patterns of partial agreement may reflect differences between problems in different contexts, as exemplified in Figure 1 by the low levels of aggressive behavior reported by all informants except Maria's mother. However, research is needed to pinpoint determinants of cross-informant agreement and to optimize the use of data from multiple sources and multiple methods. Different ways of using multi-informant data must also be tested in relation to various external criteria.

CONCLUSIONS

Assessment of psychopathology and personality requires data from multiple informants. Agreement among informants tends to be modest, but each informant may contribute useful information about different aspects of a person's functioning. Collateral reports can be easily obtained with rating forms that parallel self-report forms. Several methods are available for comparing and aggregating data from multiple sources. A key challenge for further research is how best to use data from multiple informants and from multiple methods to advance clinical assessment and the search for causes and cures for psychopathology. How best to use diverse and discrepant data is also a challenge for many other endeavors as well. Meeting such challenges requires systematic tests of how different sources and types of data can increase the overall validity of assessment.

Recommended Reading

Achenbach, T.M., Krukowski, R.A., Dumenci, L., & Ivanova, M.Y. (2005). (See References)
Achenbach, T.M., & Rescorla, L.A. (2003). (See References)
Meyer, G.J. (2002). Implications of information gathering methods for a refined taxonomy of psychopathology. In L.E. Beutler & M.L. Malik (Eds.). *Rethinking the DSM: A psychological perspective* (pp. 69–105). Washington, DC: American Psychological Association.
Piedmont, R.L., McCrae, R.R., Riemann, R., & Angleitner, A. (2000). (See References)

Acknowledgments—I am grateful for comments by Levent Dumenci, Masha Ivanova, Rebecca Krukowski, Stephanie McConaughy, Leslie Rescorla, and David Rettew.

Note

1. Address correspondence to Thomas M. Achenbach, Department of Psychiatry, University of Vermont, 1 South Prospect Street, Burlington, VT 05401; e-mail: thomas.achenbach@uvm.edu.

References

Achenbach, T.M., Krukowski, R.A., Dumenci, L., & Ivanova, M.Y. (2005). Assessment of adult psychopathology: Meta-analyses and implications of cross-informant correlations. *Psychological Bulletin, 131*, 361–382.
Achenbach, T.M., McConaughy, S.H., & Howell, C.T. (1987). Child/adolescent behavioral and emotional problems: Implications of cross-informant correlations for situational specificity. *Psychological Bulletin, 101*, 213–232.
Achenbach, T.M., Newhouse, P.A., & Rescorla, L.A. (2004). *Manual for the ASEBA Older Adult Forms & Profiles*. Burlington, VT: University of Vermont, Research Center for Children, Youth, and Families.

Achenbach, T.M., & Rescorla, L.A. (2003). *Manual for the ASEBA Adult Forms & Profiles*. Burlington, VT: University of Vermont, Research Center for Children, Youth, and Families.

American Psychiatric Association. (1980). *Diagnostic and statistical manual of mental disorders* (3rd ed.). Washington, DC: Author.

American Psychiatric Association. (1994). *Diagnostic and statistical manual of mental disorders* (4th ed.). Washington, DC: Author.

De Los Reyes, A., & Kazdin, A.E. (2005). Informant discrepancies in the assessment of childhood psychopathology: A critical review, theoretical framework, and recommendations for further study. *Psychological Bulletin, 131*, 483–509.

Dumenci, L. (2006). *The Psychometric Latent Agreement Model (PLAM) for discrete traits measured by multiple items.* Manuscript submitted for publication.

Magura, S., & Kang, S.-Y. (1996). Validity of self-reported drug use in high risk populations: A meta-analytical review. *Substance Use & Misuse, 31*, 1131–1153.

Meyer, G.J., Finn, S.E., Eyde, L.D., Kay, G.G., Moreland, K.L., Dies, R.R., Eisman, E.J., Kubiszyn, T.W., & Reed, G.M. (2001). Psychological testing and psychological assessment: A review of evidence and issues. *American Psychologist, 56*, 128–165.

Piedmont, R.L., McCrae, R.R., Riemann, R., & Angleitner, A. (2000). On the invalidity of validity scales: Evidence from self-report and observer ratings in volunteer samples. *Journal of Personality and Social Psychology, 78*, 582–593.

Rettew, D., Doyle, A., Achenbach, T.M., Dumenci, L., & Ivanova, I.M. (2006). *Meta-analyses of agreement between clinical evaluations and standardized diagnostic interviews.* Manuscript in preparation.

Section 1: Critical Thinking Questions

1. How does our current diagnostic system facilitate or impede researchers' ability to dissect disorders into more basic processes with simpler biological causes (such as those identified by Lenzenweger and Moses and Barlow)?

2. Lenzenweger describes latent risk factors, or endophenotypes, for schizophrenia, and Krueger and Markon describe latent spectra that underlie a range of common mental disorders. What are the similarities and differences between endophenotypes and internalizing/externalizing spectra?

3. Moses and Barlow argue that generalizablity of treatment effects reveals commonalities across disorders; in what other ways can findings from treatment designs yield information about the etiology and course of mental disorders?

4. Moses and Barlow identify avoidance as a characteristic shared by both depressive and anxiety disorders; how might avoidance fit into the internalizing spectrum described by Krueger and Markon?

5. Achenbach's review indicates that self and informant data on psychological disorders can often be discrepant. In those cases, how can these differing viewpoints be integrated into a more sophisticated perspective on the individual? What type of research is necessary to identify the sources of divergence between self and informant reports?

This article has been reprinted as it originally appeared in *Current Directions in Psychological Science*. Citation information for this article as originally published appears above.

Section 2: Modeling the Influence of Stress and Environmental Factors on Psychopathology

Over the past decade and a half, there has been growing excitement around research programs demonstrating genetic contributions to and biological correlates of psychopathology. Some students might suspect that these paradigms have supplanted research exploring psychosocial influences on psychopathology. To the contrary, explorations of environmental processes relevant to the development, manifestations, and treatment of psychopathology are alive and well, and becoming increasingly sophisticated. The papers in this section provide a wide view of the range of work examining the role of stress, life events, the early home environment, family relationships, and broader contextual factors in psychopathology. Importantly, they also exemplify the range of methods and theoretical models that are brought to bear in modern work on environmental influences.

First, Parent and colleagues describe an influential line of research utilizing animal models of stress in caregiving systems to understand how early home environment or parent — child relationship quality factors might produce conditions for the development of psychopathology. These studies demonstrate one potential pathway whereby decreased quality of parental care leads to greater defensive responses in physiological stress systems; changes in these systems in turn increase vulnerability for a range of physical and psychological illnesses. This paper demonstrates both the elegance and usefulness of animal models, as well as provides an excellent example of modern stress research that incorporates both psychological and biological data.

Similar to Parent et al., two papers in this section describe important aspects of family relationships that are relevant to psychopathology. Fincham reviews the extensive literature on adaptive and maladaptive marital relationships, and describes a variety of methods and paradigms that psychologists have used to understand marital interactions. This paper thoughtfully points out both the advantages and limitations of prior research on marriage, and raises important questions yet to be fully explored in the empirical literature. Hooley's paper reviews the well developed literature on the association between one important construct in the family literature (expressed emotion) and a range of psychopathologies. This review highlights the ubiquitousness of the association between psychiatric course and criticism and overinvolvement from family members. This paper pinpoints more molecular variables that may be causally involved in relapse and maintenance of treatment gains, and provides a nice example of research that with relevance cutting across both basic psychopathology and intervention.

Lucas' review describes a more traditional focus of stress research — the influence of objective life events upon subjective well-being. This paper nicely discusses the role of both individual difference factors in exposure and response to life events, as well as the ways in which life events create transitions that facilitate long-term changes within individuals.

Finally, Cutrona and colleagues introduce a much broader lens on environmental influences, reviewing studies demonstrating a correlation between characteristics of neighborhoods and levels of depression in residents. This paper introduces some possible mechanisms by which aspects of neighborhoods (such as structural resources, community support, and socioeconomic makeup) may exert an influence on depression in individuals. These findings challenge students to think about environmental influences more distal to individuals' immediate circumstances and social network, and provide an introduction to the idea of larger contextual influences on psychopathology and potential public health implications of this work.

Maternal Care and Individual Differences in Defensive Responses

Carine Parent, Tie-Yuan Zhang, Christian Caldji,
Rose Bagot, Frances A. Champagne, Jens Pruessner,
and Michael J. Meaney[1]
*McGill Program for the Study of Behavior, Genes and Environment,
Douglas Hospital Research Centre, Departments of Psychiatry
and Neurology & Neurosurgery, McGill University, Montreal,
Quebec, Canada*

Abstract

Familial transmission of mental illness is common. Recent studies in behavioral neuroscience and biological psychiatry reveal the importance of epigenetic mechanisms of transmission that center on the developmental consequences of variations in parental care. Studies with rats suggest that environmental adversity results in patterns of parent–offspring interactions that increase stress reactivity through sustained effects on gene expression in brain regions known to regulate behavioral, endocrine, and autonomic responses to stress. While such effects might be adaptive, the associated cost involves an increased risk for stress-related illness.

Keywords

maternal care; stress responses; epigenesis; stress hormones; individual differences

To explain the relation between family function and health in adulthood, researchers have proposed stress-diathesis models (Repetti, Taylor, & Seeman, 2002). These models suggest that a decreased quality of parental care alters the development of neural and endocrine systems, increasing the magnitude of emotional, autonomic, and endocrine responses to stress (collectively referred to here as defensive responses) and thus predisposing individuals to illness. The term diathesis refers to the interaction between development—including the potential influence of genetic variations—and the prevailing level of stress experienced by an individual in predicting health outcomes. Such models have considerable appeal, and could identify both the origins of illness and the nature of underlying vulnerabilities.

A critical assumption of stress-diathesis models is that the increased expression of defensive responses endangers health. In response to neural signals associated with the perception of a stressor, there is an increased release into the bloodstream of stress hormones, including glucocorticoids from the adrenal gland and catecholamines, particularly norepinephrine, from the sympathetic nervous system. These hormones increase the availability of energy (such as derived from fat and glucose metabolism) to maintain the normal cellular output and organ efficiency and protect against catastrophies such as hypotensive shock (a crash in blood pressure). These stress hormones, along with the release of catecholamines in the brain, increase vigilance and fear and enhance adaptive processes such as avoidance learning and fear conditioning. However, there are costs associated with chronic activation of stress hormones: chronically enhanced emotional arousal, persistent increases in blood sugars and fats, and disruption of sleep and normal cognitive and emotional function. For this reason, chronic activation of defensive responses can predispose individuals to illnesses such as diabetes, heart disease, and mood disorders, and individuals with enhanced stress reactivity are at greater risk for chronic illness. However, insufficient activation of defensive responses under appropriate conditions also compromises health and is associated with chronic fatigue, chronic pain, and hyperinflammation. People walk a fine line.

THE ORIGINS OF INDIVIDUAL DIFFERENCES IN DEFENSIVE RESPONSES

In the late 1950s and early 1960s, psychologists Seymore Levine and Victor Denenberg reported that postnatal handling of infant rats or mice by researchers decreased the magnitude of both behavioral and hypothalamic-pituitary-adrenal (HPA) responses to stress in adulthood (see Fig. 1). These findings demonstrated the influence of the early environment on the development of rudimentary defensive responses to threat. Levine and others suggested that the effects of handling are actually mediated by changes in maternal care. Indeed handling by the researcher increases the licking and grooming of pups by the mother (e.g., Liu et al., 1997), a major source of tactile stimulation for newborn rats. Subsequent studies examining the consequences of naturally occurring variations in pup licking and grooming among lactating rats support the maternal-mediation hypothesis. Thus, the adult offspring of mothers that naturally exhibit increased levels of pup licking and grooming (high-LG mothers) resemble postnatally handled animals on measures of behavioral and endocrine responses to stress, while those of low-LG mothers are comparable to animals that weren't handled (Liu et al., 1997; Caldji et al., 1998). Specifically, the offspring of high-LG mothers show reduced fearfulness and more modest HPA responses to stress. Cross-fostering studies, in which pups born to high-LG mothers are raised by low-LG mothers (and vice versa), suggest a direct relationship between maternal care and the postnatal development of individual differences in behavioral and HPA responses to stress (Francis, Diorio, Liu, & Meaney, 1999).

It is important to note that, in these rodent studies, the experimental design is one that maximizes the chances of detecting maternal effects. Following weaning, animals are housed under very stable laboratory conditions. Although the maternal effects are certainly reliable, the environmental complexity of a real natural setting that would normally be experienced in the post-weaning period might obscure such effects. Nevertheless, these studies also suggest that rather subtle variations within a normal range of parental care can dramatically alter development. In large measure, this is likely due to the fact that natural selection has shaped offspring to respond to subtle variations in parental behaviors as a forecast of the environmental conditions they will ultimately face following independence from the parent (Hinde 1986).

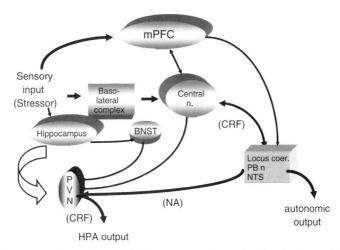

Fig. 1. Systems involving the peptide hormone corticotropin-releasing factor (CRF) that mediate defensive responses to stress in mammals. CRF is released from neurons in the paraventricular hypothalamus (PVN) into the blood supply of the pituitary, activating a hypothalamic–pituitary–adrenal (HPA) response that includes the release of pituitary adrenocorticotropin and glucocorticoids from the adrenal gland. CRF production and release is subsequently inhibited through a negative-feedback system involving the action of glucocorticoids in a number of brain regions including the hippocampus. CRF is also produced in the neurons of the central nucleus of the amygdala and the bed nucleus of the stria terminalis (BNST) that project directly to the locus coeruleus and nucleus tractus solitarius (NTS)/parabrachial nucleus (PBn), stimulating the increased release of noradrenaline (NA) throughout the forebrain, including the medial prefrontal cortex (mPFC) and the PVN.

The effects of maternal care on the development of defensive responses to stress in rats involve alterations in the production and activity of a hormone called corticotropin-releasing factor (CRF; Fig. 1) in brain regions that activate behavioral, emotional, autonomic, and endocrine responses to stressors. As adults, the offspring of high-LG mothers showed decreased CRF production in the hypothalamus, as well as reduced plasma adrenocorticotropin (ACTH) and glucocorticoid responses to acute stress, as compared with the adult offspring of low-LG mothers (Liu et al., 1997). The offspring of the high- and low-LG mothers also differed in behavioral responses to novelty (Caldji et al., 1998; Francis et al., 1999). As adults, the offspring of high-LG mothers showed decreased startle responses, substantially less fear in novel environments, and decreased defensive burying of an electrified probe placed into the home cage.

Increased pup licking and grooming is associated with enhanced sensitivity in systems that inhibit CRF expression, including the hippocampal glucocorticoid receptor and the receptor for the neurotransmitter GABA$_A$ in the amygdala. Both effects involve sustained alterations in gene expression (or activity) as a function of maternal care. The complexity of such maternal effects on gene expression is apparent in the alterations in GABA$_A$ receptor function. The adult offspring of high-LG mothers show significantly increased expression of specific proteins within this receptor that increase its function of inhibiting CRF expression; this effect is unique to the amygdala and is reversed with cross-fostering. Thus, for both the gluco-corticoid-receptor feedback system and the $GABA_A$ receptor there is an increased capacity for the inhibition of stress responses as a function of maternal licking and grooming. These findings suggest that maternal care can "program" responses to stress in the offspring through effects on the expression of genes in brain regions that mediate responses to stress. These findings provide a potential mechanism for the influence of parental care on vulnerability or resistance to stress-induced illness over the lifespan.

TRANSGENERATIONAL EFFECTS

Maternal effects might serve as a possible nongenomic, or *epigenetic*, mechanism by which selected traits are transmitted across generations. Indeed, low-LG mothers are more fearful than high-LG mothers are: Fearful mothers beget more stress-reactive offspring. The question concerns the mode of inheritance. The results of cross-fostering studies cited above indicate that individual differences in stress reactivity or in the expression of relevant genes can be directly altered by maternal behavior. A critical finding of the cross-fostering studies is that individual differences in maternal behavior are also transmitted from mothers to female offspring. Hence, the female offspring of more fearful, low-LG mothers are, as adults, more fearful, low-LG mothers. The mechanism for the intergenerational transmission of such individual differences is the difference in pup licking and grooming.

Variations in pup licking and grooming involve individual differences in estrogen-receptor-gene expression in the medial preoptic area (MPOA) of the hypothalamus, a region that is critical for maternal behavior in the rat. Estrogen increases oxytocin-receptor levels in this region; oxytocin appears to act there to facilitate the release of dopamine from neurons in another region called the ventral tegmental nucleus. The increased dopamine release activates maternal licking and grooming (Champagne, Stevenson, Gratton, & Meaney, 2004). Infusing an oxytocin-receptor antagonist directly into the brain completely eliminates the differences in maternal behavior between high- and low-LG mothers. And again, differences in estrogen-receptor expression or in oxytocin-receptor levels are reversed with cross-fostering, suggesting that maternal care regulates the activity of the estrogen receptor, forming the basis for subsequent "inherited" differences in maternal behavior (Champagne, Weaver, Diorio, Sharma, & Meaney, 2003).

ADAPTIVE VALUE OF ENHANCED STRESS
REACTIVITY IN MAMMALS

The interesting question is, why bother? Why would nature configure such a process? Why transmit individual differences in stress reactivity across generations?

Environmental adversity influences emotional well-being in parents, and these effects are reflected in alterations in parental care. In humans, parental depression and anxiety are associated with harsh, inconsistent discipline, neglect, and abuse, which can enhance stress reactivity of the offspring. In other words, the anxiety of parents is transmitted to their offspring. Since offspring usually inhabit an environment that is similar to their parents, the transmission of individual differences in traits from parent to offspring could be adaptive with respect to survival. Adversity over the adult life of the parent is likely to predict more of the same for the offspring. Under conditions of increased environmental demand, it is commonly in the animal's interest to enhance its behavioral (e.g., vigilance, fearfulness) and endocrine (HPA and metabolic/cardiovascular) responses to stress. These responses promote detection of potential threats, fear conditioning to stimuli associated with threats, and avoidance learning. Moreover, stress hormones mobilize energy reserves, essential for animals exposed to famine. Impoverished environments are also commonly associated with multiple sources of infection, and adrenal glucocorticoids are a potent defense against increased immunological activity that can lead to septic shock (organ failure). Rats with increased HPA responses to bacteria are at reduced risk for septic shock. These findings underscore the potentially adaptive value of increased HPA responses to threat.

THE EFFECTS OF STRESS ON MATERNAL BEHAVIOR IN MAMMALS

If parent–offspring interactions are to serve as a forecast for the young, then there must be a predictable relation between the quality of the environment and parental care. Perhaps the most compelling evidence for such a relation emerges from the studies of Rosenblum, Coplan, and colleagues with nonhuman primates (Coplan et al., 1996). In Bonnet macaque mother–infant pairs kept in conditions requiring extensive maternal effort to obtain food, there were severe disruptions in the quality of mother–infant interactions. Infants of mothers housed under these conditions were more timid and fearful and, even while in contact with their mothers, actually showed signs of depression commonly observed in infants who have been separated from their mothers. As adolescents, the infants reared in the more demanding conditions were more fearful and submissive and showed less social-play behavior. As expected, these conditions affected the development of neural systems that mediate behavioral and endocrine response to stress, increasing their CRF levels and their noradrenergic responses to stress. It will be fascinating to see if these traits are then transmitted to the next generation.

The critical issue is the effect of environmental adversity on maternal behavior. High-LG rat mothers exposed daily to stress during pregnancy showed a decrease in their licking and grooming to levels comparable to those of low-LG mothers. And the effects on maternal behavior were apparent in the offspring. As adults, the offspring of high-LG mothers who had been ges-tationally stressed were comparable to those of low-LG mothers on measures of behavioral responses to stress. These effects were due to a "prenatal stress" effect, as the decreased maternal licking and grooming and the same developmental scenario were apparent in a subsequent litter, even in the absence of any further experimental manipulation. The effects of gestational stress were also apparent in the maternal behavior of the female offspring. The female offspring of high-LG mothers exposed to gestational stress, even in a previous pregnancy, behaved toward their pups in a manner consistent with the behavior of their mothers; as adults, these females were low-LG mothers with reduced levels of oxytocin-receptor binding in the MPOA. Hence the effects of environmental adversity are transmitted from parent to offspring.

IMPLICATIONS

The question of vulnerability lies very much at the heart of research on anxiety disorders such as posttraumatic stress disorder (PTSD). Surprisingly, only a minority (roughly 20–30%) of people subjected to profound trauma develop PTSD, and early family life serves as a highly significant predictor of vulnerability to PTSD following trauma. These findings suggest that early-life events might alter the development of neural systems in brain regions that mediate emotional and cognitive responses to adversity and thus contribute to individual differences in vulnerability to anxiety disorders. Childhood abuse significantly alters autonomic and HPA responses to stress (Heim et al., 2000); and there is evidence for more subtle effects that do not involve stressors as extreme as persistent neglect or abuse. For example, Maternal Care scores on the Parental Bonding Index predict trait anxiety, HPA responses to stress, and stress-induced activation of the brain catecholamine system (Pruessner, Champagne, Meaney & Dagher, 2004).

There is also evidence that vulnerability to anxiety disorders may be transmitted from generation to generation. Yehuda et al. (2000) found that the adult offspring of Holocaust survivors exhibited altered HPA function and were at increased risk for PTSD. More recent studies suggest that the intergenerational transmission of the risk for PTSD in this population is mediated by alterations in parental care. This finding is consistent with earlier studies revealing that anxiety is a strong, negative predictor of maternal responsiveness in humans.

Recent studies reflect the potential for the epigenetic transmission of individual differences in behavior and gene expression from parent to offspring. Studies with humans and nonhuman primates show that variants of the serotonin-transporter gene (which metabolizes serotonin) are associated with forms of temperament that predispose individuals to depression and alcoholism (Bennett et al., 2002; Caspi et al., 2003). However, this effect is modified by environmental conditions, especially the availability of parent–offspring interactions, prevailing during early development. In macaques, normal mother–infant relations reduced the risk for impaired serotonin metabolism and impulse control that is otherwise associated with the serotonin-transporter variant. These findings remind us that measures of heritability, by definition, reflect both variation in the genome and interactions between genes and the environment.

Traits that render individuals vulnerable for psychopathology emerge as a function of the constant interaction of genes and environment over the course of development. Indeed, there is currently considerable confusion in distinguishing the characteristics of pathology from those of developmentally determined vulnerabilities. In a study involving Vietnam veterans and their twins, Gilbertson et al. (2002) found that individuals who experienced combat service in Vietnam and developed PTSD showed reduced hippocampal volume by comparison to those with a similar military history but no PTSD; importantly, the twins who never served in Vietnam or showed PTSD showed the same difference, suggesting that the reduced hippocampal volume is a trait that preceded the PTSD. These and other studies focus researchers on the developmental origins of psychopathology and on critical questions, such as how reduced hippocampal volume or other neurobiological aspects of phenotypes might render individuals vulnerable to psychopathology.

Nowhere is the interplay between genes and environment more evident than in the relationships that exist between family environment and vulnerability or resistance to chronic illness. Vulnerability for mental illness is increased by a wide range of risk factors that are common in families living in conditions of adversity, such as low socioeconomic status. These risk factors include genetic variations, complications of pregnancy and birth, familial dysfunction, child abuse and neglect, and maternal depression. Such factors define "risky" families (Repetti, Taylor, & Seeman, 2002). All forms of mental disorders are "familial"—they run in families—and the mechanisms by which vulnerability is transmitted from parent to offspring involve both genomic and epigenetic processes of transmission. The challenge is to clearly define the mechanisms of transmission; the reward would be the ability to identify remarkably effective targets for prevention. Of particular interest are the parent–child relations that define family life and the mechanisms by which the effects of family life become "biologically embedded," thereby influencing vulnerability and resistance. We (Weaver et al., 2004) recently described the effect of maternal care on the structure (not sequence) of the DNA that regulates the activity of the gene encoding for the glucocorticoid receptor in the hippocampus. These epigenetic modifications of the DNA regulate glucocorticoid-receptor expression and thus HPA responses to stress. Such findings might illustrate the processes by which a dynamic environment interacts with a fixed genome to produce a phenotype. Understanding such processes requires not only the relevant biological tools but a clear understanding of the relevant environmental signals. Obviously, such studies will require a commitment to research at the biological, psychological, and social levels of analysis.

Recommended Reading

McEwen, B.S. (1998). Protective and damaging effects of stress mediators. *New England Journal of Medicine, 338,* 171–179.
Meaney, M.J. (2001). The development of individual differences in behavioral and endocrine responses to stress. *Annual Reviews of Neuroscience, 24,* 1161–1192.
Repetti, R.L., Taylor, S.E., Seeman, T.E. (2002). (See References)

Acknowledgments—The authors' research is supported by grants from the Canadian Institutes for Health Research, the Natural Sciences and Engineering Research Council of Canada, and the National Institutes of Health, and by career awards from the Canadian Institutes for Health Research and the National Alliance for Research on Schizophrenia and Related Disorders.

Note

1. Address correspondence to Michael J. Meaney, McGill Program for the Study of Behaviour, Genes and Environment, Douglas Hospital Research Centre, 6875 boul. LaSalle, Montréal, Québec, Canada H4H 1R3; e-mail: michael.meaney@mcgill.ca.

References

Bennett, A.J., Lesch, K.P., Heils, A., Long, J.C., Lorenz, J.G., Shoaf, S.E., Champoux, M., Suomi, S.J., Linnoila, M.V., & Higley, J.D. (2002). Early experience and serotonin transporter gene variation interact to influence primate CNS function. *Molecular Psychiatry, 7*, 118–122.

Caldji, C., Tannenbaum, B., Sharma, S., Francis, D., Plotsky, P.M., & Meaney, M.J. (1998). Maternal care during infancy regulates the development of neural systems mediating the expression of behavioral fearfulness in adulthood in the rat. *Proceedings of the National Academy of Sciences USA, 95*, 5335–5340.

Caspi, A., Sugden, K., Moffitt, T.E., Taylor, A., Craig, I.W., Harrington, H., McClay, J., Mill, J., Martin, J., Braithwaite, A., & Poulton, R. (2003). Influence of life stress on depression: Moderation by a polymorphism in the 5-HTT gene. *Science, 301*, 386–390.

Champagne, F.A., Stevenson, C., Gratton, A., & Meaney, M.J. (2004). Individual differences in maternal behavior are mediated by dopamine release in the nucleus accumbens. *Journal of Neuroscience, 24*, 4113–4123.

Champagne, F.A., Weaver, I.C.G., Diorio, J., Sharma, S., & Meaney, M.J. (2003). Natural Variations in Maternal Care are associated with Estrogen Receptor Alpha Expression and Estrogen Sensitivity in the MPOA. *Endocrinology, 144*, 4720–4724.

Coplan, J.D., Andrews, M.W., Rosenblum, L.A., Owens, M.J., Friedman, S., Gorman, J.M., & Nemeroff, C.B. (1996). Persistent elevations of cerebrospinal fluid concentrations of corticotropin-releasing factor in adult nonhuman primates exposed to early-life stressors: Implications for the pathophysiology of mood and anxiety disorders. *Proceedings of the National Academy of Sciences USA, 93*, 1619–1623.

Francis, D.D., Diorio, J., Liu, D., & Meaney, M.J. (1999). Nongenomic transmission across generations in maternal behavior and stress responses in the rat. *Science, 286*, 1155–1158.

Gilbertson, M.W., Shenton, E., Ciszewski, A., Kasai, K., Lasko, N.B., Orr, S.P., & Pitman, R.K. (2002). Smaller hippocampal volume predicts pathologic vulnerability to psychological trauma. *Nature Neuroscience, 5*, 1242–1247.

Heim, C., Newport, D.J., Heit, S., Graham, Y.P., Wilcox, M., Bonsall, R., Miller, A.H., & Nemeroff, C.B. (2000). Pituitary-adrenal and autonomic responses to stress in women after sexual and physical abuse in childhood. *Journal of the American Medical Association, 284*, 592–597.

Hinde, R.A. (1986). Some implications of evolutionary theory and comparative data for the study of human prosocial and aggressive behaviour. In D. Olweus, J. Block, & M. Radke-Yarrow (Eds.), *Development of anti-social and prosocial behaviour* (pp. 13–32). Orlando: Academic Press.

Liu, D., Tannenbaum, B., Caldji, C., Francis, D., Freedman, A., Sharma, S., Pearson, D., Plotsky, P.M., & Meaney, M.J. (1997). Maternal care, hippocampal glucocorticoid receptor gene expression and hypothalamic-pituitary-adrenal responses to stress. *Science, 277*, 1659–1662.

Pruessner, J.L., Champagne, F.A., Meaney, M.J., & Dagher, A. (2004). Parental care and neuroendocrine and dopamine responses to stress in humans: A PET imaging study. *Journal of Neuroscience, 24*, 2825–2831.

Repetti, R.L., Taylor, S.E., & Seeman, T.E. (2002). Risky families: Family social environments and the mental and physical health of offspring. *Psychological Bulletin, 128*, 330–366.

Weaver, I.C.G., Cervoni, N., D'Alessio, A.C., Champagne, F.A., Seckl, J.R., Szyf, M., & Meaney, M.J. (2004). Epigenetic programming through maternal behavior. *Nature Neuroscience, 7*, 847–854.

Yehuda, R., Bierer, L.M., Schmeidler, J., Aferiat, D.H., Breslau, I., & Dolan, S. (2000). Low cortisol and risk for PTSD in adult offspring of Holocaust survivors. *American Journal of Psychiatry, 157*, 1252–1259.

This article has been reprinted as it originally appeared in *Current Directions in Psychological Science*. Citation information for this article as originally published appears above.

Marital Conflict: Correlates, Structure, and Context

Frank D. Fincham[1]
Psychology Department, University at Buffalo, Buffalo, New York

Abstract

Marital conflict has deleterious effects on mental, physical, and family health, and three decades of research have yielded a detailed picture of the behaviors that differentiate distressed from nondistressed couples. Review of this work shows that the singular emphasis on conflict in generating marital outcomes has yielded an incomplete picture of its role in marriage. Recently, researchers have tried to paint a more textured picture of marital conflict by studying spouses' backgrounds and characteristics, investigating conflict in the contexts of support giving and affectional expression, and considering the ecological niche of couples in their broader environment.

Keywords

conflict patterns; marital distress; support

Systematic psychological research on marriage emerged largely among clinical psychologists who wanted to better assist couples experiencing marital distress. In the 30 years since this development, marital conflict has assumed a special status in the literature on marriage, as evidenced by three indices. First, many of the most influential theories of marriage tend to reflect the view that "distress results from couples' aversive and ineffectual response to conflict" (Koerner & Jacobson, 1994, p. 208). Second, research on marriage has focused on what spouses do when they disagree with each other, and reviews of marital interaction are dominated by studies of conflict and problem solving (see Weiss & Heyman, 1997). Third, psychological interventions for distressed couples often target conflict-resolution skills (see Baucom, Shoham, Mueser, Daiuto, & Stickle, 1998).

IS MARITAL CONFLICT IMPORTANT?

The attention given marital conflict is understandable when we consider its implications for mental, physical, and family health. Marital conflict has been linked to the onset of depressive symptoms, eating disorders, male alcoholism, episodic drinking, binge drinking, and out-of-home drinking. Although married individuals are healthier on average than the unmarried, marital conflict is associated with poorer health and with specific illnesses such as cancer, cardiac disease, and chronic pain, perhaps because hostile behaviors during conflict are related to alterations in immunological, endocrine, and cardiovascular functioning. Physical aggression occurs in about 30% of married couples in the United States, leading to significant physical injury in about 10% of couples. Marriage is also the most common interpersonal context for homicide, and more women are murdered by their partners than by anyone else. Finally, marital conflict is associated with important family outcomes, including poor parenting, poor adjustment of children, increased likelihood of parent-child conflict, and conflict between siblings. Marital conflicts that are frequent, intense, physical, unresolved, and child related have a particularly negative influence on children, as do marital conflicts that spouses attribute to their child's behavior (see Grych & Fincham, 2001).

WHAT ARE MARITAL CONFLICTS ABOUT?

Marital conflicts can be about virtually anything. Couples complain about sources of conflict ranging from verbal and physical abusiveness to personal characteristics and behaviors. Perceived inequity in a couple's division of labor is associated with marital conflict and with a tendency for the male to withdraw in response to conflict. Conflict over power is also strongly related to marital dissatisfaction. Spouses' reports of conflict over extramarital sex, problematic drinking, or drug use predict divorce, as do wives' reports of husbands being jealous and spending money foolishly. Greater problem severity increases the likelihood of divorce. Even though it is often not reported to be a problem by couples, violence among newlyweds is a predictor of divorce, as is psychological aggression (verbal aggression and nonverbal aggressive behaviors that are not directed at the partner's body).

HOW DO SPOUSES BEHAVE DURING CONFLICT?

Stimulated, in part, by the view that "studying what people say about themselves is no substitute for studying how they behave" (Raush, Barry, Hertel, & Swain, 1974, p. 5), psychologists have conducted observational studies, with the underlying hope of identifying dysfunctional behaviors that could be modified in couple therapy. This research has focused on problem-solving discussions in the laboratory and provides detailed information about how maritally distressed and nondistressed couples behave during conflict.

During conflict, distressed couples make more negative statements and fewer positive statements than nondistressed couples. They are also more likely to respond with negative behavior when their partner behaves negatively. Indeed, this negative reciprocity, as it is called, is more consistent across different types of situations than is the amount of negative behavior, making it the most reliable overt signature of marital distress. Negative behavior is both more frequent and more frequently reciprocated in couples that engage in physical aggression than in other couples. Nonverbal behavior, often used as an index of emotion, reflects marital satisfaction better than verbal behavior, and unlike verbal behavior does not change when spouses try to fake good and bad marriages.

Are There Typical Patterns of Conflict Behavior?

The sequences of behavior that occur during conflict are more predictable in distressed than in nondistressed marriages and are often dominated by chains of negative behavior that usually escalate and are difficult for the couple to stop. One of the greatest challenges for couples locked into negative exchanges is to find an adaptive way of exiting from such cycles. This is usually attempted through responses that are designed to repair the interaction (e.g., "You're not listening to me") but are delivered with negative affect (e.g., irritation, sadness). The partners tend to respond to the negative affect, thereby continuing the cycle. This makes their interactions structured and predictable. In contrast, nondistressed couples appear to be more responsive to attempts at repair and are thereby able to exit from negative exchanges early on. For example, a spouse may respond to "Wait, you're not letting me finish" with "Sorry . . . please finish what you were saying." Their interaction therefore appears more random and less predicable.

A second important behavior pattern exhibited by maritally distressed couples is the demand-withdraw pattern, in which one spouse pressures the other with demands, complaints, and criticisms, while the partner withdraws with defensiveness and passive inaction. Specifically, behavior sequences in which the husband withdraws and the wife responds with hostility are more common in distressed than in satisfied couples. This finding is consistent with several studies showing that wives display more negative affect and behavior than husbands, who tend to not respond or to make statements suggestive of withdrawal, such as irrelevant comments. Disengagement or withdrawal is, in turn, related to later decreases in marital satisfaction. However, inferring reliable gender differences in demand-withdraw patterns would be premature, as recent research shows that the partner who withdraws varies according to which partner desires change. So, for example, when a man desires change, the woman is the one who withdraws. Finally, conflict patterns seem to be relatively stable over time (see Karney & Bradbury, 1995).

Is There a Simple Way to Summarize Research Findings on Marital Conflict?

The findings of the extensive literature on marital conflict can be summarized in terms of a simple ratio: The ratio of agreements to disagreements is greater than 1 for happy couples and less than 1 for unhappy couples. Gottman (1993) utilized this ratio to identify couple types. He observed husbands and wives during conversation, recording each spouse's positive and negative behaviors while speaking, and then calculated the cumulative difference between positive and negative behaviors over time for each spouse. Using the patterns in these difference scores, he distinguished regulated couples (increase in positive speaker behaviors relative to negative behaviors for both spouses over the course of conversation) from nonregulated couples (all other patterns). The regulated couples were more satisfied in their marriage than the non-regulated couples, and also less likely to divorce. Regulated couples displayed positive problem-solving behaviors and positive affect approximately 5 times as often as negative problem-solving behaviors and negative affect, whereas the corresponding ratio was approximately 1:1 for nonregulated couples.

Interestingly, Gottman's perspective corresponds with the findings of two early, often overlooked studies on the reported frequency of sexual intercourse and of marital arguments (Howard & Dawes, 1976; Thornton, 1977). Both showed that the ratio of sexual intercourse to arguments, rather than their base rates, predicted marital satisfaction.

Don't Research Findings on Marital Conflict Just Reflect Common Sense?

The findings described in this article may seem like common sense. However, what we have learned about marital interaction contradicts the long-standing belief that satisfied couples are characterized by a *quid pro quo* principle according to which they exchange positive behavior and instead show that it is dissatisfied spouses who reciprocate one another's (negative) behavior. The astute reader may also be wondering whether couples' behavior in the artificial setting of the laboratory is a good reflection of their behavior in the real world outside the lab. It is therefore important to note that couples who participate in such studies themselves report that their interactions in the lab are reminiscent of their typical interactions. Research also shows that conflict behavior in the lab is similar to conflict behavior in the home; however, laboratory conflicts tend to be less severe, suggesting that research findings underestimate differences between distressed and nondistressed couples.

THE SEEDS OF DISCONTENT

By the early 1980s, researchers were attempting to address the limits of a purely behavioral account of marital conflict. Thus, they began to pay attention to subjective factors, such as thoughts and feelings, which might influence behavioral interactions or the relation between behavior and marital satisfaction. For example, it is now well documented that the tendency to explain a partner's negative behavior (e.g., coming home late from work) in a way that promotes conflict (e.g., "he thinks only about himself and his needs"), rather than in less conflictual ways (e.g., "he was probably caught in traffic"), is related to less effective problem solving, more negative communication in problem-solving discussions, more displays of specific negative affects (e.g., anger) during problem solving, and steeper declines in marital satisfaction over time (Fincham, 2001). Explanations that promote conflict are also related to the tendency to reciprocate a partner's negative behavior, regardless of a couple's marital satisfaction. Research on such subjective factors, like observational research on conflict, has continued to the present time. However, it represents an acceptance and expansion of the behavioral approach that accords conflict a central role in understanding marriage.

In contrast, very recently, some investigators have argued that the role of conflict in marriage should be reconsidered. Longitudinal research shows that conflict accounts for a relatively small portion of the variability in later marital outcomes, suggesting that other factors need to be considered in predicting these outcomes (see Karney & Bradbury, 1995). In addition, studies have demonstrated a troubling number of "reversal effects" (showing that greater conflict is a predictor of improved marriage; see Fincham & Beach, 1999). It is difficult to account for such findings in a field that, for much of its existence, has focused on providing descriptive data at the expense of building theory.

Rethinking the role of conflict also reflects recognition of the fact that most of what we know about conflict behavior comes from observation of problem-solving discussions and that couples experience verbal problem-solving situations infrequently; about 80% of couples report having overt disagreements once a month or less. As a result, cross-sectional studies of distressed versus non-distressed marriages and longitudinal studies of conflict are being increasingly complemented by research designs that focus on how happy marriages become unhappy.

Finally, there is evidence that marital conflict varies according to contextual factors. For example, diary studies illustrate that couples have more stressful marital interactions at home on days of high general life stress than on other days, and at times and places where they are experiencing multiple competing demands; arguments at work are related to marital arguments, and the occurrence of stressful life events is associated with more conflictual problem-solving discussions.

NEW BEGINNINGS: CONFLICT IN CONTEXT

Although domains of interaction other than conflict (e.g., support, companionship) have long been discussed in the marital literature, they are only now emerging from the secondary status accorded to them. This is somewhat ironic given the simple summary of research findings on marital conflict offered earlier, which points to the importance of the context in which conflict occurs.

Conflict in the Context of Support Giving and Affectional Expression

Observational laboratory methods have recently been developed to assess supportive behaviors in interactions in which one spouse talks about a personal issue he or she would like to change and the other is asked to respond as she or he normally would. Behaviors exhibited during such support tasks are only weakly related to the conflict behaviors observed during the problem-solving discussions used to study marital conflict. Supportive spouse behavior is associated with greater marital satisfaction and is more important than negative behavior in determining how supportive the partners perceive an interaction to be. In addition, the amount of supportive behavior partners exhibit is a predictor of later marital stress (i.e., more supportive behavior correlates with less future marital stress), independently of conflict behavior, and when support is poor, there is an increased risk that poor skills in dealing with conflict will lead to later marital deterioration. There is also evidence that support obtained by spouses outside the marriage can influence positively how the spouse behaves within the marriage.

In the context of high levels of affectional expression between spouses, the association between spouses' negative behavior and marital satisfaction decreases significantly. High levels of positive behavior in problem-solving discussions also mitigate the effect of withdrawal or disengagement on later marital satisfaction. Finally, when there are high levels of affectional expression between spouses, the demand-withdraw pattern is unrelated to marital satisfaction, but when affectional expression is average or low, the demand-withdraw pattern is associated with marital dissatisfaction.

Conflict in the Context of Spouses' Backgrounds and Characteristics

Focus on interpersonal behavior as the cause of marital outcomes led to the assumption that the characteristics of individual spouses play no role in those outcomes. However, increasing evidence that contradicts this assumption has generated recent interest in studying how spouses' backgrounds and characteristics might enrich our understanding of marital conflict.

The importance of spouses' characteristics is poignantly illustrated in the intergenerational transmission of divorce. Although there is a tendency for individuals whose parents divorced to get divorced themselves, this tendency varies depending on the offspring's behavior. Divorce rates are higher for offspring who behave in hostile, domineering, and critical ways, compared with offspring who do not behave in this manner.

An individual characteristic that is proving to be particularly informative for understanding marriage comes from recent research on attachment, which aims to address questions about how the experience of relationships early in life affects interpersonal functioning in adulthood. For example, spouses who tend to feel secure in relationships tend to compromise and to take into account both their own and their partner's interests during problem-solving interactions; those who tend to feel anxious or ambivalent in relationships show a greater tendency to oblige their partner, and focus on relationship maintenance, than do those who tend to avoid intimacy in relationships. And spouses who are preoccupied with being completely emotionally intimate in relationships show an elevated level of marital conflict after an involuntary, brief separation from the partner.

Of particular interest for understanding negative reciprocity are the findings that greater commitment is associated with more constructive, accommodative responses to a partner's negative behavior and that the dispositional tendency to forgive is a predictor of spouses' responses to their partners' transgressions; spouses having a greater tendency to forgive are less likely to avoid the partner or retaliate in kind following a transgression by the partner. Indeed, spouses themselves acknowledge that the capacity to seek and grant forgiveness is one of the most important factors contributing to marital longevity and satisfaction.

Conflict in the Context of the Broader Environment

The environments in which marriages are situated and the intersection between interior processes and external factors that impinge upon marriage are important to consider in painting a more textured picture of marital conflict. This is because problem-solving skills and conflict may have little impact on a marriage in the absence of external stressors. External stressors also may influence marriages directly. In particular, non-marital stressors may lead to an increased number of negative interactions, as illustrated by the fact that economic stress is associated with marital conflict. There is a growing need to identify the stressors and life events that are and are not influential for different couples and for different stages of marriage, to investigate how these events influence conflict, and to clarify how individuals and marriages may inadvertently generate stressful events. In fact, Bradbury, Rogge, and Lawrence (2001), in considering the ecological niche of the couple (i.e., their life events, family constellation, socioeconomic standing, and stressful circumstances), have recently argued that it may be "at least as important to examine the struggle that exists between the couple . . . and the environment they inhabit as it is to examine the interpersonal struggles that are the focus of our work [observation of conflict]" (p. 76).

CONCLUSION

The assumption that conflict management is the key to successful marriage and that conflict skills can be modified in couple therapy has proved useful in propelling the study of marriage into the mainstream of psychology. However, it may have outlived its usefulness, and some researchers are now calling for greater attention to other mechanisms (e.g., spousal social support) that might be responsible for marital outcomes. Indeed, controversy over whether conflict has beneficial or detrimental effects on marriage over time is responsible, in part, for the recent upsurge in longitudinal research on marriage. Notwithstanding diverse opinions on just how central conflict is for understanding marriage, current efforts to study conflict in a broader marital context, which is itself seen as situated in a broader ecological niche, bode well for advancing understanding and leading to more powerful preventive and therapeutic interventions.

Recommended Reading

Bradbury, T.N., Fincham, F.D., & Beach, S.R.H. (2000). Research on the nature and determinants of marital satisfaction: A decade in review. *Journal of Marriage and the Family, 62,* 964–980.
Fincham, F.D., & Beach, S.R. (1999). (See References)
Grych, J.H., & Fincham, F.D. (Eds.). (2001). (See References)
Karney, B.R., & Bradbury, T.N. (1995). (See References)

Acknowledgments—This article was written while the author was supported by grants from the Templeton, Margaret L. Wendt, and J.M. McDonald Foundations.

Note

1. Address correspondence to Frank D. Fincham, Department of Psychology, University at Buffalo, Buffalo, NY 14260.

References

Baucom, D.H., Shoham, V., Mueser, K.T., Daiuto, A.D., & Stickle, T.R. (1998). Empirically supported couple and family interventions for marital distress and adult mental health problems. *Journal of Consulting and Clinical Psychology, 66,* 53–88.
Bradbury, T.N., Rogge, R., & Lawrence, E. (2001). Reconsidering the role of conflict in marriage. In A. Booth, A.C. Crouter, & M. Clements (Eds.), *Couples in conflict* (pp. 59–81). Mahwah, NJ: Erlbaum.
Fincham, F.D. (2001). Attributions and close relationships: From balkanization to integration. In G.J. Fletcher & M. Clark (Eds.), *Blackwell handbook of social psychology* (pp. 3–31). Oxford, England: Blackwell.
Fincham, F.D., & Beach, S.R. (1999). Marital conflict: Implications for working with couples. *Annual Review of Psychology, 50,* 47–77.
Gottman, J.M. (1993). The roles of conflict engagement, escalation, and avoidance in marital interaction: A longitudinal view of five types of couples. *Journal of Consulting and Clinical Psychology, 61,* 6–15.

Grych, J.H., & Fincham, F.D. (Eds.). (2001). *Interpa-rental conflict and child development: Theory, research, and applications.* New York: Cambridge University Press.

Howard, J.W., & Dawes, R.M. (1976). Linear prediction of marital happiness. *Personality and Social Psychology Bulletin, 2,* 478–480.

Karney, B.R., & Bradbury, T.N. (1995). The longitudinal course of marital quality and stability: A review of theory, method, and research. *Psychological Bulletin, 118,* 3–34.

Koerner, K., & Jacobson, N.J. (1994). Emotion and behavior in couple therapy. In S.M. Johnson & L.S. Greenberg (Eds.), *The heart of the matter: Perspectives on emotion in marital therapy* (pp. 207–226). New York: Brunner/Mazel.

Raush, H.L., Barry, W.A., Hertel, R.K., & Swain, M.A. (1974). *Communication, conflict, and marriage.* San Francisco: Jossey-Bass.

Thornton, B. (1977). Toward a linear prediction of marital happiness. *Personality and Social Psychology Bulletin, 3,* 674–676.

Weiss, R.L., & Heyman, R.E. (1997). A clinical-research overview of couple interactions. In W.K. Halford & H. Markman (Eds.), *The clinical handbook of marriage and couples interventions* (pp. 13–41). Brisbane, Australia: Wiley.

This article has been reprinted as it originally appeared in *Current Directions in Psychological Science*. Citation information for this article as originally published appears above.

Do Psychiatric Patients Do Better Clinically if They Live with Certain Kinds of Families?

Jill M. Hooley[1]
Harvard University

Abstract

Many forms of severe mental illness have biological origins. Nonetheless, the kinds of family environments that psychiatric patients live in are reliably associated with how likely patients are to relapse. This article describes some characteristics of families that place patients at increased risk for relapse, and outlines the behaviors that such families engage in. Behavior in these families is not especially pathological, but because psychiatric patients may be especially sensitive to stress, even fairly common characteristics of family life may trigger underlying biological vulnerabilities that could eventually culminate in relapse.

Keywords

mental disorders; relapse; families; expressed emotion

Among the most serious challenges that can confront any family is coping with severe mental illness. Unfortunately, this is a challenge faced by large numbers of families. Mental disorders are not uncommon. The prevalence of schizophrenia is just under 1%, and it directly affects the lives of approximately 2 million people in the United States. Mood disorders are even more prevalent, affecting around 5% of the population, or more than 10 million people in any given year (Narrow, Rae, Robins, & Regier, 2002). As these numbers illustrate, the lives of many people are influenced directly or indirectly by severe mental illness.

Research over the past several decades has confirmed that many forms of psychiatric disorders have biological origins. Given this, it might at first glance seem surprising that the kinds of family environments that psychiatric patients live in have any bearing on how those patients fare clinically. However, a large literature now attests to the importance of the family environment in the course of disorders such as schizophrenia and depression, and even substance abuse and anxiety. This article provides an overview of what is known about the most important family variable in this regard—a measure of the family environment called expressed emotion (or EE).

WHAT IS EXPRESSED EMOTION AND WHY IS IT IMPORTANT?

EE is a measure of family atmosphere assessed by an interview with the patient's most important family members. Each interview is conducted individually with the relative without the patient present. During the interview (which is always audio-taped for later coding), the relative is asked a series of semistructured and open-ended questions. The main focus of the interview is to provide the relative with an opportunity to talk about the development of the patient's difficulties, as well as his or her current symptoms.

After the interview, a trained rater makes ratings of the three key elements of EE: criticism, hostility, and emotional overinvolvement (EOI). The most important element is criticism. Criticism is rated whenever the relative makes a comment stating explicitly that he or she dislikes or disapproves of something the patient does (e.g., "It really annoys me when he hangs around the house smoking all day."). Criticism is also rated whenever changes in the pitch, rate, or inflection of the relative's voice indicate a critical attitude toward the patient.

The second element of EE is hostility. Hostility can be regarded as a more extreme form of criticism. Hostile remarks criticize the patient as a person, rather than something that he or she specifically does (e.g., "She has such a bad attitude about everything. She's always negative."). Remarks that indicate rejection of the patient (e.g., "I breathe a sigh of relief every time he goes out.") are also rated as hostile. Finally an entirely different aspect of the relative's attitude toward the patient is assessed in the rating of EOI. EOI reflects a dramatic, overprotective, excessively devoted, or self-sacrificing style toward the patient. A comment such as "I hate to leave him home alone even for an hour or two; I worry constantly about him" would be rated as high in EOI.

These characteristics of family members are important for one reason. When measured during a period of crisis (i.e., during a hospitalization or period of exacerbation of symptoms), high levels of EE (i.e., high levels of criticism or hostility, or marked EOI) are a reliable predictor of later relapse in psychiatric patients. Patients with schizophrenia or mood disorders who live with high-EE family members have a risk of relapse that is 2 to 3 times higher than the relapse risk found in patients who live with families who do not show these characteristics (Butzlaff & Hooley, 1998). The association between high EE and relapse is also true for patients with substance-abuse problems (O'Farrell, Hooley, Fals-Stewart, & Cutter, 1998). High levels of family EE have also been linked to less favorable treatment outcomes for patients with anxiety disorders and posttraumatic stress disorder (Chambless & Steketee, 1999; Tarrier, Sommerfield, & Pilgrim, 1999). It is important to note that the link between EE and relapse does not seem to be explained by clinical differences in the patients themselves (Hooley, Rosen, & Richters, 1995).

WHAT DO HIGH-EE RELATIVES DO?

Studies that have examined the behavior of high- and low-EE relatives during their face-to-face interactions with patients have consistently demonstrated that high-EE relatives tend to behave more negatively toward patients than do low-EE relatives. At the most general level, high-EE relatives talk more and listen less than low-EE relatives (Kuipers, Sturgeon, Berkowitz, & Leff, 1983). They also tend to criticize patients more when they interact with them, disagree with patients more, and generally show less accepting behavior toward them (e.g., Miklowitz, Goldstein, Falloon, & Doane, 1984).

Another characteristic of high-EE relatives is that compared with low-EE relatives, they have a tendency to be more behaviorally controlling (Hooley & Campbell, 2002). According to their own reports, when they want the patient to do something, they are likely to issue demands or to become directly coercive (e.g., "I pulled the plate out of her hand to make her stop eating."). In contrast, low-EE relatives tend to make more mild requests (e.g., "I asked her please to hang up her coat.").

Finally, studies that have examined the sequencing of behaviors in high- and low-EE families have suggested that there is less reciprocated positivity and more reciprocated negativity in high-EE interactions than in low-EE interactions. In other words, when an interaction involves a high-EE relative, negative behavior by one person tends to be followed by negative behavior in the recipient, regardless of who was negative first. In contrast, in interactions that involve patients and their low-EE relatives, negativity is much less likely to be reciprocated, and negative interaction sequences, when they do occur, are quickly ended (Hahlweg et al., 1989).

WHY DOES HIGH EE DEVELOP?

If you have read to this point, you might have concluded that high-EE attitudes are rare and that high-EE relatives are unpleasant people who care little about their psychiatrically ill family member. Both of these conclusions are incorrect, however. Far from being rare, high-EE attitudes are common. Somewhere between 45% and 75% of relatives of patients with schizophrenia, for example, are rated as high in EE (Hooley & Gotlib, 2000). It is also the case that the overwhelming majority of these family members care deeply about the welfare and well-being of their psychiatrically ill family member. In their own ways, they try hard to help him or her. Unfortunately, coping with serious mental illness is a difficult and often frustrating task. Progress is typically slow, and setbacks are common. Somewhat ironically, the roots of high EE may lie in the determination of relatives to help patients manage their illnesses better.

An important difference between high- and low-EE relatives is reflected in the way they talk about the patient and his or her problems. Whereas low-EE relatives often make remarks indicating acceptance of the current situation ("For the moment, I think he is doing all he can."), high-EE relatives often have quite specific ideas about what the patient could or should do. High-EE relatives are inclined to make remarks such as, "If she would take her medication, she would be a whole lot better." In other words, they show a tendency to believe that the patient, by changing certain aspects of his or her behavior (e.g., taking medication, getting out more, taking up a hobby, exercising more, drinking less caffeine), could do something (even if it is minor) to make a bad situation better.

Research studies have confirmed that relatives who show critical or hostile attitudes are more likely than low-EE relatives to have an underlying belief that patients can do more to control some of their life difficulties, symptoms, and problems. Of course, this should not be taken to mean that high-EE relatives believe that patients can, by exercising more control and willpower, simply make their psychiatric disorders go away. However, high-EE relatives seem highly inclined to try to help by making direct suggestions, offering ideas, or, in more extreme cases, applying coercion.

The accepted theoretical model of EE assumes that differences in EE arise from differences in relatives' beliefs about the patients' illness (see Hooley &

Gotlib, 2000). Quite possibly, some of the differences in the beliefs of high- and low-EE relatives are linked to underlying personality differences in the relatives themselves. Compared with low-EE relatives, high-EE relatives tend to be less tolerant and less flexible. High-EE relatives also tend to have a more *internally based locus of control* than low-EE relatives. This means that they tend to be less fatalistic, less accepting of the status quo, and more likely to believe that they can, by taking action, make a difference in their world. Although an internal, action-oriented approach to life is highly valued in U.S. culture and often leads to successful outcomes, such an approach may create difficulties when the challenge is mental illness. In this case, the well-meaning efforts of high-EE relatives to effect change may lead to frustration for the relatives themselves and stress for the very patients they are so motivated to help. This stress may trigger biological changes in the patients and may help explain why high EE is a risk factor for relapse.

HELPING FAMILIES HELP PATIENTS

Knowledge about the association between high family levels of EE and increased risk of relapse in patients has led to the development of family-based approaches to the treatment of schizophrenia and other psychiatric disorders. These interventions are used in conjunction with other clinical approaches, such as medications for patients. In general, the common elements of such treatment approaches are to provide relatives with education about the illness, to improve patterns of communication within the family, and to facilitate the development of more effective problem-solving skills. When their families receive interventions of this kind, 9- to 12-month rates of relapse in patients with schizophrenia, for example, fall to approximately 10%. In comparison, when an active family treatment is not provided, rates of relapse are around 50%. Clearly, providing families with skills to help them cope better with severe mental illness in a close relative greatly improves the long-term outcome of patients with disorders such as schizophrenia (see McFarlane, Link, Dushay, Marchal, & Crilly, 1995).

CURRENT DIRECTIONS IN RESEARCH

The link between EE in relatives and poor clinical outcome in patients should not be interpreted to mean that families are to blame for the fact that patients relapse. Criticism, the most important element of the EE measure, is not exclusively found in families that contain a psychiatric patient. Rather, it can be regarded as a normative interpersonal stressor that is part of most people's routine experience. In light of how ubiquitous criticism is, perhaps what is most important to learn is how it is processed—both in emotionally healthy people and in those who are susceptible to disorders such as depression and schizophrenia. One of the most influential heuristics for understanding psychopathology is the diathesis-stress model. This model views psychopathology as the consequence of stress interacting with an underlying predisposition (biological, psychosocial, or sociocultural) to produce a specific disorder. Studying responses to a stressor such as criticism provides researchers with an opportunity to learn more about the nature of vulnerability within a familiar diathesis-stress framework.

In our current work, my research group is bringing together two previously unrelated areas of investigation—psychosocial stress and functional neuroimaging (an imaging technique that allows for the study of the brain at work). By taking criticism, a psychosocial stressor known to predict relapse, and using it as a stimulus in a functional magnetic resonance imaging (fMRI) paradigm, we hope to learn much about the nature of biological vulnerability to psychopathology and the neuroanatomy involved in psychiatric relapse.

So far, the main focus of our research has concerned vulnerability to depression. In the first study of its kind, we used fMRI to study focal (i.e., specific and localized) activation changes in the brains of healthy control participants who had never experienced any psychiatric difficulties and a group of participants who had been clinically depressed in the past but who were fully recovered (see Hooley, Gruber, Scott, Hiller, & Yurgelun-Todd, 2004). The novel feature of our research design was that while they were in the scanner, all participants heard their own mothers making comments about them. Some of the comments involved criticism; others involved praise.

When they heard their mothers criticizing them, the healthy control participants showed an increase in activation in dorsolateral pre-frontal cortex (DLPFC). This is an area of the brain that has been implicated as being involved in both emotional processing and depression. Compared with the healthy control group, however, participants with a vulnerability to depression showed a significant failure to activate DLPFC when they were exposed to criticism. In other words, activity in this brain area decreased rather than increased. This finding is all the more noteworthy because the formerly depressed participants had been depression free for almost 3 years on average and scored no differently on a current measure of depression than did the control participants.

Results such as this provide potentially important clues about the links between interpersonal experience and the neurobiology of emotionally relevant stimuli. Given current thinking about the possible role of higher brain areas (e.g., prefrontal cortex) in the inhibition of brain areas involved in emotion (e.g., the limbic system, and particularly the amygdala; Davidson, 2000), our findings raise the possibility that vulnerability to depression may be characterized by a failure to engage prefrontal cortex in response to a personally significant psychosocial challenge like criticism. The long-term consequences of this failure remain unexplored.

Integrating EE research with functional neuroimaging techniques may lead to progress in understanding the neurobiology of relapse. Criticism is an empirically validated psychosocial stressor that has obvious real-world validity, can be manipulated experimentally, and can be used within an imaging paradigm. EE-based social-challenge studies hold the potential to provide valuable information concerning the processing of emotional stimuli in general, as well as insights into the neural correlates of psychosocial stress in psychopathology.

Recommended Reading

Butzlaff, R.L., & Hooley, J.M. (1998). (See References)
Hooley, J.M., & Gotlib, I.H. (2000). (See References)

Leff, J., & Vaughn, C. (1985). *Expressed emotion in families*. New York: Guilford Press.

Pilling, S., Bebbington, P., Kuipers, E., Garety, P., Geddes, J., Orbach, G., & Morgan, C. (2002). Psychological treatments in schizophrenia: I. Meta-analysis of family intervention and cognitive behavior therapy. *Psychological Medicine, 32*, 763–782.

Acknowledgments—Support for this research was provided by grants from the National Institute of Mental Health (MH42782 and MH66746), as well as the Milton Fund of Harvard University.

Note

1. Address correspondence to Jill M. Hooley, Department of Psychology, Harvard University, 33 Kirkland St., Cambridge, MA 02138; e-mail: jmh@wjh.harvard.edu.

References

Butzlaff, R.L., & Hooley, J.M. (1998). Expressed emotion and psychiatric relapse. *Archives of General Psychiatry, 55*, 547–552.

Chambless, D.L., & Steketee, G. (1999). Expressed emotion and behavior therapy outcome: A prospective study with obsessive-compulsive and agoraphobic outpatients. *Journal of Consulting and Clinical Psychology, 67*, 658–665.

Davidson, R.J. (2000). The functional anatomy of affective style. In R.D. Lane & L. Nadel (Eds.), *Cognitive neuroscience of emotion* (pp. 371–388). New York: Oxford University Press.

Hahlweg, K., Goldstein, M.J., Nuechterlein, K.H., Magaña, A.B., Mintz, J., Doane, J.A., Miklowitz, D.J., & Snyder, K.S. (1989). Expressed emotion and patient-relative interaction in families of recent onset schizophrenics. *Journal of Consulting and Clinical Psychology, 57*, 11–18.

Hooley, J.M., & Campbell, C. (2002). Control and controllability: Beliefs and behavior in high expressed emotion relatives. *Psychological Medicine, 32*, 1091–1099.

Hooley, J.M., & Gotlib, I.H. (2000). A diathesis-stress conceptualization of expressed emotion and clinical outcome. *Applied and Preventive Psychology, 9*, 135–151.

Hooley, J.M., Gruber, S.A., Scott, L.A., Hiller, J.B., & Yurgelun-Todd, D.A. (2004). *Activation in dorsolateral prefrontal cortex in response to maternal criticism and praise in recovered depressed and healthy control participants*. Manuscript submitted for publication.

Hooley, J.M., Rosen, L.R., & Richters, J.E. (1995). Expressed emotion: Toward clarification of a critical construct. In G. Miller (Ed.), *The behavioral high-risk paradigm in psychopathology* (pp. 88–120). New York: Springer-Verlag.

Kuipers, L., Sturgeon, D., Berkowitz, R., & Leff, J. (1983). Characteristics of expressed emotion: Its relationship to speech and looking in schizophrenic patients and their relatives. *British Journal of Clinical Psychology, 22*, 257–264.

McFarlane, W.R., Link, B., Dushay, R., Marchal, J., & Crilly, J. (1995). Psychoeducational multiple family groups: Four year relapse outcome in schizophrenia. *Family Process, 34*, 127–144.

Miklowitz, D.J., Goldstein, M.J., Falloon, I.R., & Doane, J.A. (1984). Interactional correlates of expressed emotion in the families of schizophrenics. *British Journal of Psychiatry, 144*, 482–487.

Narrow, W.E., Rae, D.S., Robins, L.N., & Regier, D.A. (2002). Revised prevalence estimates of mental disorders in the United States. *Archives of General Psychiatry, 59*, 115–123.

O'Farrell, T.J., Hooley, J.M., Fals-Stewart, W., & Cutter, H.S.G. (1998). Expressed emotion and relapse in alcoholic patients. *Journal of Consulting and Clinical Psychology, 66*, 744–752.

Tarrier, N., Sommerfield, C., & Pilgrim, H. (1999). Relatives' expressed emotion (EE) and PTSD treatment outcome. *Psychological Medicine, 29*, 801–811.

Adaptation and the Set-Point Model of Subjective Well-Being: Does Happiness Change After Major Life Events?

Richard E. Lucas[1]
Michigan State University and German Institute for Economic Research, Berlin

Abstract

Hedonic adaptation refers to the process by which individuals return to baseline levels of happiness following a change in life circumstances. Dominant models of subjective well-being (SWB) suggest that people can adapt to almost any life event and that happiness levels fluctuate around a biologically determined set point that rarely changes. Recent evidence from large-scale panel studies challenges aspects of this conclusion. Although inborn factors certainly matter and some adaptation does occur, events such as divorce, death of a spouse, unemployment, and disability are associated with lasting changes in SWB. These recent studies also show that there are considerable individual differences in the extent to which people adapt. Thus, happiness levels do change, and adaptation is not inevitable.

Keywords

happiness; subjective well-being; adaptation; set-point theory

People's greatest hopes and fears often center on the possible occurrence of rare but important life events. People may dread the possibility of losing a loved one or becoming disabled, and they may go to great lengths to find true love or to increase their chances of winning the lottery. In many cases, people strive to attain or avoid these outcomes because of the outcomes' presumed effect on happiness. But do these major life events really affect long-term levels of subjective well-being (SWB)? Dominant models of SWB suggest that after experiencing major life events, people inevitably adapt. More specifically, set-point theorists posit that inborn personality factors cause an inevitable return to genetically determined happiness set points. However, recent evidence from large-scale longitudinal studies challenges some of the stronger conclusions from these models.

ADAPTATION RESEARCH AND THEORY

Although the thought that levels of happiness cannot change may distress some people, researchers believe that adaptation processes serve important functions (Frederick & Loewenstein, 1999). For one thing, these processes protect people from potentially dangerous psychological and physiological consequences of prolonged emotional states. In addition, because adaptation processes allow unchanging stimuli to fade into the attentional background, these processes ensure that change in the environment receives extra attention. Attention to environmental change is advantageous because threats that have existed for prolonged periods of time are likely to be less dangerous than novel threats. Similarly, because rewards that have persisted are less likely to disappear quickly than are novel rewards, it will often be advantageous to attend and react more strongly to these novel rewards. Finally, by reducing emotional reactions over time, adaptation processes allow individuals to disengage from goals that have little chance of success. Thus, adaptation can be beneficial, and some amount of adaptation to life circumstances surely occurs.

Yet many questions about the strength and ubiquity of adaptation effects remain, partly because of the types of evidence that have been used to support adaptation theories. In many cases, adaptation is not directly observed. Instead, it must be inferred from indirect evidence. For instance, psychologists often cite the low correlation between happiness and life circumstances as evidence for adaptation effects. Factors such as income, age, health, marital status, and number of friends account for only a small percentage of the variance in SWB (Diener, Suh, Lucas, & Smith, 1999). One explanation that has been offered for this counterintuitive finding is that these factors initially have an impact but that people adapt over time. However, the weak associations between life circumstances and SWB themselves provide only suggestive evidence for this explanation.

Additional indirect support for the set-point model comes from research that takes a personality perspective on SWB. Three pieces of evidence are relevant (Lucas, in press-b). First, SWB exhibits moderate stability even over very long periods of time and even in the face of changing life circumstances. Recent reviews suggest that approximately 30 to 40% of the variance in life-satisfaction measures is stable over periods as long as 20 years. Second, a number of studies have shown that well-being variables are about 40 to 50% heritable. These heritability estimates appear to be even higher (about 80%) for long-term levels of happiness (Lykken & Tellegen, 1996). Finally, personality variables like extroversion and neuroticism are relatively strong predictors of happiness, at least when compared to the predictive power of external factors. The explanation for this set of findings is that events can influence short-term levels of happiness, but personality-based adaptation processes inevitably move people back to their genetically determined set point after a relatively short period of time.

More direct evidence for hedonic adaptation comes from studies that examine the well-being of individuals who have experienced important life events. However, even these studies can be somewhat equivocal. For instance, one of the most famous studies is that of Brickman, Coates, and Janoff-Bulman (1978) comparing lottery winners and patients with spinal-cord injuries to people in a control group. Brickman et al. showed that lottery winners were not significantly happier than the control-group participants and that individuals with spinal-cord injuries "did not appear nearly as unhappy as might be expected" (p. 921). This study appears to show adaptation to even the most extreme events imaginable. What is often not mentioned, however, is that although the participants with spinal-cord injuries were above neutral on the happiness scale (which is what led Brickman et al. to conclude that they were happier than might be expected), they were significantly less happy than the people in the control group, and the difference between the groups was actually quite large. Individuals with spinal-cord injuries were more than three quarters of a standard deviation below the mean of the control group. This means that the average participant from the control group was happier than approximately 78% of participants with spinal-cord injuries. This result has now been replicated quite often—most existing studies show relatively large differences between individuals with spinal-cord injuries and healthy participants in control groups (Dijkers, 1997).

In addition to problems that result from the interpretation of effect sizes, methodological limitations restrict the conclusions that can be drawn from many existing studies of adaptation. Most studies are not longitudinal, and even fewer are prospective (though there are some notable exceptions; see e.g., Bonanno, 2004; Caspi et al., 2003). Because participants' pre-event levels of SWB are not known, it is always possible that individuals who experienced an event were more or less happy than average before the event occurred. Certain people may be predisposed to experience life events, and these predisposing factors may be responsible for their happiness levels being lower than average. For instance, in a review of the literature examining the well-being of children who had lost limbs from various causes, Tyc (1992) suggested that those who lost limbs due to accidents tended to have higher levels of premorbid psychological disorders than did those who lost limbs due to disease. Thus, simply comparing the well-being of children who lost limbs to those who did not might overestimate the effect of the injury. Psychologists have demonstrated that level of happiness predicts the occurrence of a variety of events and outcomes (Lyubomirsky, King, & Diener, 2005), and therefore, studies that compare individuals who have experienced a particular event with those who have not but that do not take into account previous happiness level must be interpreted cautiously.

A second methodological concern relates to what are known as demand characteristics. When researchers recruit participants specifically because they have experienced a given life event, participants may over- or underreport SWB. These reports may occur because people believe the life event should have an impact, because they want to appear well-adjusted, or simply because the context of the study makes the event more salient. For instance, Smith, Schwarz, Roberts, and Ubel (2006) showed that patients with Parkinson's disease reported lower life satisfaction when the study instructions indicated that Parkinson's disease was a focus than when the instructions indicated that the study focused on the general population.

USING LARGE-SCALE PANEL STUDIES TO ASSESS ADAPTATION TO LIFE EVENTS

Recently, my colleagues and I have turned to archival data analysis using large, nationally representative panel studies to address questions about adaptation to life events. These studies have a number of advantages over alternative designs. First, they are prospective, which means that pre-event levels of SWB are known. Second, they are longitudinal, which means that change over time can be accurately modeled. Third, very large samples are often involved, which means that even rare events are sampled. Finally, because designers of these studies often recruit nationally representative samples, and because the questionnaires often focus on a variety of issues, demand characteristics are unlikely to have much of an effect.

We have used two such panel studies—the German Socioeconomic Panel Study (GSOEP) and the British Household Panel Study (BHPS)—to examine the amount of adaptation that occurs following major life events. The GSOEP includes almost 40,000 individuals living in Germany who have been assessed yearly for up to 21 years. The BHPS includes more than 27,000 individuals living in Great Britain who have been assessed yearly for up to 14 years. We have used these data sets to examine the extent to which people adapt to events such as marital transitions (Lucas, 2005; Lucas, Clark, Georgellis, & Diener, 2003), bouts of unemployment (Lucas, Clark, Georgellis, & Diener, 2004), and the onset of a disability (Lucas, in press-a). At least three important findings have emerged (see Diener, Lucas, & Scollon, 2006, for a more detailed review).

First, long-term levels of SWB do change, and adaptation is not inevitable. In fact, these studies show that there is no single answer to the question of whether people adapt to life events. Instead, the pattern of adaptation varies across different events. Figure 1 shows the average within-person trajectories for life satisfaction before and after various life events. These data show that although the average person adapts to marriage (and this adaptation tends to occur within just a couple of years; Lucas et al., 2003), adaptation to other events is often very slow or incomplete. Widows and widowers return very close (within about .15 points) to the level of life satisfaction that they reported before their spouse died, but this process of adaptation takes approximately 7 years (Lucas et al., 2003). Individuals who get divorced or experience unemployment report what appear to be permanent changes in life satisfaction following these events (Lucas, 2005; Lucas et al., 2004). Furthermore, these changes can sometimes be very large. Individuals who acquire a severe disability report life-satisfaction levels that are more than a full standard deviation below their baseline levels, and these levels do not appear to rebound over time (Lucas, in press-a).

A second important finding is that, for all events we have studied, there are large individual differences in the amount of adaptation that occurs. To demonstrate, it is possible to calculate the variability in within-person change that occurs before and after the event. In the case of marriage, very little change occurs on average. However, the standard deviation for the amount of change that occurs was approximately 1.0 (for responses derived from an 11-point scale). This means that approximately 30% of participants reported lasting changes in satisfaction of between a half and a full point, and an additional 32% reported lasting changes of more than a full point. These effects are quite large in relation to the amount of variance that exists in baseline levels of well-being. A participant who began the study with an average level of life satisfaction but experienced a change that was one standard deviation above the mean change would move to the 74th percentile overall in level of life satisfaction. Similarly, someone who experienced a change that was one standard deviation below the mean would move to the 26th percentile overall. These individual differences in reaction and adaptation likely result both from variability in the nature of the event (some marriages are better than others) and from variability in people's reactions to similar events. In either case, the average trajectory does not tell the whole story about the potential for life events to have a major impact on people's long-term levels of SWB.

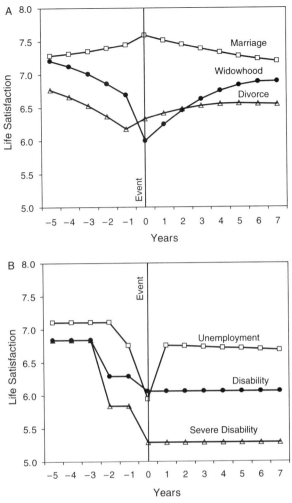

Fig. 1. Average within-person trajectories for life satisfaction before and after various life events. Panel A shows reaction and adaptation to marriage, death of a spouse, and divorce. Panel B shows reaction and adaptation to unemployment and the onset of varying degrees of disability. Adapted from Lucas (2005), Lucas (in press-a), Lucas, Clark, Georgellis, and Diener (2003), and Lucas, Clark, Georgellis, and Diener (2004).

A third major finding is that people who will eventually experience a major life event often differ from people who will not, even before the event occurs. Therefore prospective longitudinal studies are necessary to separate pre-existing differences from longitudinal change. For instance, cross-sectional studies have consistently shown that married people are happier than single, divorced, or widowed people; yet our studies showed that marriage was not associated with lasting increases in happiness. Instead, people who eventually married were happier than average (or at least happier than those who married and then divorced) even more than 5 years before the marriage (Lucas, 2005; Lucas et al., 2003).

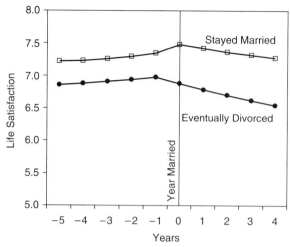

Fig. 2. Trajectories of life satisfaction before and after marriage for individuals who remain married and those who eventually divorce. Adapted from Lucas (2005).

People who eventually divorced, on the other hand, started out with lower levels of well-being than those who did not divorce, and they reported lasting changes following this event. These findings are illustrated in Figure 2, in which levels of life satisfaction before and after marriage are plotted for participants who eventually divorced and for those who stayed married. These results suggest that about half of the difference that is typically found between married and divorced individuals in cross-sectional studies is the result of selection effects, and half is the result of lasting changes that follow divorce.

FUTURE DIRECTIONS

Although large-scale, nationally representative panel studies are an important tool for answering questions about adaptation, they are not without limitations. The set of psychological variables that has been assessed thus far is relatively limited. This lack of information about psychological characteristics means that moderators and process variables cannot be examined. Future research on adaptation should focus on achieving the following three goals.

First, sophisticated methodologies to assess adaptation to a wide variety of events must be used, so that researchers can develop a clear picture of the events to which people can and cannot adapt. As these events are catalogued, hypotheses about the characteristics that distinguish these events can be formulated and tested. For instance, Frederick and Loewenstein (1999) suggested that people may be able to adapt to one-time events like the loss of a spouse or the onset of an unchanging medical condition but may be less able to adapt to conditions that change or worsen over time.

A second goal is that programmatic research should lead to greater insight into the processes that underlie hedonic adaptation. Adaptation may result from physiological processes that reduce emotional reactivity to constant stimuli, or it could result from psychological processes that change the way people think about events that have occurred in their lives. For instance, adaptation effects may emerge when people disengage from goals that have become unattainable and set new goals toward which they can strive, or it may occur as people develop strengths or acquire new skills that enable them to deal more effectively with less-than-ideal life circumstances.

A third research goal is to clarify the individual-level characteristics that promote or prevent adaptation. Our studies (Lucas, 2005, in press-a; Lucas et al., 2003, 2004) show that there are considerable individual differences in the amount of adaptation that occurs. One fruitful avenue for understanding these individual differences is to look for personality variables that moderate adaptation effects over time. For instance, Bonanno and colleagues have identified distinct trajectories of distress following major traumatic life events like the loss of a spouse or a child (Bonanno, 2004). Notably, characteristics including hardiness, self-enhancement, and positive emotions have been shown to be associated with the most resilient pattern of reactions. In addition, Caspi and colleagues have shown that interactions between stressful life events and specific genes predict the onset of depression (Caspi et al., 2003). It is possible that similar gene-by-environment interactions would also affect reaction and adaptation to life events. Future research must identify additional demographic, social, and personality factors that promote positive reactions to major life events.

IS THERE A HAPPINESS SET POINT?

The studies reviewed in this paper do not refute the set-point model of happiness. Instead, they put the empirical findings that have emerged from that model in a broader context. What does it mean to an individual that happiness is 50% or even 80% heritable? What does it mean that 35% of the variance in well-being is stable over time? Do these empirical facts mean that long-term levels of happiness do not change? The results reviewed in this paper show that the answer to this question is no. They confirm that although happiness levels are moderately stable over time, this stability does not preclude large and lasting changes. Happiness levels do change, adaptation is not inevitable, and life events do matter.

Recommended Reading

Bonanno, G. (2004). (See References)
Diener, E., Lucas, R.E., & Scollon, C.N. (2006). (See References)
Frederick, S., & Loewenstein, G. (1999). (See References)

Note

1. Address correspondence to Richard E. Lucas, Department of Psychology, Michigan State University, East Lansing, MI 48823; e-mail: lucasri@msu.edu.

References

Bonanno, G.A. (2004). Loss, trauma, and human resilience: Have we underestimated the human capacity to thrive after extremely aversive events? *American Psychologist*, 59, 20–28.

Brickman, P., Coates, D., & Janoff-Bulman, R. (1978). Lottery winners and accident victims: Is happiness relative? *Journal of Personality & Social Psychology, 36*, 917–927.

Caspi, A., Sugden, K., Moffitt, T.E., Taylor, A., Craig, I.W., Harrington, H., et al. (2003). Influence of life stress on depression: Moderation by a polymorphism in the 5-HTT gene. *Science, 301*, 386–389.

Diener, E., Lucas, R.E., & Scollon, C. (2006). Beyond the hedonic treadmill: Revising the adaptation theory of well-being. *American Psychologist, 61*, 305–314.

Diener, E., Suh, E.M., Lucas, R.E., & Smith, H.L. (1999). Subjective well-being: Three decades of progress. *Psychological Bulletin, 125*, 276–302.

Dijkers, M. (1997). Quality of life after spinal cord injury: A meta analysis of the effects of disablement components. *Spinal Cord, 35*, 829–840.

Frederick, S., & Loewenstein, G. (1999). Hedonic adaptation. In D. Kahneman, E. Diener, & N. Schwarz (Eds.), *Well-being: The foundations of hedonic psychology* (pp. 302–329). New York: Sage.

Lucas, R.E. (2005). Time does not heal all wounds: A longitudinal study of reaction and adaptation to divorce. *Psychological Science, 16*, 945–950.

Lucas, R.E. (in press-a). Long-term disability is associated with lasting changes in subjective well-being: Evidence from two nationally representative longitudinal studies. *Journal of Personality and Social Psychology*.

Lucas, R.E. (in press-b). Personality and subjective well-being. In M. Eid & R.J. Larsen (Eds.), *The science of subjective well-being*. New York: Guilford.

Lucas, R.E., Clark, A.E., Georgellis, Y., & Diener, E. (2003). Reexamining adaptation and the set point model of happiness: Reactions to changes in marital status. *Journal of Personality & Social Psychology, 84*, 527–539.

Lucas, R.E., Clark, A.E., Georgellis, Y., & Diener, E. (2004). Unemployment alters the set point for life satisfaction. *Psychological Science, 15*, 8–13.

Lykken, D., & Tellegen, A. (1996). Happiness is a stochastic phenomenon. *Psychological Science, 7*, 186–189.

Lyubomirsky, S., King, L., & Diener, E. (2005). The benefits of frequent positive affect: Does happiness lead to success? *Psychological Bulletin, 131*, 803–855.

Smith, D.M., Schwarz, N., Roberts, T.R., & Ubel, P.A. (2006). Why are you calling me? How study introductions change response patterns. *Quality of Life Research, 15*, 621–630.

Tyc, V.L. (1992). Psychosocial adaptation of children and adolescents with limb deficiencies: A review. *Clinical Psychology Review, 2*, 275–291.

Neighborhood Characteristics and Depression: An Examination of Stress Processes

Carolyn E. Cutrona,[1] Gail Wallace, and Kristin A. Wesner
Iowa State University

Abstract

Neighborhoods with poor-quality housing, few resources, and unsafe conditions impose stress, which can lead to depression. The stress imposed by adverse neighborhoods increases depression above and beyond the effects of the individual's own personal stressors, such as poverty and negative events within the family or workplace. Furthermore, adverse neighborhoods appear to intensify the harmful impact of personal stressors and interfere with the formation of bonds between people, again increasing risk for depression. Neighborhoods do not affect all people in the same way. People with different personality characteristics adjust in different ways to challenging neighborhoods. As a field, psychology should pay more attention to the impact of contextual factors such as neighborhoods. Neighborhood-level mental health problems should be addressed at the neighborhood level. Public housing policies that contribute to the concentration of poverty should be avoided and research should be conducted on the most effective ways to mobilize neighborhood residents to meet common goals and improve the context in which they live.

Keywords

neighborhood; community; depression; poverty

Most theories relating depression to stress focus on events that occur within peoples' immediate lives, such as relationship problems or work stressors. Recent research reveals that depression may be linked to characteristics of the neighborhoods in which people live. Research has only recently undertaken to understand the ways in which neighborhoods affect depression and other forms of mental illness. Much less has been written about how neighborhoods influence mental health compared to the large amount that has been written about how neighborhoods influence problem behaviors like delinquency, crime, drug use, and adolescent childbearing (Leventhal & Brooks-Gunn, 2000).

It is important to understand the role of neighborhoods in the development of depression for at least three reasons: (a) People often do not realize that they are affected by the context around them and thus mistakenly blame themselves for the invisible stressors that affect their well-being; (b) outsiders also fail to realize that residents of adverse neighborhoods are influenced by their surroundings (high rates of mental health problems in poor neighborhoods may be blamed on the personal characteristics or race of residents rather than on the neighborhoods themselves); and (c) when threats to public health are caused by characteristics of entire communities, it is more efficient to address these threats at the community level rather than to treat each affected individual separately. Thus, it is important to raise public awareness of the mental health risks that accompany adverse neighborhoods.

Issues of neighborhood quality have immediate practical implications. The New Orleans neighborhoods most severely damaged by Hurricane Katrina in 2005 were areas of concentrated poverty; if they are rebuilt as before, with poor-quality resources and little integration with more prosperous families, a wide range of social problems, including threats to mental health, will reappear. As we will describe in more detail, the hopelessness of individual poverty is compounded by community impoverishment.

The question addressed in this article is how psychological health, specifically depression, is affected by residence in a specific neighborhood, beyond the strains of low family income and other personal factors that heighten risk for depression. All of the studies summarized in this review examined the effects of neighborhood characteristics on depression after statistically eliminating the effects of individual and family characteristics, such as income, education, employment status, age, and race, that may increase personal vulnerability to depression.

WHAT IS A NEIGHBORHOOD?

Most often, neighborhoods are defined as census tracts. The U.S. Census works with local residents to identify meaningful neighborhood units when it decides on tract boundaries. A census tract typically has 4,000 to 6,000 people and includes approximately nine city blocks. Some researchers use smaller units, called block groups, which are smaller areas within census tracts. A few researchers use very small areas, called face blocks (both sides of the street for one block). The impact of neighborhood characteristics on mental health does not depend much on the neighborhood unit that is used in a particular study (Sampson, Morenoff, & Gannon-Rowley, 2002).

NEIGHBORHOOD CHARACTERISTICS

Physical features of neighborhoods, such as quality of housing and the presence or absence of basic resources, including hospitals, reliable public transportation, and retail stores, can be important determinants of well-being. More research has been conducted on the influence of the people who live in neighborhoods than on the physical characteristics of neighborhoods. Two types of "person" characteristics have received research attention: *structural* and *functional*. Aspects of the population makeup of a neighborhood are termed structural characteristics. They include, but are not limited to, the percent of neighborhood residents who are poor, jobless, well-educated, or members of an ethnic minority group. Information about structural aspects of neighborhoods is almost always derived from the U.S. Census.

Aspects of how people in a neighborhood behave are termed functional characteristics. Examples of negative functional characteristics include the extent to which neighborhood residents behave in an uncivil or threatening manner and tolerate or engage in unlawful behavior ("social disorder"). Although not everyone in the neighborhood may engage in a specific behavior, if the behavior is sufficiently prevalent and affects a large number of residents, it may be viewed as a functional characteristic of that neighborhood. Functional characteristics are assessed through surveys of neighborhood residents or by systematic observation by researchers (e.g., counting the number of teenagers who hang out on the street late at night).

THEORETICAL FRAMEWORK

Stress plays a central role in theories that link neighborhood characteristics and depression. Characteristics of the neighborhoods in which people live influence the stress process in three different ways (see Fig. 1). First, neighborhood characteristics influence the level of daily stress imposed upon residents. Second, neighborhood characteristics influence people's vulnerability to depression following negative events in their lives (Elliott, 2000). In a highly adverse neighborhood, the same event is more likely to trigger depression than in a good-quality neighborhood. Third, neighborhood characteristics interfere with the formation of bonds among people. In turn, disrupted bonds lead to depression through several different pathways including lower levels of informal social control, inadequate social support, and poor family-role performance.

Daily Level of Stress

Neighborhood stressors may be imposed by physical characteristics of the neighborhood (e.g., lack of resources and unpleasant physical surroundings) or by the people who inhabit the neighborhood (e.g., threats to physical safety).

Lack of Resources and Physical Stressors   Many physical features of high-poverty neighborhoods impose stress on the lives of their residents, including low-quality housing, high traffic density, and undesirable commercial operations (e.g., adult bookstores). Observer ratings of housing quality predicted depression beyond the effects of family income in a study of low- and middle-income rural women (Evans, Wells, Chan, & Saltzman, 2000). Furthermore, women who moved from poor-quality apartments to single-family homes through Habitat for Humanity showed significant decreases in depressive symptoms (Evans et al., 2000). Low-income neighborhoods lack many resources, including health care, retail stores, and recreational facilities. Lack of access to needed resources is demoralizing because of the extra effort required to meet daily needs (Sampson et al., 2002).

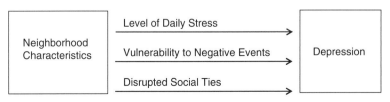

Fig. 1. Three pathways from neighborhood characteristics to depression.

79

Very few studies have quantified neighborhood resources. More refined measures that capture type, accessibility, and distance to community resources are needed.

The People in the Neighborhood   A potent source of stress is fear of victimization (Hill, Ross, & Angel, 2005). There is evidence that social disorder, not poverty per se, is the neighborhood characteristic that most directly causes depression (Ross, 2000). People who live in neighborhoods with high rates of crime must cope with anxiety over their safety and that of their possessions. Neighborhood social disorder is associated with depressive symptoms in both children and adults (Aneshensel & Sucoff, 1996; Hill et al., 2005). By contrast, neighborhood poverty without social disorder does not show a consistent effect on depression in adults (Cutrona, Russell, Hessling, Brown, & Murry, 2000), although its effects on children appear to be more consistent (Xue, Leventhal, Brooks-Gunn, & Earls, 2005).

Vulnerability to Depression Following Negative Events

A second way that adverse neighborhoods engender depression is by intensifying the harmful mental health impact of negative events in people's lives (Cutrona et al., 2005). Someone who experiences a negative event (e.g., job loss) in a poor neighborhood is more likely to become depressed than is one who experiences the same event in a more advantaged neighborhood. Among African American women, all of whom had experienced at least one severe negative life event in the past year, only 2% of those who lived in low-stress neighborhoods experienced the onset of a major depressive episode, as compared to 12% of those who lived in high-stress neighborhoods. Reasons for this heightened vulnerability may include lack of resources, the absence of role models who provide hope for personal success, and local norms that promote ineffective coping and negative interpretations of events (Elliott, 2000).

Neighborhood Effects on Interpersonal Relationships

Neighborhood characteristics influence the probability that people will form ties with each other (Sampson et al., 2002). When residential turnover is high, people are less likely to form relationships. Similarly, people do not tend to form relationships when they live in neighborhoods high in social disorder, because they mistrust their neighbors (Hill et al., 2005). Relationship disruption may have several different consequences relevant to depression, including lower levels of informal social control, inadequate social support, and poor family-role performance.

Informal Social Control   When people do not know each other, they do not monitor or control each others' behavior, and norms that permit antisocial or maladaptive behavior may arise (Sampson et al., 2002). When people engage in maladaptive behavior, problems often result, such as job loss or unintended pregnancy, which in turn lead to depression. By contrast, in neighborhoods where people know and trust one another, they are more likely to discourage problem behaviors that might lead to depression (e.g., through disapproval, telling parents, alerting authorities, or forming neighborhood-watch groups).

Social Support   People who live in high-social-disorder neighborhoods have fewer ties with their neighbors and perceive their relationships with their closest friends and relatives as being less supportive than do people in better neighborhoods (Aneshensel & Sucoff, 1996), perhaps because support providers themselves are highly burdened. Residence in an economically disadvantaged neighborhood appears to weaken the protective power of social resources in people's lives. Among adolescents, a close supportive relationship with parents only protected against depression in higher-income neighborhoods, not in lower-income neighborhoods (Wickrama & Bryant, 2003). Similarly, among adults, frequent contact with friends and involvement in community organizations protected against depression in higher- but not in lower-income neighborhoods (Elliott, 2000).

Family-Role Performance   Some neighborhoods provide few role models for competent fulfillment of family roles; thus marriages and parenting processes may suffer, resulting in depression among both adults and children (Cutrona et al., 2003; Wickrama & Bryant, 2003). Neighborhood poverty predicted lower-quality parenting behaviors, including lower observed warmth, in parents of adolescents (Wickrama & Bryant, 2003). Poor parenting, in turn, predicted depression among the adolescents. In another observational study, residents of high-poverty neighborhoods behaved less warmly toward their spouses than residents of low-poverty neighborhoods did (Cutrona et al., 2003). Low warmth may lead to marital problems, which have been widely shown to predict depression.

DIFFERENCES IN REACTIONS TO NEIGHBORHOODS

The impact of neighborhood characteristics on people's psychological adjustment varies noticeably, depending on people's personal traits and circumstances (Cutrona et al., 2000). In one study of women who lived in high-social-disorder neighborhoods, levels of distress were extremely high if the women were high on the personality trait of negative affectivity (a tendency to strong emotional reactions; see Fig. 2). By contrast, women who scored high on optimism and personal mastery were relatively immune to the negative mental health impact of neighborhood social disorder (Cutrona et al., 2000). Some people with particularly resilient personalities can cope successfully, even in dangerous and disorderly neighborhoods. However, other people are highly vulnerable to depression when they live in adverse surroundings. It may be that living in a disadvantaged and disorderly neighborhood eventually erodes optimism and replaces it with hopelessness and negativity.

CONCLUSIONS AND FUTURE DIRECTIONS

The field of psychology has paid insufficient attention to the impact of contextual factors on well-being. Neighborhood context affects important psychological processes, above and beyond personal and family stressors, by increasing stress load, intensifying reactivity to negative life events, and damaging the quality of interpersonal relationships. Furthermore, psychological characteristics appear to moderate the impact of neighborhoods on adjustment. Some people with

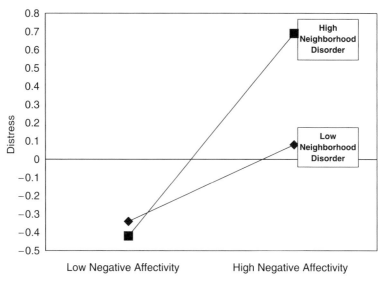

Fig. 2. Effect of neighborhood social disorder on distress for women high on negative affectivity versus for women low on negative affectivity. (Lines are plotted for 1 standard deviation above and one standard deviation below the sample mean on neighborhood social disorder; the y-axis is labeled in standard deviation units.) From "Direct and Moderating Effects of Community Context on the Psychological Well-Being of African American Women," by C.E. Cutrona, D.W. Russell, R.M. Hessling, & P.A. Brown, 2000, *Journal of Personality and Social Psychology, 79*, p. 1097. Copyright 2000 by the American Psychological Association. Reprinted with permission.

particularly resilient personalities cope effectively with neighborhood stressors, but others appear to be significantly harmed psychologically. The influence of contexts on a wide range of psychological processes merits further study.

Better methods for separating the mental health impact of people's personal characteristics from those of their neighborhoods are needed. Social experiments in which low-income people are given rent subsidies and randomly assigned to live in different kinds of neighborhoods have shown that youth and adults show better mental health when they move from impoverished neighborhoods to middle-class neighborhoods (e.g., Rosenbaum & Harris, 2001). These studies demonstrate clearly that some of the problems associated with low-income people should actually be attributed to low-income environments.

Duncan and Raudenbush (2001) offered a number of suggestions for how to improve the design of survey-based neighborhood studies. These include analyzing family characteristics that might mistakenly be attributed to neighborhoods; examining the similarity between siblings, neighbors, and non-neighbors on mental health outcomes to sort out the contributions of family characteristics from those of neighborhood characteristics; and using separate samples of neighborhood residents to obtain information about the neighborhood (e.g., degree of social disorder) and outcome measures (e.g., level of depression).

The most efficient way to improve mental health in impoverished neighborhoods is to improve the quality of neighborhoods. A number of projects are currently underway around the country to help residents of impoverished inner-city neighborhoods organize to improve the quality of life in their neighborhoods (e.g., Jason, 2006). Research is needed to determine the best strategies for empowering local residents to take effective action. Techniques are needed to study processes of change in neighborhoods and the factors that facilitate change.

Decisions about where to build subsidized housing for low-income families are critically important. There is evidence that economically integrated neighborhoods are beneficial and that concentrating low-income housing in the poorest neighborhoods perpetuates problems of social disorder and resource deprivation. As noted earlier, rebuilding New Orleans presents the opportunity to avoid concentrations of poverty, which breed hopelessness and depression as well as other social problems. It is important that policymakers have access to empirical data that will help them make informed decisions about housing and economic-development issues. Greater collaboration across the disciplines of city planning, economics, sociology, and psychology are needed in generating such data.

Recommended Reading

Brooks-Gunn, J., Duncan, G.J., & Aber, J.L. (Eds.). (1997). *Neighborhood poverty, Vol. 1: Context and consequences for children*. New York: Russell Sage Foundation.

Jencks, C., & Mayer, S.E. (1990). The social consequences of growing up in a poor neighborhood. In L.E. Lynn & M.G.H. McGeary (Eds.), *Adolescents at risk: Medical and social perspectives* (pp. 19–34). Boulder, CO: Westview Press.

Massey, D.S., & Denton, N.A. (1993). *American apartheid: Segregation and the making of the underclass*. Cambridge, MA: Harvard University Press.

Pearlin, L. (1999). The stress process revisited: Reflections on concepts and their relationships. In C. Aneshensel & J. Phelan (Eds.), *Handbook of the sociology of mental health*. New York: Plenum Press.

Sampson, R.J. (2001). How do communities undergird or undermine human development? Relevant contexts and social mechanisms. In A. Booth & A.C. Crouter (Eds.), *Does it take a village? Community effects on children, adolescents, and families* (pp. 3–30). Mahwah, NJ: Erlbaum.

Note

1. Address correspondence to Carolyn E. Cutrona, Institute for Social and Behavioral Research, 2625 N. Loop Dr. Suite 500, Ames, IA 50010; e-mail: ccutrona@iastate.edu.

References

Aneshensel, C., & Sucoff, C.A. (1996). The neighborhood context of adolescent mental health. *Journal of Health and Social Behavior, 37*, 293–310.

Cutrona, C.E., Russell, D.W., Abraham, W.T., Gardner, K.A., Melby, J.N., Bryant, C., & Conger, R.D. (2003). Neighborhood context and financial strain as predictors of marital interaction and marital quality in African American couples. *Personal Relationships, 10*, 389–409.

Cutrona, C.E., Russell, D.W., Brown, P.A., Clark, L.A., Hessling, R.M., & Gardner, K.A. (2005). Neighborhood context, personality, and stressful life events as predictors of depression among African American women. *Journal of Abnormal Psychology, 114*, 3–15.

Cutrona, C.E., Russell, D.W., Hessling, R.M., Brown, P.A., & Murry, V. (2000). Direct and moderating effects of community context on the psychological well-being of African American women. *Journal of Personality and Social Psychology, 79*, 1088–1101.

Duncan, G.J., & Raudenbush, S.W. (2001). Neighborhoods and adolescent development: How can we determine the links? In A. Booth & A.C. Crouter (Eds.), *Does it take a village? Community effects on children, adolescents, and families* (pp. 105–136). Mahwah, NJ: Erlbaum.

Elliott, M. (2000). The stress process in neighborhood context. *Health & Place, 6,* 287–299.

Evans, G.W., Wells, N.M., Chan, H.Y.E., & Saltzman, H. (2000). Housing quality and mental health. *Journal of Consulting and Clinical Psychology, 68,* 526–530.

Hill, T.D., Ross, C.E., & Angel, R.J. (2005). Neighborhood disorder, psychophysiological distress, and health. *Journal of Health & Social Behavior, 46,* 170–186.

Jason, L.A. (2006). Benefits and challenges of generating community participation. *Professional Psychology: Research and Practice, 37,* 132–139.

Leventhal, T., & Brooks-Gunn, J. (2000). The neighborhoods they live in: The effects of neighborhood residence upon child and adolescent outcomes. *Psychological Bulletin, 126,* 309–337.

Rosenbaum, J.E., & Harris, L.E. (2001). Low-income families in their new neighborhoods. *Journal of Family Issues, 22,* 183–210.

Ross, C.E. (2000). Neighborhood disadvantage and adult depression. *Journal of Health and Social Behavior, 41,* 177–187.

Sampson, R.J., Morenoff, J.D., & Gannon-Rowley, T. (2002). Assessing "Neighborhood Effects": Social processes and new directions in research. *Annual Review of Sociology, 28,* 443–478.

Wickrama, K.A.S., & Bryant, C.M. (2003). Community context of social resources and adolescent mental health. *Journal of Marriage and Family, 65,* 850–866.

Xue, Y., Leventhal, T., Brooks-Gunn, J., & Earls, F.J. (2005). Neighborhood residence and mental health problems of 5- to 11-year-olds. *Archives of Genetic Psychiatry, 62,* 554–563.

Section 2: Critical Thinking Questions

1. Lucas described a number of findings demonstrating that (a) life transitions can alter subjective well-being, and (b) that there are important psychological differences between those who do and do not go on to experience particular life events. How might different kinds of life transitions play a role in the development or maintenance of psychopathology, and how may psychopathology or risk factors for psychopathology influence exposure to particular life events?

2. Cutrona et al.'s paper states that it is important for studies of neighborhood influences on depression to explore whether their effects are partially attributable to family characteristics. Might adverse neighborhood conditions result in family processes similar to those described by Parent et al.? Are there characteristics of individuals or their family environment that might protect them against the adverse effects of negative neighborhood characteristics?

3. Lenzenweger's paper on risk for schizophrenia in section 1 described heritable personality traits that are involved in the disorder and which are also present in nonaffected relatives of those with schizophrenia. How might these characteristics be related to the negative family processes of expressed emotion described by Hooley?

4. What are some of the advantages and limitations of using animal models to study psychopathology?

This article has been reprinted as it originally appeared in *Current Directions in Psychological Science.* Citation information for this article as originally published appears above.

Section 3: The Intersection of Biology and Psychology

A number of studies in this reader describe research exploring biological markers of psychopathology and biological mechanisms involved in etiological pathways to a variety of disorders. Recent advances in this field have widened the range of biological systems now known to have meaningful associations with psychological disorders. These empirical findings have challenged traditional divisions between the study of physical and mental health, and stimulated transdisciplinary theoretical advances. Moreover, a new paradigm in behavior genetics has emerged that explores interactions among genetic polymorphisms and environmental conditions in the prediction of psychopathology. This exciting new avenue of research has challenged the dichotomy between environmental and genetic contributions to mental health, and illuminated the interplay between inherited individual differences and the environments in which individuals function. While it is perhaps too early to speculate whether these findings will revolutionize thinking about the genetics of mental illness, they have inspired new excitement about modeling environmental influences on disorders.

Modern work on the biological components of psychopathology is characterized by a transdisciplinary focus, linking models and methods across a variety of research literatures. The novelty of some of the constructs and methods that characterize this work may prove challenging for some students of abnormal psychology. The papers in this section provide excellent introductions to some of the issues involved in research of this nature and should evoke an appreciation for the usefulness of models that address psychological phenomena with an understanding of their place within the larger biopsychosocial sphere of human functioning. The first two papers (by Kemeny and Miller and Blackwell) convey some of the central questions facing psychology, including the question of how environmental events and influences "get under the skin" to impact physiological systems that in turn play a role in medical and psychological disorders.

Kemeny provides a succinct overview of the literature on autonomic, hormonal, and immune systems involved in stress responsivity. The paper also describes how adaptive stress responsivity mechanisms may go awry in a variety of ways, leading to increased vulnerability for physical and psychological maladaptation. Of note, Kemeny proposes that existing models of the body's response to stress may need to be revised to consider psychological mediators of the association between type of stressor and the quality and type of ensuing physiological response. This model proposes that a full understanding of physiological stress components must incorporate psychological mechanisms such as cognitive appraisals.

Miller and Blackwell's review describes cutting edge research exploring immunological mechanisms that now appear to play a role in both heart disease and depressive disorders, and their comorbidity. Their paper proposes an overarching theory of how chronic stress leads to inflammation, which in turn sets into motion pathways to both depression and heart disease. This work is exciting and creative, and should stimulate students' appreciation of the remaining as yet unidentified biological cascades the lie between an individual's environment and their responses to it.

The final two papers in this section describe exciting new findings demonstrating that the effects of particular genetic polymorphisms in genes relevant to neurotransmitter functioning depend upon particular environmental circumstances. Fox and colleagues review findings on interactions between various markers of environmental stress and polymorphisms in the serotonin transporter gene. They propose that phenotypic differences in traits related to internalizing disorders may develop from a complex interplay between children's genotype and their early rearing environment. Similarly, Reis' paper elucidates some of the fascinating findings from genetically informative studies demonstrating how individuals' genes and their environments are intertwined in ways that question traditional and simplistic divisions between constructs that reside within the individual and those that are outside of the individual. Reiss clearly explicates how many measures of the family environment are in fact correlated with genotype (in biological families) or represent processes evoked or eliciting by individual difference factors emerging from these genotypes.

The Psychobiology of Stress

Margaret E. Kemeny[1]

Department of Psychiatry, University of California, San Francisco, San Francisco, California

Abstract

Stressful life experience can have significant effects on a variety of physiological systems, including the autonomic nervous system, the hypothalamic-pituitary-adrenal axis, and the immune system. These relationships can be bidirectional; for example, immune cell products can act on the brain, altering mood and cognition, potentially contributing to depression. Although acute physiological alterations may be adaptive in the short term, chronic or repeated provocation can result in damage to health. The central dogma in the field of stress research assumes a stereotyped physiological response to all stressors (the generality model). However, increasing evidence suggests that specific stressful conditions and the specific way an organism appraises these conditions can elicit qualitatively distinct emotional and physiological responses (the integrated specificity model). For example, appraisals of threat (vs. challenge), uncontrollability, and negative social evaluation have been shown to provoke specific psychobiological responses. Emotional responses appear to have specific neural substrates, which can result in differentiated alterations in peripheral physiological systems, so that it is incorrect to presume a uniform stress response.

Keywords

stress; endocrine; autonomic; immune; physiology; emotion; cognitive

The term stress is used in the scientific literature in a vague and inconsistent way and is rarely defined. The term may refer to a stimulus, a response to a stimulus, or the physiological consequences of that response. Given this inconsistency, in this review I avoid using the term stress (except when discussing the field of stress research) and instead differentiate the various components of stress. *Stressors*, or stressful life experiences, are defined as circumstances that threaten a major goal, including the maintenance of one's physical integrity (physical stressors) or one's psychological well-being (psychological stressors; Lazarus & Folkman, 1984). *Distress* is a negative psychological response to such threats and can include a variety of affective and cognitive states, such as anxiety, sadness, frustration, the sense of being overwhelmed, or helplessness. Researchers have proposed a number of stressor taxonomies, most of which differentiate threats to basic physiological needs or physical integrity, social connectedness, sense of self, and resources. A number of properties of stressful circumstances can influence the severity of the psychological and physiological response. These properties include the stressor's controllability (whether responses can affect outcomes of the stressor), ambiguity, level of demand placed on the individual, novelty, and duration.

PHYSIOLOGICAL EFFECTS OF EXPOSURE TO STRESSFUL LIFE EXPERIENCE

Extensive research in humans and other animals has demonstrated powerful effects of exposure to stressors on a variety of physiological systems. These specific changes are believed to have evolved to support the behaviors that allow the organism to deal with the threat (e.g., to fight or flee). In order for the organism to respond efficiently, physiological systems that are needed to deal with threats are mobilized and physiological systems that are not needed are suppressed. For example, when responding to a threat, the body increases available concentrations of glucose (an energy source) to ready the organism for physical activity; at the same time, the body inhibits processes that promote growth and reproduction. Although the body is adapted to respond with little ill effect to this acute mobilization, chronic or repeated activation of systems that deal with threat can

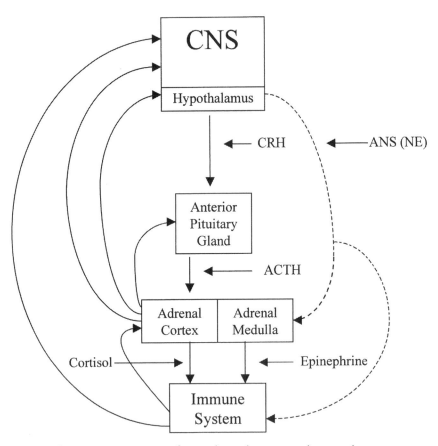

Fig. 1. Schematic representation of interrelationships among the central nervous system (CNS), the hypothalamic-pituitary-adrenal axis, the autonomic nervous system (ANS), and the immune system. Dashed lines indicate ANS neural pathways, and solid lines indicate hormonal pathways. ACTH = adrenocorticotropic hormone; CRH = corticotropin-releasing hormone; NE = norepinephrine.

have adverse long-term physiological and health effects (McEwen, 1998; Sapolsky, 1992). A wide array of physiological systems have been shown to change in response to stressors; in this section, I summarize the effects on the three most carefully studied systems (Fig. 1).

Impact on the Autonomic Nervous System

Since Walter Cannon's work on the fight-or-flight response in the 1930s, researchers have been interested in the effects of stressful experience on the sympathetic adrenomedullary system (the system is so named because the sympathetic nervous system and adrenal medulla are its key components; see Fig. 1). Cannon correctly proposed that exposure to emergency situations results in the release of the hormone epinephrine from the adrenal medulla (the core of the adrenal gland, located above the kidney). This effect was shown to be accomplished by the activity of the autonomic nervous system (ANS). The ANS has two components: the *parasympathetic nervous system*, which controls involuntary resting functions (activation of this system promotes digestion and slows heart rate, e.g.), and the *sympathetic nervous system,* which comes into play in threatening situations and results in increases in involuntary processes (e.g., heart rate and respiration) that are required to respond to physical threats. Fibers of the sympathetic nervous system release the neurotransmitter norepinephrine at various organ sites, including the adrenal medulla, causing the release of epinephrine (also known as adrenaline) into the bloodstream.

Research has demonstrated that exposure to a variety of stressors can activate this system, as manifested by increased output of norepinephrine and epinephrine, as well as increases in autonomic indicators of sympathetic arousal (e.g., increased heart rate). This extremely rapid response system can be activated within seconds and results in the "adrenaline rush" that occurs after an encounter with an unexpected threat.

Impact on the Hypothalamic-Pituitary-Adrenal Axis

A large body of literature suggests that exposure to a variety of acute psychological stressors (e.g., giving a speech, doing difficult cognitive tasks), for relatively short durations, can cause an increase in the levels of the hormone cortisol in the blood, saliva, and urine. This increase is due to activation of the hypothalamic-pituitary-adrenal (HPA) axis (see Fig. 1). Neural pathways link perception of a stressful stimulus to an integrated response in the hypothalamus, which results in the release of corticotropin-releasing hormone. This hormone stimulates the anterior part of the pituitary gland to release adrenocorticotropic hormone, which then travels through the blood stream to the adrenal glands and causes the adrenal cortex (the outer layer of the adrenal gland) to release cortisol (in rodents this hormone is called corticosterone). The activation of this entire system occurs over minutes rather than seconds (as in the case of the ANS). The peak cortisol response occurs 20 to 40 min from the onset of acute stressors. Recovery, or the return to baseline levels, occurs 40 to 60 min following the end of the stressor on average (Dickerson & Kemeny, 2002).

Impact on the Immune System

Exposure to stressful experiences can diminish a variety of immune functions. For example, stressful life experiences, such as bereavement, job loss, and even taking exams, can reduce circulating levels of classes of immunological cells called lymphocytes; inhibit various lymphocyte functions, such as the ability to proliferate when exposed to a foreign substance; and slow integrated immune responses, such as wound healing (Ader, Felten, & Cohen, 2001). Individuals' autonomic reactivity to stressors correlates with the degree to which their immune system is affected by acute laboratory stressors. Extensive evidence that autonomic nerve fibers innervate (enter into) immune organs and alter the function of immune cells residing there supports the link between the ANS and the immune system. In addition, some of the immunological effects of stressors are due to the potent suppressive effects of cortisol on immunological cells. Cortisol can inhibit the production of certain cytokines (chemical mediators released by immune cells to regulate the activities of other immune cells) and suppress a variety of immune functions.

Exposure to stressors can also enhance certain immune processes, for example, those closely related to inflammation. Inflammation is an orchestrated response to exposure to a pathogen that creates local and systemic changes conducive to destroying it (e.g., increases in core body temperature). However, chronic, inappropriate inflammation is at the root of a host of diseases, including certain autoimmune diseases such as rheumatoid arthritis, and may play a role in others, such as cardiovascular disease. There is a great deal of current interest in factors that promote inappropriate inflammation outside the normal context of infection. Exposure to some psychological stressors can increase circulating levels of cytokines that promote inflammation, perhaps because stressful experience can reduce the sensitivity of immune cells to the inhibitory effects of cortisol (Miller, Cohen, & Ritchey, 2002).

Not only can the brain and peripheral neural systems (systems that extend from the brain to the body—e.g., the ANS and HPA axis) affect the immune system, but the immune system can affect the brain and one's psychological state. In rodents, certain cytokines can act on the central nervous system, resulting in behavioral changes that resemble sickness (e.g., increases in body temperature, reduction in exploratory behavior) but also appear to mimic depression (e.g., alterations in learning and memory, anorexia, inability to experience pleasure, reductions in social behavior, alterations in sleep, behavioral slowing). Emerging data indicate that these cytokines can induce negative mood and alter cognition in humans as well. These effects may explain affective and cognitive changes that have been observed to be associated with inflammatory conditions. They may also explain some depressive symptoms associated with stressful conditions (Maier & Watkins, 1998).

Health Implications

Activation of these physiological systems during exposure to a stressor is adaptive in the short run under certain circumstances but can become maladaptive if the systems are repeatedly or chronically activated or if they fail to shut down when the threat no longer exists. McEwen (1998) has coined the term *allostatic load* to refer to the cumulative toll of chronic overactivation of the physiological systems that are designed to respond to environmental perturbations. For example, evidence suggests that chronic exposure to stressors or distress (as in posttraumatic stress disorder and chronic depression) can cause atrophy in a part of the brain called the hippocampus, resulting in memory loss. Chronic exposure to stressful circumstances has also been shown to increase vulnerability to upper respiratory infections in individuals exposed to a virus. Researchers have observed effects on other health outcomes as well, but complete models of stress and health that document all the mediating mechanisms from the central nervous system to the pathophysiological processes that control disease are not yet available (Kemeny, 2003).

GENERALITY VERSUS SPECIFICITY IN THE PHYSIOLOGICAL RESPONSE TO STRESSORS

The central dogma of most stress research today is that stressors have a uniform effect on the physiological processes I have just described. Hans Selye shaped the thinking of generations of researchers when he argued that the physiological response to stressful circumstances is nonspecific, meaning that all stressors, physical and psychological, are capable of eliciting the triad of physiological changes he observed in his rodent research: shrinking of the thymus (a central immune organ), enlargement of the adrenal gland (which produces corticosterone), and ulceration of the gastrointestinal tract. Very little research has directly tested this *generality model* by determining whether or not differences in stressful conditions are associated with distinctive physiological effects in humans. Modern versions of the generality model propose that if stressors lead to the experience of distress (or perceived stress), then a stereotyped set of physiological changes will be elicited in the systems I have described. These models also emphasize the important role of a variety of psychological and environmental factors that can moderate the relationships among stressor exposure, distress, and physiological activation (see Fig. 2). However, these newer versions are essentially generality models because all of the

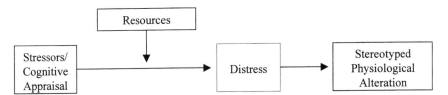

Fig. 2. The generality model of stress. This model proposes that exposure to stressors and the cognitive appraisals of those events can lead to distress. The nature of this relationship depends on the resources available to deal with the stressors (e.g., coping skills, social support, personality factors, genetics, environmental resources). Elevations in distress cause a stereotyped physiological alteration in stressresponsive systems. Bidirectional relationships between many components of the model are assumed but are not indicated here.

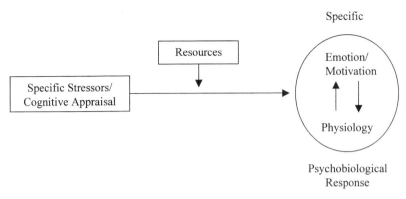

Specific

Resources

Specific Stressors/
Cognitive Appraisal

Emotion/
Motivation

Physiology

Psychobiological
Response

Fig. 3. The integrated specificity model of stress. This model proposes that exposure to specific stressful conditions and cognitive appraisals of those conditions shape the specific nature of an integrated psychobiological response (including emotion-motivation and physiology) to promote adaptive responses to the threat. For example, threats that are appraised as uncontrollable may lead to an integrated psychobiological response that includes disengagement from the goal that is threatened by the stressor (manifested in withdrawal, inactivity, and reduced effort), related affective states (e.g., depression), and physiological changes that support disengagement. Threats appraised as controllable may lead to an integrated response involving engagement with the threat and physiological responses supporting active coping processes. As in the generality model, resources available to deal with the stressors can moderate this relationship.

factors are considered relevant to the extent that they buffer against or exacerbate the experience of distress, without considering that different kinds of distress (e.g., different emotional responses) might have distinctive physiological correlates. According to these models, distress has a uniform relationship to physiology.

There is, however, increasing evidence for specificity in the relationship between stressors and physiology. Weiner (1992) advocated an integrated specificity model of stressor physiology, arguing that "organisms meet . . . challenges and dangers by integrated behavioral, physiological patterns of response that are appropriate to the task" (p. 33). According to this model, both behavior and physiology are parts of an integrated response to address a specific environmental condition (see Fig. 3), and specific conditions or environmental signals elicit a patterned array of hormonal and neural changes that are designed to ready the organism to deal with the specific nature of the threat. In animals, specific neural and peripheral changes occur in concert with behaviors such as fighting, fleeing, defending, submitting, exerting dominance, and hunting prey, among others. Distinctive behaviors (fight, flight, and defeat) have also been elicited by activating specific regions of the brain with excitatory amino acids.

COGNITIVE APPRAISALS SHAPE PHYSIOLOGICAL RESPONSES

Cognitive appraisal processes can profoundly shape the specific nature of the physiological response to stressful circumstances and play a central role in the integrated specificity model. Cognitive appraisal is the process of categorizing a situation in terms of its significance for well-being (Lazarus & Folkman, 1984). Primary appraisal relates to perceptions of goal threat, whereas secondary appraisal relates to perceptions of resources available to meet the demands of the circumstance (e.g., intellectual, social, or financial resources). Three categories of cognitive appraisals have been shown to elicit distinctive affective and physiological responses.

Threat Versus Challenge

According to Blascovich and Tomaka (1996), the experience of threat results when the demands in a given situation are perceived to outweigh the resources. When resources are perceived to approximate or exceed demands, however, the individual experiences a challenge response. These two motivational states are associated with distinctive ANS alterations. In situations that require active responses to obtain a goal, challenge is associated with increases in sympathetic arousal (increased cardiac performance) coupled with reduced or unchanged peripheral resistance (resistance to blood flow). These changes parallel those observed with metabolically demanding aerobic exercise. Threat, in contrast, although also associated with sympathetic arousal involving increased cardiac performance, is associated with *increased* peripheral resistance, leading to increased blood pressure. Thus, different cognitive appraisals can result in distinctive patterns of ANS reactivity with potentially distinguishable implications for health. The issue here is not degree of activation of the sympathetic nervous system, but rather distinctive qualities of activation depending on the specific nature of the cognitive appraisal process.

Perceived Control

Animal and human research demonstrates that uncontrollable circumstances, or those perceived as uncontrollable, are more likely to activate key stressor-relevant systems than are circumstances that the organism perceives to be controllable. For example, when rodents with and without control over exposure to identical stressors are compared, those with control show a reduced cortisol response. A meta-analysis (a statistical analysis that summarizes findings across studies) has demonstrated that humans who are exposed to stressors in an acute laboratory context are significantly more likely to experience HPA activation if the stressors are uncontrollable than if they are controllable (Dickerson & Kemeny, 2002). Threats that are appraised as controllable but in fact are uncontrollable have been shown to elicit less severe physiological alterations (e.g., in the immune system) than those appraised as uncontrollable.

Social Cognition

The social world has a powerful effect on stress-relevant physiological systems (Cacioppo, 1994). For example, social isolation has a very significant effect on health, which is likely mediated by the physiological systems described here. Other social processes can regulate physiological systems as well. For example, place in a dominance hierarchy has a significant effect on physiological systems. Subordinate animals, who have low social status, demonstrate a more activated

HPA axis, higher levels of cytokines that promote inflammation, and other physiological changes compared with their dominant counterparts. A meta-analytic review has demonstrated that demanding performance tasks elicit HPA activation when one's social status or social self-esteem is threatened by performance failures, but these effects are greatly diminished when this social-status threat is not present (Dickerson & Kemeny, 2002). Cognitive appraisals of social status and social self-esteem appear to play an important role in these effects (Dickerson, Gruenewald, & Kemeny, in press).

CONCLUSIONS

The research findings on cognitive appraisal and physiological systems lead to two important conclusions. First, depending on the nature of the eliciting conditions, different patterns of physiological response can occur. Second, when cognitive appraisals of conditions are manipulated, distinctive physiological effects can be observed within the same context. Therefore, the way the individual thinks about the situation may override the impact of the specific nature of the conditions themselves.

In the integrated specificity model of stressful experience, stressful conditions and appraisals of them elicit integrated psychobiological responses (including emotion and physiology) that are tied to the nature of the threat experienced. A number of researchers have found that different neural and autonomic pathways are activated during different emotional experiences. Thus, specific emotions, in all likelihood, play a central role in the nature of the physiological response to stressful conditions. A more intensive evaluation of the role of distinct emotions would be an important contribution to future stress research. It is most likely that distinctions will be observed when researchers evaluate patterns of physiological change across systems, rather than relying on single response systems (e.g., cortisol level), and when emotional behavior is assessed in conjunction with self-report data.

Recommended Reading

Dickerson, S.S., & Kemeny, M.E. (2002). (See References)
Kemeny, M.E., & Gruenewald, T.L. (2000). Affect, cognition, the immune system and health. In E.A. Mayer & C. Saper (Eds.), *The biological basis for mind body interactions* (pp. 291–308). Amsterdam: Elsevier Science.
Lazarus, R.S., & Folkman, S. (1984). (See References)
Sapolsky, R.M. (1992). (See References)
Weiner, H. (1992). (See References)

Acknowledgments—This article is dedicated to the memory of Herbert Weiner, a pioneer in the field of stress research, who profoundly shaped the thinking of the generations of stress researchers he trained.

Note

1. Address correspondence to Margaret E. Kemeny, Health Psychology Program, Department of Psychiatry, Laurel Heights Campus, University of California, 3333 California St., Suite 465, San Francisco, CA 94143.

References

Ader, R., Felten, D.L., & Cohen, N. (2001). *Psychoneuroimmunology* (3rd ed.). New York: Academic Press.

Blascovich, J., & Tomaka, J. (1996). The biopsychosocial model of arousal regulation. *Advances in Experimental Social Psychology, 28,* 1–51.

Cacioppo, J.T. (1994). Social neuroscience: Autonomic, neuroendocrine, and immune responses to stress. *Psychophysiology, 31,* 113–128.

Dickerson, S.S., Gruenewald, T.L., & Kemeny, M.E. (in press). When the social self is threatened: Shame, physiology and health. *Journal of Personality.*

Dickerson, S.S., & Kemeny, M.E. (2002). *Acute stressors and cortisol responses: A theoretical integration and synthesis of laboratory research.* Manuscript submitted for publication.

Kemeny, M.E. (2003). An interdisciplinary research model to investigate psychosocial cofactors in disease: Application to HIV-1 pathogenesis. *Brain, Behavior & Immunity, 17,* 562–572.

Lazarus, R.S., & Folkman, S. (1984). *Stress, appraisal, and coping.* New York: Springer.

Maier, S.F., & Watkins, L.R. (1998). Cytokines for psychologists: Implications of bidirectional immune-to-brain communication for understanding behavior, mood, and cognition. *Psychological Review, 105,* 83–107.

McEwen, B.S. (1998). Protective and damaging effects of stress mediators. *New England Journal of Medicine, 338,* 171–179.

Miller, G.E., Cohen, S., & Ritchey, A.K. (2002). Chronic psychological stress and the regulation of proinflammatory cytokines: A gluco-corticoid resistance model. *Health Psychology, 21,* 531–541.

Sapolsky, R.M. (1992). Neuroendocrinology of the stress-response. In J.B. Becker, S.M. Breedlove, & D. Crews (Eds.), *Behavioral endocrinology* (pp. 287–324). Cambridge, MA: MIT Press.

Weiner, H. (1992). *Perturbing the organism: The biology of stressful experience.* Chicago: University of Chicago Press.

This article has been reprinted as it originally appeared in *Current Directions in Psychological Science*. Citation information for this article as originally published appears above.

Turning Up the Heat: Inflammation as a Mechanism Linking Chronic Stress, Depression, and Heart Disease

Gregory E. Miller[1] and Ekin Blackwell

Department of Psychology, University of British Columbia

Abstract

Mounting evidence indicates that chronic stressors and depressive symptoms contribute to morbidity and mortality from cardiac disease. However, little is known about the underlying mechanisms responsible for these effects or about why depressive symptoms and cardiac disease co-occur so frequently. In this article we outline a novel model that seeks to address these issues. It asserts that chronic stressors activate the immune system in a way that leads to persistent inflammation. With long-term exposure to the products of inflammation, people develop symptoms of depression and experience progression of atherosclerosis, the pathologic condition that underlies cardiac disease.

Keywords

stress; depression; inflammation; atherosclerosis

Though people have long believed that certain thoughts and feelings are toxic for their health, only in the past 30 years has convincing evidence accumulated to support this view. This research indicates that while not all negative thoughts and feelings are bad for health, specific cognitive and emotional processes do contribute to the development and progression of medical illness. In this article we focus on two of the best-studied culprits, chronic stressors and depressive symptoms, and how they "get under the skin" to influence disease. We focus on coronary heart disease (CHD), the leading cause of mortality in developed countries and the context in which mind–body connections are best documented.

STRESSORS, DEPRESSION, AND CHD RISK

Chronic stressors come in different packages, ranging from troubled marriages to difficult workplaces. What they have in common is the tendency to be appraised as threatening and unmanageable. They can involve situations in which the troubling stimulus persists over a long time (an abusive boss), as well as situations in which the event is brief but the threat persists longer (a sexual assault). Research indicates that exposure to chronic stress generally increases vulnerability to CHD. In a study of 12,000 healthy males followed over 9 years, those facing chronic difficulties at work or home were 30% more likely to die of CHD (Matthews & Gump, 2002). Another project measured adverse childhood experiences in 17,000 adults and found a dose–response relationship with CHD incidence. Those who reported a variety of adverse experiences such as neglect, domestic violence, and parental criminal behavior were 3.1 times more likely to develop CHD (Dong et al., 2004).

Depression can take the form of a low mood or a clinical syndrome. In both cases it typically involves sadness and anhedonia, which may be accompanied by disturbances in eating, sleeping, and cognition. Depression is common in CHD. About 20% of patients meet criteria for a clinical diagnosis, and even more have symptoms below the diagnostic threshold. These symptoms diminish quality of life and contribute to poorer medical outcomes. For example, in a study of 900 patients interviewed in the hospital following a heart attack, high levels of depressive symptoms were associated with a threefold increase in cardiac mortality over 5 years (Lesperance, Frasure-Smith, Talajic, & Bourassa, 2002). There is also evidence that in healthy young adults, depressive symptoms can accelerate the development of CHD. For example, in a 27-year study of middle-aged adults, those with high levels of depressive symptoms at baseline were 1.7 times more likely to have a fatal heart attack (Barefoot & Schroll, 1996).

Although these findings provide compelling evidence of mind–body connections in CHD, they also raise challenging questions that researchers are just starting to address. One has to do with the underlying mechanisms linking mind and body. How can nebulous patterns of thinking and feeling "get inside the body" in a way that alters disease trajectories? A second question has to do with the high rate of comorbidity between depression and CHD. There are other serious medical conditions, such as cancer, for which the rates of depression are much lower (Dew, 1998). Why is it especially common in cardiac patients? Another question researchers struggle with concerns theoretical integration. Though most studies have focused on chronic stress or depressive symptoms, these states are likely to be closely related and to influence disease through similar pathways. So an important challenge involves conceptually integrating literatures that have evolved separately and determining where the "action" really is.

AN INTEGRATIVE CONCEPTUAL FRAMEWORK

We have developed a conceptual framework to begin answering these questions (Fig. 1). It begins with the notion that chronic stressors activate the immune system in a way that leads to persistent inflammation. This refers to a molecular and cellular cascade the body uses to eliminate infections and resolve injuries. The model suggests that with long-term exposure to the products of inflammation, people develop symptoms of depression and experience accelerated CHD progression. This occurs because the signaling molecules deployed to orchestrate inflammation—pro-inflammatory cytokines—elicit adaptations in the brain that are manifested as symptoms of depression. These molecules also promote growth of plaques in blood vessels and stimulate processes that lead those plaques to rupture. In doing so, they bring about heart attacks. The model goes on to assert that the excessive inflammation is responsible for bidirectional connections between depression and atherosclerosis. That is, cytokines are viewed as a mechanism through which depression fosters CHD progression, and at the same time as the reason cardiac patients experience high rates of affective difficulties. It should be noted that although chronic stress is depicted as the model's starting point, a person could enter the cascade as a result of depressive symptoms or coronary disease; chronic stress is sufficient, but not necessary, to initiate the model's processes.

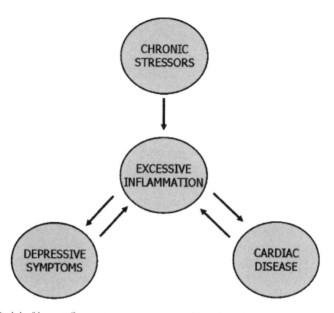

Fig. 1. Model of how inflammatory processes mediate the relations among chronic stressors, depressive symptoms, and cardiac disease. Stressors activate the immune system in a way that leads to persistent inflammation. With long-term exposure to the molecular products of inflammation, people are expected develop symptoms of depression and experience progression of cardiac disease. Excessive inflammation is also viewed as responsible for the bidirectional relationship between depression and atherosclerosis. (Some pathways in the model are excluded for the sake of brevity and simplicity—for example, the likely bidirectional relationship between chronic stressors and depressive symptoms.

WHAT IS INFLAMMATION?

When the immune system detects invading microbes like viruses or bacteria, it launches an inflammatory response, which causes white blood cells to accumulate at the site of infection. These cells attempt to eliminate the pathogen, rid the body of cells that have been infected with it, and repair any tissue damage that it has caused. This entire process is orchestrated by inflammatory cytokines, which are signaling molecules secreted by white blood cells. The most critical cytokines are interleukin-1β, interleukin-6 (IL-6), and tumor necrosis factor-α, and they have wide-ranging functions that include directing cells toward infections, signaling them to divide, and activating their killing mechanisms. Because these molecules are released when the immune system is active, researchers use their presence as a rough index of the magnitude of inflammation in the body. This is also done by measuring C-reactive protein (CRP), a molecule produced by the liver in response to IL-6.

DOES CHRONIC STRESS TRIGGER INFLAMMATION?

What evidence is there to support the idea that chronic stressors activate the immune system in a way that promotes inflammation? Over the past few years a number of studies have found that among persons facing serious chronic stressors, concentrations of inflammatory molecules such as IL-6 and CRP are significantly elevated (Segerstrom & Miller, 2004). One project followed older adults caring for a relative with dementia. Caregiving is a potent chronic stressor that presents challenges in nearly every domain of life, and it does so at a time of life when coping resources are often waning. Over a 6-year follow-up, caregivers displayed marked increases in IL-6 and did so at a rate that was four times more rapid than controls (Kiecolt-Glaser et al., 2003). This pattern of findings was initially puzzling to researchers, because chronic stressors were believed to suppress immune functions. But it is now clear that the immune system responds to any given stressor in a complex fashion; some of its functions are activated at the same time as others are disabled (Segerstrom & Miller, 2004).

Researchers are now seeking to understand the mechanisms through which chronic stressors bring about inflammation. Some evidence indicates that chronic stressors "prime" the immune system to respond to challenges in an especially aggressive fashion. Another hypothesis is that chronic stressors interfere with the immune system's capacity to shut down after a challenge has been minimized. One signal the body uses to do this is cortisol; at high levels, this hormone dampens the release of cytokines. However, chronic stressors interfere with this process. In parents whose children were being treated for cancer, for example, cortisol's ability to suppress IL-6 production was markedly diminished (Miller, Cohen, & Ritchey, 2002). This suggests that chronic stressors "take the brakes off" inflammation. Another intriguing possibility derives from animal research showing that stressors like social isolation can bring about inflammation in the brain (Maier, Watkins, & Nance, 2001). This process has been shown, in turn, to activate inflammation in the periphery. So, in humans, chronic stressors may trigger a cytokine cascade that starts in the brain and then makes its way to other areas of the body.

DEPRESSION AND INFLAMMATION

Can inflammation bring about depression? To answer this question, researchers have exposed rodents to bacterial products that trigger inflammation and shown that the animals develop symptoms resembling depression—symptoms known as "sickness behaviors." These include declines in food intake, motor activity, grooming behavior, and social exploration, as well as a lack of interest in hedonic activities such as sex (Yirmiya, 1996). It has been difficult to examine this process directly in humans, because they cannot safely be exposed to inflammatory substances. However, researchers have been able to address this question indirectly in cancer patients, who are administered cytokines with the hope that they will boost immune functions. About 50% of patients treated with cytokines develop symptoms, such as dysphoria, anhedonia, fatigue, anorexia, and cognitive impairment, that are consistent with a diagnosis of major depression (Musselman et al., 2001). The extent of these symptoms is directly related to the dose of cytokine therapy, and prophylactic treatment with antidepressant medications can often prevent them from arising. Although these findings suggest that inflammation brings about adaptations that resemble depression, further research is necessary to determine whether these conditions are one and the same or merely "lookalikes." It may also be the case that sickness behavior underlies some cases of depression—like those that arise in CHD and other inflammatory conditions—but is not responsible for affective difficulties more generally.

Researchers are still attempting to understand how and why sickness behaviors emerge. They may be an evolved strategy to maximize the chances of survival after infection (Maier & Watkins, 1998). When infected, an organism's survival depends on its capacity to mount a vigorous defense and to avoid contact with pathogens and predators that might capitalize on its vulnerability. Organisms must initiate a febrile response, which interferes with pathogens' capacity to reproduce, and mobilize their immune systems to fight. These responses, however, pose significant metabolic demands. By spending more time sleeping and withdrawing from activities, the organism conserves energy and avoids contact with pathogens and predators. When viewed from this perspective, the "depressive" symptoms that arise following inflammation are behavioral adaptations that evolved to maximize the chances of survival during infection.

And can depression provoke inflammation? Cross-sectional studies indicate that among patients suffering from clinical depression, concentrations of CRP and IL-6 are increased by 40% to 50% (Miller, Stetler, Carney, Freedland, & Banks, 2002). These effects do not seem to be limited to clinical depression; similar patterns are found in patients with depressive symptoms, even when they are not severe enough to warrant a diagnosis. But it is difficult to rigorously evaluate whether depression provokes inflammation, because humans cannot be randomly assigned to experience affective difficulties. To overcome this difficulty, researchers have studied patients before and after treatment and have shown that cytokine volumes decrease after depressive symptoms have been ameliorated. These findings suggest that depression operates causally. How it does so remains unclear. Depressive symptoms could prime the immune system to respond aggressively to challenges; alternatively, they could initiate a cytokine cascade in the brain that spreads elsewhere. They also could foster maladaptive behaviors that themselves activate inflammatory processes. The best data to date are consistent with the latter hypothesis; much of the inflammation in depression is attributable to excess weight and sleeping disturbances (Miller, Stetler, et al., 2002; Motivala & Irwin, in press).

INFLAMMATION CONTRIBUTES TO CHD

CHD begins when infections and injuries damage the arteries supplying the heart, causing an influx of white blood cells that are seeking to repair the lesion. These cells accumulate in the vessel wall, where they become engorged with cholesterol, and eventually contribute to formation of plaque. Much later in the disease process, these cells help to destabilize the plaque. When this occurs, the plaque can rupture, and its remnants can block blood flow in the vessel. This process deprives the heart of nutrients, and results in death of cardiac tissues, an outcome known as myocardial infarction, or heart attack. Because inflammation is centrally involved in the progression of CHD, studies have examined whether the presence of inflammatory molecules forecasts disease. This work shows that high levels of such molecules, particularly CRP and IL-6, confer risk for later CHD morbidity and mortality (Libby, 2002).

WHERE DO WE GO FROM HERE?

While several of the model's basic predictions have been confirmed, more work needs to be done before its overall utility can be evaluated. The first step in the process should entail testing the model's mediational hypotheses. Do stressful experiences foster depressive symptoms and cardiac disease by triggering inflammation? Does inflammation operate as a bidirectional pathway linking depression and atherosclerosis? To answer these questions, researchers will need to conduct multiwave prospective investigations assessing constructs frequently. If the model's predictions turn out to be accurate, it will become important to further differentiate its constructs so that their most toxic elements are revealed. Must stressors be severe, like caregiving, to bring about inflammation? Or can more day-to-day concerns such as deadlines and traffic elicit the same processes? There are also nagging questions about the depression construct. Do the symptoms of depression have a unique capacity to initiate the cascades depicted in the model, or is their effect attributable to a broader cluster of negative emotions that also includes anger and anxiety (Suls & Bunde, 2005)? For the model to be maximally valuable as a research tool, the next wave of studies will have to distill these constructs. Fortunately, there are some good leads to guide this work. For example, an intriguing program of research indicates that when stressors elicit feelings of shame, they are especially potent triggers of inflammation and have a special capacity to bring about depressive episodes (Dickerson, Gruenewald, & Kemeny, 2004; Kendler, Hettema, Butera, Gardner, & Prescott, 2003). As time goes on it will also become important to incorporate additional mechanisms linking the model's constructs. Research has already identified a number of candidate pathways. In focusing our discussion on inflammation, we do not mean to imply that these pathways are unimportant; we simply view inflammation as the best candidate for pulling together the disparate literatures we have discussed. Of course, for the model to be complete, these other pathways must be integrated. To the extent that the next wave of studies can meet these challenges, researchers will be able to develop convincing mechanistic explanations for the age-old belief that the mind and body are connected.

Recommended Reading

Irwin, M.R. (2002). Psychoneuroimmunology of depression: Clinical implications. *Brain, Behavior and Immunity, 16*, 1–16.
Kop, W.J. (1999). Chronic and acute psychological risk factors for clinical manifestations of coronary artery disease. *Psychosomatic Medicine, 61*, 476–487.
Maier, S.F., & Watkins, L.R. (1998). (See References)

Acknowledgments—The authors thank Dr. Edith Chen for helpful feedback on this manuscript, and the Michael Smith Foundation for Health Research and the Heart and Stroke Foundation of Canada for supporting this work.

Note

1. Address correspondence to Dr. Gregory Miller, Department of Psychology, University of British Columbia, 2136 West Mall Avenue, Vancouver BC V6T 1Z4 Canada; e-mail: gemiller@psych.ubc.ca.

References

Barefoot, J.C., & Schroll, M. (1996). Symptoms of depression, acute myocardial infarction, and total mortality in a community sample. *Circulation, 93,* 1976–1980.

Dew, M.A. (1998). Psychiatric disorder in the context of physical illness. In B.P. Dohrenwend (Ed.), *Adversity, stress, and psychopathology* (pp. 177–218). New York: Oxford University Press.

Dickerson, S.S., Gruenewald, T.L., & Kemeny, M.E. (2004). When the social self is threatened: Shame, physiology, and health. *Journal of Personality, 72,* 1191–1216.

Dong, M., Giles, W.H., Felitti, V.J., Dube, S.R., Williams, J.E., Chapman, D.P., & Anda, R.F. (2004). Insights into causal pathways for ischemic heart disease: Adverse childhood experiences study. *Circulation, 110,* 1761–1766.

Kendler, K.S., Hettema, J.M., Butera, F., Gardner, C.O., & Prescott, C.A. (2003). Life event dimensions of loss, humiliation, entrapment, and danger in the prediction of onsets of major depression and generalized anxiety. *Archives of General Psychiatry, 60,* 789–796.

Kiecolt-Glaser, J.K., Preacher, K.J., MacCallum, R.C., Atkinson, C., Malarkey, W.B., & Glaser, R. (2003). Chronic stress and age-related increases in the proinflammatory cytokine IL-6. *Proceedings of the National Academy of Sciences, U.S.A., 100,* 9090–9095.

Lesperance, F., Frasure-Smith, N., Talajic, M., & Bourassa, M.G. (2002). Five-year risk of cardiac mortality in relation to initial severity and one-year changes in depression symptoms after myocardial infarction. *Circulation, 105,* 1049–1053.

Libby, P. (2002). Atherosclerosis: The new view. *Scientific American, 286,* 46–55.

Maier, S.F., & Watkins, L.R. (1998). Cytokines for psychologists: Implications of bidirectional immune-to-brain communication for understanding behavior, mood, and cognition. *Psychological Review, 105,* 83–107.

Maier, S.F., Watkins, L.R., & Nance, D.M. (2001). Multiple routes of action of IL-1 on the nervous system. In R. Ader, D. Felten, & N. Cohen (Eds.), *Psychoneuroimmunology* (3rd ed., pp. 563–579). New York: Academic Press.

Matthews, K., & Gump, B.B. (2002). Chronic work stress and marital dissolution increase risk of posttrial mortality in men from the Multiple Risk Factor Intervention Trial. *Archives of Internal Medicine, 162,* 309–315.

Miller, G.E., Cohen, S., & Ritchey, A.K. (2002). Chronic psychological stress and the regulation of pro-inflammatory cytokines: A glucocorticoid resistance model. *Health Psychology, 21,* 531–541.

Miller, G.E., Stetler, C.A., Carney, R.M., Freedland, K.E., & Banks, W.A. (2002). Clinical depression and inflammatory risk markers for coronary heart disease. *The American Journal of Cardiology, 90,* 1279–1283.

Motivala, S.J., & Irwin, M.R. (in press). Sleep and immunity: Cytokine pathways linking sleep and health outcomes. *Current Directions in Psychological Science.*

Musselman, D.L., Lawson, D.H., Gumnick, J.F., Manatunga, A.K., Penna, S., Goodkin, S., Greiner, K., Nemeroff, C.B., & Miller, A.H. (2001). Paroxetine for the prevention of depression induced by high-dose interferon alfa. *New England Journal of Medicine, 344,* 961–966.

Segerstrom, S.C., & Miller, G.E. (2004). Psychological stress and the immune system: A meta-analytic study of 30 years of inquiry. *Psychological Bulletin, 130,* 601–630.

Suls, J., & Bunde, J. (2005). Anger, anxiety, and depression as risk factors for cardiovascular disease: The problems and implications of overlapping affective dispositions. *Psychological Bulletin, 131,* 260–300.

Yirmiya, R. (1996). Endotoxin produces a depressive-like episode in rats. *Brain Research, 711,* 163–174.

Plasticity for Affective Neurocircuitry: How the Environment Affects Gene Expression

Nathan A. Fox[1]
University of Maryland, College Park

Amie A. Hane
Williams College

Daniel S. Pine
The National Institutes of Health

Abstract

We (Fox et al., 2005) recently described a gene-by-environment interaction involving child temperament and maternal social support, finding heightened behavioral inhibition in children homozygous or heterozygous for the serotonin transporter (5HTTLPR) gene short allele whose mothers reported low social support. Here, we propose a model, Plasticity for Affective Neurocircuitry, that describes the manner in which genetic disposition and environmental circumstances may interact. Children with a persistently fearful temperament (and the 5HTTLPR short allele) are more likely to experience caregiving environments in which threat is highlighted. This in turn will exacerbate an attention bias that alters critical affective neurocircuitry to threat and enhances and maintains anxious behavior in the child.

Keywords

temperament; gene × environment interaction; attention bias to threat; parenting

Individual differences in the stress response represent stable aspects of behavior that emerge early in life and reflect aspects of brain function. While behavioral-genetic studies implicate genes and the environment in these differences, the manner in which specific genes and environmental events shape specific aspects of brain function remains poorly specified. Recent work provides important clues, however, concerning these specific pathways. In particular, emerging findings suggest that specific genes associated with the function of the neurotransmitter serotonin (5-HT) interact with social stressors during development to shape function in a neural circuit implicated in the stress response.

RESEARCH ON GENE × ENVIRONMENT INTERACTIONS

A series of recent research reports provides evidence for gene-by-environment (denoted gene × environment) interactions with a protein crucially involved in the effects of 5-HT on behavior. This protein regulates the fate of 5-HT released from neurons. Each of the genetically derived variants in this protein is known as an expression of a serotonin transporter protein polymorphism (5HTTLPR; Caspi et al., 2003; Kaufman et al., 2004). The 5HTTLPR gene has two major functional alleles: a long and a short, as well as another long-variant allele that behaves, functionally, like the short allele. Individuals who are homozygous have two copies of either the long or the short. Individuals who are heterozygous have one copy of each. In general, studies of gene × environment interaction with this particular gene suggest that individuals who are homozygous for the short allele of the 5HTTLPR and who are exposed to significant stress are more likely to exhibit significant maladaptive behavior than are individuals who are homozygous for the long allele and are exposed to similar levels of stress. Individuals who are heterozygous, having one copy of the long and one of the short allele, usually fall somewhere in the middle, exhibiting more maladaptive outcomes compared to individuals homozygous for the long, and somewhat fewer than individuals who are homozygous for the short allele.

For example, Caspi et al. (2003) found that individuals homozygous for the short allele of 5-HTTLPR and exposed to five or more stressful life events were more likely to experience a major depressive episode, compared to individuals homozygous for the long allele exposed to such stress. Kaufman et al. (2004) reported that children carrying the short allele who had a history of abuse were more likely to evidence depression if their caregivers reported that they themselves were under high stress. Both of these studies reported psychiatric outcomes as a result of this particular gene × environment interaction. Caspi et al. (2003) examined the probability of major depression. Kaufman et al. (2004) reported on depressive symptoms in the subjects.

In a recent paper, we (Fox et al., 2005) reported on a similar gene × environment interaction in young children who were selected for the temperamental characteristic of behavioral inhibition. Signs of behavioral inhibition are detectable within the first months of life. For example, infants displaying high motor reactivity and negative affect when presented with novel auditory and visual stimuli are more likely to display behavioral inhibition as toddlers and preschoolers (Fox, Henderson, Rubin, Calkins, & Schmidt, 2001). Behaviorally inhibited children cease their ongoing activity and withdraw to their caregiver's proximity when confronted with novel events. They are also likely to isolate themselves when confronted with unfamiliar peers or adults. This behavioral style appears early in life, is associated with physiological markers of stress, social reticence with unfamiliar peers, low self-concept in childhood, and may be a risk factor for later psychopathology (Perez-Edgar & Fox, 2005).

We examined the relationship between childhood behavior and two variants of the 5-HTTLPR. As noted above, this protein mediates 5-HT influences on behavior by regulating the fate of 5-HT released from neurons into the synaptic cleft, the space that separates two communicating neurons. We found that children with lower-activity variants of the 5-HTTLPR whose mothers reported experiencing low social support were more likely to display behavioral inhibition at age 7, relative to children with similar 5-HT genetics but whose mothers reported more social support. The gene × environment interaction suggested that children with high-activity forms of the gene were "protected" from manifesting inhibition, even if their mothers reported experiencing low social support. Moreover, while child 5HTTLPR strongly related to inhibition in children with low levels of social support, for children with high levels of social support, no such relationship with 5HTTLPR emerged.

These data extend the findings of previous work, reporting the interaction of environmental stress and genes in predicting behavioral outcomes. Unlike other studies, though, the Fox et al. (2005) study presents data on a sample of typically developing children with nonpsychiatric outcomes. But like the other papers it does not address the mechanisms or processes by which the environmental stressor(s) affect variations in genotype to create the particular phenotypic outcome.

NEUROBIOLOGY OF 5HTTLPR

The short and long forms of the 5HTTLPR produce proteins known as reuptake transporters. These proteins lie within the synapse, the space separating two communicating neurons, and they function to remove serotonin from the synapse after it has been released. 5-HT neurons removed from the brain and studied in the laboratory revealed that the different forms of 5-HT reuptake transporters associated with distinct genotypes act differently. This early work clearly demonstrated functional consequences of the 5HTTLPR. More recent work has begun to describe possible influences of the different polymorphisms or variations in the 5HTTLPR in the neural-system function of living primates and humans.

5-HT neurons, like neurons for other modulatory neurotransmitters, make connections with broadly distributed networks in the brain. 5-HT influences on behavior are thought to emerge through the neurotransmitter's effects on information processing. The neural architecture engaged in the service of processing dangerous stimuli has been mapped in particularly precise detail, and 5-HT is thought to modulate functioning in this circuit (Gross & Hen, 2004). The circuit encompasses the ventral prefrontal cortex (vPFC), an area involved in decision making, and the amygdala, a structure involved in the detection of salient events such as those that are novel or threatening. Both structures receive strong 5-HT innervations. Thus, the amygdala, vPFC, and connections between them constitute a neural circuit that has been labeled "vPFC–amygdala circuitry." Consistent with the laboratory evidence of its effects on serotonin reuptake, the 5HTTLPR also predicts functional aspects of this ventral prefrontal–amygdala circuitry (Pezawas et al., 2005).

One of the most important issues to resolve concerns the mapping of these 5-HT influences across development. Neuroimaging studies in humans demonstrate robust developmental influences on prefrontal–amygdala circuitry (Monk et al., 2003). Studies in animal models suggest that these influences result from developmental changes in 5-HT function (Gross & Hen, 2004). This suggests that the relationship between the 5HTTLPR and prefrontal–amygdala function is likely to change across development. Neuroimaging studies have yet to examine this issue.

Interestingly, animal models suggest that 5-HT effects on neural development emerge through interactions with the environment (Gross & Hen, 2004). Given these data, how then precisely does the action of the environment interact with the 5HTTLPR to shape brain function and behavior? In the specific case of behavioral inhibition, how does the mother's report of her social support influence the expression of her child's 5-HTT gene in a way that ultimately impacts the child's tendency to display inhibited behavior? We propose a model, called Plasticity for Affective Neurocircuitry, and suggest two possible complementary mechanisms, based upon work in the area of anxiety and our own developmental studies. The first deals with the manner in which caregivers interact with behaviorally inhibited children; the second, with the attention bias that may develop as a result of temperamental disposition, caregiver influence, or their interaction.

CAREGIVER BEHAVIOR AND SOCIAL SUPPORT

Research suggests that reported level of social support correlates with quality of caregiver behavior. Mothers who report high levels of social support tend to be more sensitive toward their infants (Crockenberg & McCluskey, 1986) and more satisfied with their role as a parent (Thompson & Walker, 2004). Additional evidence indicates that level of social support may be particularly important for mothers of temperamentally distress-prone infants. Crockenberg and her colleagues found that the positive association between social support and maternal sensitivity was only significant for irritable infants (Crockenberg & McCluskey, 1986). Pauli-Pott, Mertesacker, and Beckmann (2004) found that maternal insensitivity was predicted by the joint effect of infant negative emotionality and low social support. Hence, social support is a factor contributing to the quality of maternal caregiving behavior, particularly for inhibited children who have a history of negative reactivity in infancy and early childhood.

An emergent body of research indicates that the quality of the mother–child relationship mitigates the relation between early and later forms of behavioral inhibition, such that some parents of behaviorally inhibited children interact with their children in a manner that appears to exacerbate or maintain their child's temperament. In our own research, we have identified a unique group of children who consistently withdraw from novelty at age 4 months and who receive insensitive maternal caregiving due to this proneness to distress. For instance, Ghera, Hane, Malesa, and Fox (2006) found that infants who responded negatively to novel stimuli at age 4 months and who were viewed by their mothers as difficult to soothe received low levels of maternal sensitivity. Hane, Fox, Henderson, and Marshall (2006) found that 9-month-old infants who showed high levels of behavioral avoidance to ominous stimuli and a corresponding pattern of right frontal electroencephalogram (EEG) asymmetry (itself a determinant of continued inhibition across early childhood; see Fox et al., 2001), received low levels of maternal sensitivity. Hane and Fox (2006) reported that infants who received low-quality maternal caregiving behavior showed more fearfulness and less sociability in the laboratory, more negative affect while interacting in the home with their mothers, and a pattern of right frontal EEG asymmetry. Taken together, this research suggests that quality of maternal caregiving behavior shapes the development of behavioral inhibition, perhaps by altering the neural systems that underlie reactivity to stress and novelty (see a review by Parent et al., 2005, for parallels in research with rodents).

ATTENTION BIAS TO THREAT

A second mechanism through which experience may affect the neural systems underlying behavioral inhibition involves the development of attention bias to threat. A variety of data using a number of different experimental paradigms suggest that individuals who self-report a high degree of anxious symptoms or who are diagnosed with a number of different anxiety disorders display an attention bias to threat. When presented with visual stimuli reflecting threat, anxious individuals are more vigilant toward these stimuli and take longer to disengage from visual attention to them (Mogg, Millar, & Bradley, 2000). In humans, as in other species, the ability to detect threatening stimuli in the environment appears to provide an important adaptive advantage for safety and survival. The neural systems that are involved in threat detection have been well described in nonhuman primates, rats, and, through the use of functional neuroimaging, in humans (Monk et al., 2006). These systems encompass prefrontal–amygdala circuitry previously tied to threat responses and 5HTTLPR in humans.

An enhanced sensitivity to threat has been suggested as an underlying mechanism in anxiety disorders (MacLeod, Rutherford, Campbell, Ebsworthy, & Holker, 2002). A recent meta-analysis (Bar-Haim, Lamy, Pergamin, Bakermans-Kraneburg, & van IJzendoorn, 2007) suggests that the distribution of attention in anxious individuals may be part of a resource-allocation system that biases the individual to pay close attention to threat. Such biases may develop over time and be the result of a person's ongoing transaction with threatening or aversive stimuli. Moreover, studies using experimental approaches, at least in adults, suggest that these attention biases are causally implicated in the genesis of anxiety following exposure to stress (MacLeod et al., 2002). From this perspective, children born with a disposition to react intensively and with negative affect to stress or novelty may go on to show different patterns of behavior, depending on the degree to which they are exposed to overzealous, intrusive maternal behavior as opposed to a more sensitive, nurturing style.

The Plasticity for Affective Neurocircuitry model that we propose suggests that early temperament influences quality of the caregiving environment and quality of the environment in turn shapes attention bias to threat and mediates the relation between early temperament and later inhibition (see Fig. 1). Rubin, Burgess, and Hastings (2002) showed that the relation between behavioral inhibition as a toddler and reticence at age 4 was significant and positive only for those children whose mothers were psychologically overcontrolling and derisive. Thus it appears that caregivers who highlight or identify negative events in their child's environment (often in an effort to control their child's behavior) may in fact be inadvertently promoting attention bias in the child. Evidence from studies of interactions between mothers and children with anxiety disorders supports this position. For example, Barrett, Rapee, and Dadds (1996) found that parental discussion of ambiguous situations was associated with increased perception of threat and the creation of avoidant plans of action in anxious children. Thus, from within the caregiving environment, children disposed to respond with negative affect to novelty or uncertainty may be further reinforced to bias their attention toward threat during the course of interactions with caregivers.

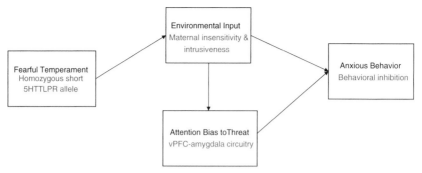

Fig. 1. Plasticity for Affective Neurocircuitry model. A child's genetically disposed fearful temperament (due to homozygosity for the short allele of the serotonin transporter, 5HTTLPR, gene) elicits and is elicited by caregiver behavior (maternal insensitivity and intrusiveness) to shape attention bias to threat and the underlying neural circuitry (in the ventral prefrontal cortex, vPFC, and amygdala) supporting this bias. Exaggerated attention bias contributes to the emergence and maintenance of anxious behaviors.

CONCLUSIONS

At the present time, there are preciously few data on the development of attention biases to evocative, threatening, or stressful stimuli. Research in this area is clearly needed in order to understand the development of these attention processes and their effects on social behavior.

Research in the area of behavioral inhibition already highlights the importance of both biological dispositions and caregiving environments in shaping the social responses of the young child. Evidence of gene × environment interactions in this group of children marks another important step toward understanding the developmental mechanisms involved in the emergence of important variations in social behavior. The next steps involve process-focused research. Studies that carefully model the development of gene × environment interactions and the factors that mitigate the relevance of such interactions to key social outcomes are warranted; such studies would elucidate the mechanisms by which the environment influences the phenotypic expression of critical genes such as the 5HTTLPR and the degree to which phenotypes change across development. Hane and Fox (in press) suggest that early environmental experiences not only change the phenotypic expression of stress reactivity, but also prime the child to respond with a similar behavioral repertoire upon encountering like environmental stressors in the future. Hence, the child who is genetically vulnerable to anxiety and who has also developed a tendency to focus on threat vis à vis interactions with his or her caregivers may develop a strong attention threat bias that maintains anxious behavior well into adulthood.

Recommended Reading

Fox, N.A., Henderson, H.A., Marshall, P.J., Nichols, K.E., & Ghera, M.M. (2005). Behavioral inhibition: Linking biology and behavior within a developmental framework. *Annual Reviews of Psychology*, 56, 235–262.

Perez-Edgar, K., & Fox, N.A. (2005). Temperament and anxiety disorders. *Child Adolescent Clinics of North America, 14*, 681–705.

Pine, D.S., Cohen, P., Gurley, D., Brook, J., & Ma, Y. (1998). The risk of early-adulthood anxiety disorders in adolescents with anxiety and depressive disorders. *Archives of General Psychiatry, 55*, 56–64.

Pine, D.S., Klein, R.G., Mannuzza, S., Moulton, J.L., Lissek, S., Guardino, M., & Woldehawariat, G. (2005). Face-emotion processing in offspring at-risk for panic disorder. *Journal of the American Academy of Child and Adolescent Psychiatry, 44*, 664–672.

Note

1. Address correspondence to Nathan A. Fox, Department of Human Development, University of Maryland, College Park, MD 20742; e-mail: fox@umd.edu.

References

Bar Haim, Y., Lamy, D., Pergamin, L., Bakermans-Kraneburg, M.J., & van IJzendoorn, M.H. (2007). Threat-related attentional bias in anxious and non-anxious individuals: A meta-analytic study. *Psychological Bulletin, 133*, 1–24.

Barrett, P.M., Rapee, R.M., & Dadds, M.M. (1996). Family enhancement of cognitive style in anxious and aggressive children. *Journal of Abnormal Child Psychology, 24*, 187–203.

Caspi, A., Snugden, K., Moffitt, T.E., Taylor, A., Craig, I.W., & Harrington, H., et al. (2003). Influence of life stress on depression: Moderation by a polymorphism in the 5-HTT gene. *Science, 301*, 386–389.

Crockenberg, S., & McCluskey, K. (1986). Change in maternal behavior during the baby's first year of life. *Child Development, 57*, 746–753.

Fox, N.A., Henderson, H.A., Rubin, K.H., Calkins, S.D., & Schmidt, L.A. (2001). Continuity and discontinuity of behavioral inhibition and exuberance: Psychophysiological and behavioral influences across the first four years of life. *Child Development, 72*, 1–21.

Fox, N.A., Nichols, K.E., Henderson, H.A., Rubin, K., Schmidt, L., Hamer, D., Ernst, M., & Pine, D.S. (2005). Evidence for a gene–environment interaction in predicting behavioral inhibition in middle childhood. *Psychological Science, 16*, 921–926.

Ghera, M.M., Hane, A.A., Malesa, E.M., & Fox, N.A. (2006). The role of infant soothability in the relation between infant negativity and maternal sensitivity. *Infant Behavior and Development, 29*, 289–293.

Gross, C., & Hen, R. (2004). The developmental origins of anxiety. *Nature Reviews Neuroscience, 5*, 545–552.

Hane, A.A., & Fox, N.A. (2006). Ordinary variations in maternal caregiving of human infants influence stress reactivity. *Psychological Science, 17*, 550–556.

Hane, A.A., & Fox, N.A. (in press). A closer look at the transactional nature of early social development: The relations among early caregiving environments, temperament, and early social development and the case for phenotypic plasticity. In F. Santoianni & C. Sabatano (Eds.), *Brain development in learning environments: Embodied and perceptual advancements.*

Hane, A.A., Fox, N.A., Henderson, H.A., & Marshall, P.J. (2006). *Setting the trajectories to social competence: The relations among temperamental reactivity, frontal EEG asymmetry and social behavior in infancy.* Unpublished manuscript.

Kaufman, J., Yang., B., Douglas-Palomberi, H., Houshyar, S., Lipschitz, D., Krystal, J.H., & Gerlernter, J. (2004). Social supports and serotonin transporter gene moderate depression in maltreated children. *Proceedings of the National Academy of Sciences, 101*, 17316–17321.

MacLeod, C., Rutherford, E., Campbell, L., Ebsworthy, G., & Holker, L. (2002). Selective attention and emotional vulnerability: Assessing the causal basis of their association through the experimental manipulation of attentional bias. *Journal of Abnormal Psychology, 111*, 107–123.

Mogg, K., Millar, N., & Bradley, B.P. (2000). Biases in eye movements to threatening facial expressions in generalized anxiety disorder and depressive disorder. *Journal of Abnormal Psychology, 109*, 695–704.

Monk, C., McClure, E.B., Nelson, E.B., Zarahn, E., Bilder, R.M., Leibenluft, E., Charney D.S., Ernst, M., & Pine, D.S. (2003). Adolescent immaturity in attention-related brain engagement to emotional facial expressions. *NeuroImage, 20*, 420–428.

Monk, C.S., Nelson, E.E., McClure, E.B., Mogg, K., Bradley, B.P., Leibenluft, E., Blair, R.J., Chen, G., Charney, D.S., Ernst, M., & Pine, D.S. (2006). Ventrolateral prefrontal cortex activation and attentional bias in response to angry faces in adolescents with generalized anxiety disorder. *American Journal of Psychiatry, 163*, 1091–1097.

Parent, C., Zhang, T., Caldji, C., Bagot, R., Champagne, F.A., Pruessner, J., Meaney, M.J. (2005). Maternal care and individual differences in defensive responses. *Current Directions in Psychological Science, 14*, 229–233.

Pauli-Pott, U., Mertesacker, B., & Beckmann, D. (2004). Predicting the development of infant emotionality from maternal characteristics. *Development and Psychopathology, 16*, 19–42.

Perez-Edgar, K., & Fox, N.A. (2005). A behavioral and electrophysiological study of children's selective attention under neutral and affective conditions. *Journal of Cognition and Development, 6*, 89–118.

Pezawas, L., Meyer-Lindenberg, A., Drabant, E.M., Verchinski, B.A., Munoz, K.E., Kolachana, B.S., Egan, M.F., Mattay, V.S., Hariri, A.R., & Weinberger, D.R. (2005). 5-HTTLPR polymorphism impacts human cingulated–amygdala interactions: A genetic susceptibility mechanism for depression. *Nature Neuroscience, 8*, 828–834.

Rubin, K.H., Burgess, K.B., & Hastings, P.D. (2002). Stability and social-behavioral consequences of toddlers' inhibited temperament and parenting behaviors. *Child Development, 73*, 483–495.

Thompson, S.D., & Walker, A.C. (2004). Satisfaction with parenting: A comparison between adolescent mothers and fathers. *Sex Roles, 50*, 677–687.

This article has been reprinted as it originally appeared in *Current Directions in Psychological Science*. Citation information for this article as originally published appears above.

The Interplay Between Genotypes and Family Relationships: Reframing Concepts of Development and Prevention

David Reiss[1]

Center for Family Research, Department of Psychiatry and Behavioral Sciences, George Washington University

Abstract

Children's genotypes and their social relationships are correlated throughout their development. Heritable characteristics of children evoke strong and specific responses from their parents; frequently, these same heritable characteristics also influence the children's adjustment. Moreover, parental heritable traits that influence their parenting are also transmitted to children and influence their children's adjustment. Thus, genetically influenced evocative processes from children and parental-transmission mechanisms influence the covariances between measures of family relationships and child development. These findings suggest new targets for preventing adverse development: altering parental responses to heritable characteristics of children and influencing the genetically influenced ontogeny of parenting.

Keywords

genotype; relationships; parenting; prevention

Conventional models of psychological development acknowledge that genetic and social factors both play a role. Older models assumed that these two influences were independent from each other and that differences among individuals in personality development, cognitive development and psychological development could be explained by adding their effects together. More recently, it has become clear that, in many cases, the social environment interacts with genetic influences. For example, the genetic risk for schizophrenia seems to be fully expressed only when children at genetic risk grow up in families with high conflict, emotional restriction, and chaotic intergenerational boundaries (Tienari et al., 2004). Such a perspective still allows social and genetic variables to be thought of as relatively distinct: Genetic factors render individuals susceptible to adverse social environments; then, at some point—perhaps in early childhood or much later in development—unfavorable social factors elicit behavioral difficulties.

Recent data suggest that genetic and social influences are even more intertwined, however. From early development through adulthood, genetic and social factors are *correlated*; that is, individuals' genotypes are associated with many specific characteristics of their environment. This association occurs in two ways. First, as can be inferred from twin, sibling, and adoption studies, heritable characteristics of children can evoke highly specific responses from the social environment. For example, certain heritable characteristics of children evoke warmth and involvement from their parents. More importantly, the same genetic factors that evoke parental warmth also contribute to a child's social responsibility, including adherence to community norms and helping and sharing behaviors. In the research of my colleagues and I, almost all of the covariance between maternal warmth and child social responsibility is due to these genetic influences common to both parenting and child development (Reiss, Neiderhiser, Hetherington, & Plomin, 2000).

The second way such associations may occur is that heritable traits that influence a mother's or father's parenting may be genetically transmitted to their children. Those same traits in children may make them vulnerable to psychopathology. For example, a recent twin study suggests that heritable factors influence maternal smoking during pregnancy and, when transmitted to children, increase the childrens' likelihood of having conduct problems. These data raise questions about whether fetal exposure to tobacco products is the main cause of their postnatal conduct problems (Maughan, Taylor, Caspi, & Moffitt, 2004).

In behavioral genetics, associations between individuals' genotypes and their environment are called *genotype–environment correlations*. When a correlation is due to the effects of heritable features stimulating responses from the environment, it is called an *evocative* genotype–environment correlation. When it is due to genes transmitted by parents to their children, the term is *passive* genotype–environment correlation. Use of the word *genotype* in this type of research signifies the cumulative effect of all genetic influences on a particular trait, as examined in studies that usually use twin, sibling, or adoption designs.

GENOTYPE–ENVIRONMENT CORRELATIONS AND MECHANISMS OF DEVELOPMENT

Parent–Child Relationships May Amplify Genetic Influences

Rowe (1981) first reported data suggesting evocative genotype–parenting correlations. Monozygotic (i.e. derived from a single egg and genetically identical) twins' reports of how accepted they were by their parents were correlated more than twice as highly as the reports of dizygotic (i.e. from different eggs and 50% genetically related) twins. Figure 1 illustrates how monozygotic–dizygotic comparisons are used to make inferences about such correlations. Rowe's finding was subsequently replicated many times using different methods of assessing parent–child relationships: interviews of parents (Goodman & Stevenson, 1991), parental self-reports, and direct observation of parent–child relationships (O'Connor, Hetherington, Reiss, & Plomin, 1995). These findings do not reflect parental bias due to their knowledge of whether their twins were monozygotic or dizygotic, since the findings also hold where monozygotic twins have been misdiagnosed as dizygotic (Goodman & Stevenson, 1991).

Adoption studies have confirmed the importance of evocative genotype–parenting correlations: The behavior of an adoptive parent toward his or her child can be predicted from patterns of behavior in the birth parent. For example, two separate studies predicted adoptive parents' degree of harsh discipline and hostility toward their children from the level of aggressive behavior in the birth parents. These studies suggest that inherited externalizing (including aggressive and delinquent) behavior in the children evoked the response in the adoptive

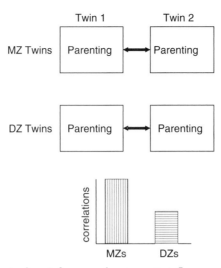

Fig. 1. Diagram showing how inferences about genetic influences on variation of a measured variable, in this case parenting, may be drawn from twin data. Boxes represent measured variable in a comparison of monozygotic (MZ) and dizygotic (DZ) child twins; the arrows represent correlations. The bar graph at the bottom of the figure represents example findings. The example finding shows MZ child twins correlate much more strongly than DZ child twins, enabling the inference that heritable characteristics of the child influence parenting (Reiss, Neiderhiser, Hetherington, & Plomin, 2000).

parents (Ge et al., 1996; O'Connor, Deater-Deckard, Fulker, Rutter, & Plomin, 1998).

Heritable evoked parental responses have been reported from age 1 through late adolescence. For example, one study compared nonadoptive siblings, who share 50% of their individual-differences genes, with siblings adopted from different birth parents. Data gathered at age 1 and again at age 2 suggested that children's genotypes greatly influenced how much intellectual stimulation their parents provided to them: Parental behavior correlated much higher toward the nonadoptive siblings than toward the adoptive siblings (Braungart, Plomin, Fulker, & DeFries, 1992). Other studies have reported on genetic influences on parenting at age 3, in middle childhood, and in adolescence. One longitudinal twin study suggested that heritable evocative effects increase across adolescence; this increase across age was particularly marked for fathers (Elkins, McGue, & Iacono, 1997).

To study heritable evocative effects, the Nonshared Environment in Adolescent Development study (NEAD; Reiss et al., 2000) combined a twin design with a stepfamily design. We drew genetic inferences from comparisons among monozygotic twins, dizygotic twins, full siblings, half siblings (e.g., a mother brings a child from a previous marriage and has a child with her new husband) and unrelated siblings (i.e., each parent brings a child from a previous marriage). NEAD showed that heritable evocative effects may be quite specific. For example, genetic factors that evoke maternal warmth are distinct from those that evoke paternal warmth.

Additional findings reveal that heritable effects go beyond evocative effects on parents. The same genetic factors in a child that evoke particular parenting responses also influence many dimensions of their own adjustment during childhood and adolescence. Inferences about these influences are drawn by comparing *cross correlations* across sibling types (see Fig. 2). For example, a mother's harsh parenting towards sibling A can be correlated with the level of antisocial behavior of sibling B. Genetic influences on covariance are inferred when these cross correlations decline systematically from monozygotic twins at the highest to dizygotic twins and full siblings in the middle to unrelated siblings at the lowest.

NEAD found that over 70% of the covariance between a mother's hostile parenting and her adolescents' antisocial behavior was accounted for by genetic influences common to both. These findings have been confirmed by several subsequent studies (e.g., Burt, Krueger, McGue, & Iacono, 2003). NEAD found sizable genetic contributions to many other covariances including mothers' hostile parenting with impairment in adolescents' cognitive performance, fathers' warmth with adolescents' social responsibility, and fathers' hostility with adolescents' depression. NEAD, using longitudinal data collected from earlier and later adolescence, found

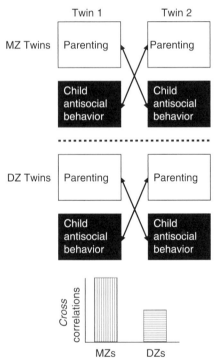

Fig. 2. Example cross correlation of parenting and child adjustment across sibling types. Parenting in one twin cross correlates with antisocial behavior in the other, more highly for monozygotic (MZ) twins than for dizygotic (DZ) twins. This suggests that the covariation between parenting and child antisocial behavior can be attributed to genetic influences common to both variables (Reiss et al., 2000).

that, in many cases, the child's heritable impact on parental response preceded the development of the behavior in question. For example, genetic influence on hostile parenting preceded the evolution of antisocial behavior.

Evocative genotype–parenting correlations may amplify more direct genetic influences on the child's problem behavior. Indeed, it is possible that parental responses to their children's heritable characteristics—responses to which the parents themselves are insensible—are critical for transforming heritable influences on children's temperaments into problems requiring clinical attention. To verify this hypothesis and test its significance for preventive intervention, my colleagues and I are currently conducting a prospective adoption study. We are following birth- and adoptive parents and adopted toddlers from age 9 months. This Early Growth and Development Study (EGADS) will allow us to pinpoint exactly what heritable noxious behaviors in the child evoke adverse parental responses and the consequence of these parental responses for subsequent child development.

The Heritable Development of Parenting

Evidence for passive genotype–parenting correlation requires evidence that (a) the parents' genes influence their parenting and (b) genetic factors that influence parenting are transmitted to their children and influence important dimensions of the children's adjustment. Evidence of this kind provides clues to childhood origins of parenting styles. For example, suppose it is observed that the same genetic factors that influence lack of warmth in mothers also influence depressive symptoms in their children. This would suggest that genetic factors link childhood internalizing with reduced maternal warmth, thereby offering clues about how genetically influenced parenting patterns unfold over the long term. Evidence for these passive effects comes from two sources.

First, studies using twins who are parents have shown genetic influences on dimensions of parenting. Our Twin Mom study investigated a sample of monozygotic and dizygotic twins who were mothers of adolescents. It showed that mothers' reports of their own warmth, hostility, and monitoring of the whereabouts of their children were more highly correlated for monozygotic than for dizygotic twins. A similar pattern of findings was shown using observer ratings for mothers' warmth and for children's ratings of their mothers' monitoring (Neiderhiser et al., 2004).

Second, adoption studies have found evidence for passive genetic links between parenting and the adjustment of children both in early childhood and in later adolescence. The correlation between parenting and child adjustment in birth families reflects evocative genotype–parenting correlations, environmental mechanisms, and passive genotype–parenting correlations. The last type are missing in adoptive families. Thus, by comparing correlations between parenting and child adjustment between the two groups it is possible to estimate—by elimination—the strength of passive genotype–parenting correlations. For example, one adoption study assessed parents' ratings of cohesiveness, lack of conflict, and open expression of feelings in their family during the time their children were 1 to 5 years old. For boys but not for girls, these ratings predicted teacher ratings of child delinquency and aggression at age 7, but only for boys raised by their own birth parents (Braungart-Rieker, Rende, Plomin, & DeFries, 1995). The correlations between parenting and teacher-rated aggression were insignificant in adoptive families. The correlations between adolescent problems and ratings of the quality of family relationships by their mothers were higher in families in which parents reared their own children than in adoptive families (McGue, Sharma, & Benson, 1996).

Taken together, these finding suggest that genotypic differences among parents influence their parenting and that these genotypic differences are transmitted to children, in whom they are manifested by psychiatric symptoms. We are currently investigating whether there are specific genetic links between childhood behavioral characteristics and patterns of parenting. For example, might internalizing problems in childhood be genetically linked to parental withdrawal and lack of support? Might childhood externalizing be genetically linked to aggressive and hostile parenting styles?

Highlighting Relationship Influences

Genetically informed studies highlight two sorts of family relationships that are linked with child psychological development independently of children's genotypes. Parent–child relationships are the first sort of such relationships identified by behavioral genetic data. For example, NEAD found that maternal rapport and affection was linked to adolescent autonomy and sociability. This is the case no matter what the child's genotype. Moreover, siblings within the same family are similar in their autonomy and sociability whether they are dizygotic or monozygotic twins or unrelated siblings. In contrast to parent hostility, the amount of maternal warmth received is also similar across both types of twins and unrelated siblings. Thus, taken together, our data suggest that mothers are relatively consistent in the positive feelings they show to children in their family and that all children benefit, no matter their genotype (Reiss et al., 2000).

Second, behavioral genetic data have highlighted nonparental family relationships that appear to influence childrens' development independently of their genotype. For example, NEAD showed that hostility and conflict in sibling relationships was strongly associated with adolescent antisocial behavior and depression. Conflict and hostility were highly reciprocal in adolescent siblings and put both siblings at equal risk for psychiatric symptoms independently of their genotypes. Moreover, NEAD showed a strong association between marital conflict and parent–child conflict on the one hand and sibling hostility on the other. More importantly, these links across family subsystems were independent of child genotype. Thus, in adolescence, hostility between siblings may be an indirect route through which family discord increases the vulnerability of children regardless of their genotype (Reiss et al., 2000).

Because it included the partners of the sisters who were the biological parents of the adolescent children, the Twin Mom study was able to yield valuable data on the role of adult genotypes in marital relationships. The study found that although genetic factors had a substantial influence on marital quality, as reported by both the twin siblings and their husbands, genetic factors explained little of the covariance between marital satisfaction and levels of wives' depressive symptoms. Rather, in this association, the dynamics of the marital relationships may play a central role (Spotts et al., 2004). These findings extend nongenetic studies of adult development that appeared to show that good marriages protect against depression and other behavior difficulties. However, nongenetic studies may miss heritable features of individuals that lead to both sustained, high-quality marriages and invulnerability to depression. Yet if the TwinMoms data is replicated, heritable features will seem unlikely to play a significant role in how marriages protect the marital partners.

IMPLICATIONS: NEW TARGETS FOR PREVENTION

Data on genotypes and family relationships offer three novel opportunities to design preventive interventions to forestall the development of serious problem behaviors and psychopathology.

First, findings suggesting that parent–child relationships amplify maladaptive genetic influences offer some of the most promising leads in preventing the expression of unfavorable genetic influences on many domains of child and adolescent adjustment. EGADS is designed to specify particular targets for intervention: parents' responses to heritable difficulties in their children. Numerous studies show that highly focused interventions can produce sustained changes in how parents respond to challenging children (Bakermans-Kranenburg, van Ijzendoorn, & Juffer, 2003). EGADS is designed to ascertain whether such interventions might suppress the parental amplification process and thus diminish adverse genetic influences.

Second, findings on passive genotype correlations provide a new target for interventions: promoting favorable parenting. The discovery of genetic links between childhood behavior and parenting suggests some childhood and adolescent origins of parenting behavior that should be addressed in efforts to prevent risky parental behavior such as drug abuse during pregnancy or hostile and abusive parenting subsequently. For example, efforts to prevent the early emergence of conduct problems may prevent later serious antisocial behavior as well as abusive parenting.

Finally, studies of genotype–environment correlation suggest new psychosocial targets for preventing psychological and behavioral disorders: siblings and marriages. Techniques already developed for clinical interventions with maladaptive sibling relationships and with marriages might be refashioned for preventing psychological disorders in the siblings or marital partners.

Recommended Reading

Maughan, B., Taylor, A., Caspi, A., & Moffitt, T.E. (2004). (See References)

Reiss, D., Pedersen, N.L., Cederblad, M., Lichtenstein, P., Hansson, K., Neiderhiser, J.M., et al. (2001). Genetic probes of three theories of maternal adjustment: I. Recent evidence and a model. *Family Process, 40,* 247–259.

Rutter, M., Pickles, A., Murray, R., & Eaves, L. (2001). Testing hypotheses on specific environmental causal effects on behavior. *Psychological Bulletin, 127,* 291–324.

Note

1. Address correspondence to David Reiss, Center for Family Research, Department of Psychiatry and Behavioral Sciences, George Washington University, 2300 K Street, NW, Washington, DC 20037; e-mail: cfrdxr@gwumc.edu.

References

Bakermans-Kranenburg, M.J., van Ijzendoorn, M.H., & Juffer, F. (2003). Less is more: Meta-analyses of sensitivity and attachment interventions in early childhood. *Psychological Bulletin, 129*, 195–215.

Braungart, J.M., Plomin, R., Fulker, D.W., & DeFries, J.C. (1992). Genetic mediation of the home environment during infancy: A sibling adoption study of the HOME. *Developmental Psychology, 28*, 1048–1055.

Braungart-Rieker, J., Rende, R.D., Plomin, R., & DeFries, J.C. (1995). Genetic mediation of longitudinal associations between family environment and childhood behavior problems. *Development & Psychopathology, 7*, 233–245.

Burt, S., Krueger, R.F., McGue, M., & Iacono, W. (2003). Parent–child conflict and the comorbidity among childhood externalizing disorders. *Archives of General Psychiatry, 60*, 505–513.

Elkins, I.J., McGue, M., & Iacono, W.G. (1997). Genetic and environmental influences on parent–son relationships: Evidence for increasing genetic influence during adolescence. *Developmental Psychology, 33*, 351–363.

Ge, X., Conger, R.D., Cadoret, R.J., Neiderhiser, J.M., Yates, W., Troughton, E., & Stewart, M.A. (1996). The developmental interface between nature and nurture: A mutual influence model of child antisocial behavior and parent behaviors. *Developmental Psychology, 32*, 574–589.

Goodman, R., & Stevenson, J. (1991). Parental criticism and warmth towards unrecognized monozygotic twins. *Behavior and Brain Sciences, 14*, 394–395.

Maughan, B., Taylor, A., Caspi, A., & Moffitt, T.E. (2004). Prenatal smoking and early childhood conduct problems: Testing genetic and environmental explanations of the association. *Archives of General Psychiatry, 61*, 836–843.

McGue, M., Sharma, A., & Benson, P. (1996). The effect of common rearing on adolescent adjustment: Evidence from a U.S. adoption cohort. *Developmental Psychology, 32*, 604–613.

Neiderhiser, J.M., Reiss, D., Pedersen, L., Lichtenstein, P., Spotts, E.L., Hansson, K., Cederblad, M., & Elthammar, O. (2004). Genetic and environmental influences on mothering of adolescents: A comparison of two samples. *Developmental Psychology, 40*, 335–351.

O'Connor, T.G., Deater-Deckard, K., Fulker, D., Rutter, M., & Plomin, R. (1998). Genotype-environment correlations in late childhood and early adolescence: Antisocial behavioral problems and coercive parenting. *Developmental Psychology, 34*, 970–981.

O'Connor, T.G., Hetherington, E.M., Reiss, D., & Plomin, R. (1995). A twin-sibling study of observed parent–adolescent interactions. *Child Development, 66*, 812–829.

Reiss, D., Neiderhiser, J., Hetherington, E.M., & Plomin, R. (2000). *The relationship code: Deciphering genetic and social patterns in adolescent development.* Cambridge, MA: Harvard University Press.

Rowe, D.C. (1981). Environmental and genetic influences on dimensions of perceived parenting: A twin study. *Developmental Psychology, 17*, 203–208.

Spotts, E.L., Neiderhiser, J.M., Ganiban, J., Reiss, D., Lichtenstein, P., Hansson, K., Cederblad, M., & Pedersen, N. (2004). Accounting for depressive symptoms in women: A twin study of associations with interpersonal relationships. *Journal of Affective Disorders, 82*, 101–111.

Tienari, P., Wynne, L.C., Sorri, A., Lahti, I., Laksy, K., Moring, J., Naarala, M., Nieminen, P., & Wahlberg, K. (2004). Genotype-environment interaction in schizophrenia spectrum disorder. *British Journal of Psychiatry, 184*, 216–222.

Section 3: Critical Thinking Questions

1. Kemeny argues that there is specificity of the body's response to particular types of stressors. Given that stress has been linked to a variety of

118

psychopathologies, how might specificity of stress type-physiological response account for why some individuals develop one form of disorder following stress (e.g., depression) while others develop a different disorder (e.g., PTSD)?

2. The papers in this section describe how acute and chronic stressors elicit physiological responses causally related to psychopathology, primarily anxiety and depression. Might other pathways to these disorders involve similar physiological mechanisms? What other other forms of psychopathology also be linked to maladaptive stress responses?

3. How do findings demonstrating that genes interact with environmental factors to predict psychopathology and risk for psychopathology challenge traditional notions of the nature-nurture debate?; What kinds of environmental measures might be most fruitful for understanding how gene x environment interactions influence risk for psychopathology?

4. Reiss' review describes how the family environment is saturated with effects originating from genetic sources, including measures of parenting and family relationships. Many effects may be attributable to child characteristics eliciting particular kinds of interactions and behaviors from their parents. It is often easier to think of adults as having an impact on children's behavior, but Reiss' paper describes how the effects may also run in the other direction; how does this occur, and why might it be an adaptive feature of human functioning? If there aren't "parenting genes," what do you think the genetic effects on parenting and family relationships consist of?

This article has been reprinted as it originally appeared in *Current Directions in Psychological Science*. Citation information for this article as originally published appears above.

Section 4: Internalizing Disorders (Anxiety, Depression, and Eating Disorders)

The spectrum of disorders characterized by negative emotions/misery (see Krueger and Markon's paper in the first section of this reader) is the subject of considerable research from a broad range of approaches. The papers in this section provide a cross-section of the kinds of questions currently being asked about internalizing psychopathology and describe the notable progress made over the past decade in understanding their origins.

The five reviews in this section address issues related to anxiety, anxiety disorders, and stressors related to anxiety. First, Ohman and Mineka review their influential model of evolutionarily prepared phobias, focusing specifically on the origins of snake phobias in primates. This paper describes a sophisticated series of studies supporting a model of an evolved fear module involved in governing responses to recurrent environmental threats in the evolutionary past (including snakes) and which continue to allow stimuli previously associated with those threats ready access to attentional and emotional systems that produce fear responses. Davis and colleagues describe novel findings regarding the neural mechanisms that influence extinction of previously learned fear responses. Their paper clearly explicates central aspects of extinction learning, and the abnormal fear learning processes that are involved in posttraumatic stress disorder (PTSD). Exciting findings indicate that a particular compound (d-cycloserine) binds to a receptor involved in consolidation of extinction learning, thus facilitating extinction learning and producing improvements over exposure therapy alone. This paper is an excellent example of how basic science can be harnessed to improve existing interventions and potentially lead to the development of new interventions.

Three other papers in this section also deal with PTSD and related concepts. Many lay readers may assume that the experience of trauma is sufficient for the development of PTSD. However, as thoughtfully reviewed by Ozer and Weiss, individuals differ in their likelihood of developing this disorder following traumatic events. Their paper raises crucial questions about how trauma is conceptualized, and the kinds of intervening psychological variables that contribute to individual differences in response to traumatic events. In a similar vein, Bonanno provides a compelling argument that resilience in the face of trauma is a common outcome of exposure to difficult life events, and stimulates interesting questions about the kinds of characteristics that might promote such resilience. Finally, McNally's important paper confronts some of the most controversial issues concerning a particular traumatic event, childhood sexual abuse. This review describes the clinical literature on individuals who report having repressed and recovered memories of prior abuse, and details a number of laboratory paradigms that have been employed to explore this phenomenon.

Rottenberg's paper also describes laboratory paradigms for exploring psychopathological processes, specifically, emotional reactivity among individuals with depressive disorders. Although the clinical presentation of depression is characterized by high levels of negative emotions, Rottenberg describes a series of studies documenting that depressed individuals exhibit blunted emotional reactivity to standardized probes, compared to nondepressed individuals.

Finally, Klump and Culbert describe recent work exploring genetic contributions to eating disorders (anorexia and bulimia). Importantly, they illustrate the importance of theoretically motivated molecular genetic studies that explore genes relevant to the systems implicated in the disorder under study.

The Malicious Serpent: Snakes as a Prototypical Stimulus for an Evolved Module of Fear

Arne Öhman[1]

Department of Clinical Neuroscience, Karolinska Institute, Stockholm, Sweden (A.Ö.)

Susan Mineka

Department of Psychology, Northwestern University, Evanston, Illinois (S.M.)

Abstract

As reptiles, snakes may have signified deadly threats in the environment of early mammals. We review findings suggesting that snakes remain special stimuli for humans. Intense snake fear is prevalent in both humans and other primates. Humans and monkeys learn snake fear more easily than fear of most other stimuli through direct or vicarious conditioning. Neither the elicitation nor the conditioning of snake fear in humans requires that snakes be consciously perceived; rather, both processes can occur with masked stimuli. Humans tend to perceive illusory correlations between snakes and aversive stimuli, and their attention is automatically captured by snakes in complex visual displays. Together, these and other findings delineate an evolved fear module in the brain. This module is selectively and automatically activated by once-threatening stimuli, is relatively encapsulated from cognition, and derives from specialized neural circuitry.

Keywords

evolution; snake fear; fear module

Snakes are commonly regarded as slimy, slithering creatures worthy of fear and disgust. If one were to believe the Book of Genesis, humans' dislike for snakes resulted from a divine intervention: To avenge the snake's luring of Eve to taste the fruit of knowledge, God instituted eternal enmity between their descendants. Alternatively, the human dislike of snakes and the common appearances of reptiles as the embodiment of evil in myths and art might reflect an evolutionary heritage. Indeed, Sagan (1977) speculated that human fear of snakes and other reptiles may be a distant effect of the conditions under which early mammals evolved. In the world they inhabited, the animal kingdom was dominated by awesome reptiles, the dinosaurs, and so a prerequisite for early mammals to deliver genes to future generations was to avoid getting caught in the fangs of Tyrannosaurus rex and its relatives. Thus, fear and respect for reptiles is a likely core mammalian heritage. From this perspective, snakes and other reptiles may continue to have a special psychological significance even for humans, and considerable evidence suggests this is indeed true. Furthermore, the pattern of findings appears consistent with the evolutionary premise.

THE PREVALENCE OF SNAKE FEARS IN PRIMATES

Snakes are obviously fearsome creatures to many humans. Agras, Sylvester, and Oliveau (1969) interviewed a sample of New Englanders about fears, and found snakes to be clearly the most prevalent object of intense fear, reported by 38% of females and 12% of males.

Fear of snakes is also common among other primates. According to an exhaustive review of field data (King, 1997), 11 genera of primates showed fear-related responses (alarm calls, avoidance, mobbing) in virtually all instances in which they were observed confronting large snakes. For studies of captive primates, King did not find consistent evidence of snake fear. However, in direct comparisons, rhesus (and squirrel) monkeys reared in the wild were far more likely than lab-reared monkeys to show strong phobiclike fear responses to snakes (e.g., Mineka, Keir, & Price, 1980). That this fear is adaptive in the wild is further supported by independent field reports of large snakes attacking primates (M. Cook & Mineka, 1991).

This high prevalence of snake fear in humans as well as in our primate relatives suggests that it is a result of an ancient evolutionary history. Genetic variability might explain why not all individuals show fear of snakes. Alternatively, the variability could stem from differences in how easily individuals learn to fear reptilian stimuli when they are encountered in aversive contexts. This latter possibility would be consistent with the differences in snake fear between wild- and lab-reared monkeys.

LEARNING TO FEAR SNAKES

Experiments with lab-reared monkeys have shown that they can acquire a fear of snakes vicariously, that is, by observing other monkeys expressing fear of snakes. When nonfearful lab-reared monkeys were given the opportunity to observe a wild-reared "model" monkey displaying fear of live and toy snakes, they were rapidly conditioned to fear snakes, and this conditioning was strong and persistent. The fear response was learned even when the fearful model monkey was shown on videotape (M. Cook & Mineka, 1990).

When videos were spliced so that identical displays of fear were modeled in response to toy snakes and flowers, or to toy crocodiles and rabbits (M. Cook & Mineka, 1991), the lab-reared monkeys showed substantial conditioning to toy snakes and crocodiles, but not to flowers and toy rabbits. Toy snakes and flowers served equally well as signals for food rewards (M. Cook & Mineka, 1990), so the selective effect of snakes appears to be restricted to aversive contexts. Because these monkeys had never seen any of the stimuli used prior to these experiments, the results provide strong support for an evolutionary basis to the selective learning.

A series of studies published in the 1970s (see Öhman & Mineka, 2001) tested the hypothesis that humans are predisposed to easily learn to fear snakes. These studies used a discriminative Pavlovian conditioning procedure in which various pictures served as conditioned stimuli (CSs) that predicted the presence and absence of mildly aversive shock, the unconditioned stimulus (US). Participants for whom snakes (or spiders) consistently signaled shocks showed stronger and more lasting conditioned skin conductance responses (SCRs; palmar sweat responses that index emotional activation) than control participants for whom flowers or mushrooms signaled shocks. When a nonaversive US was used, however, this difference disappeared. E.W. Cook, Hodes, and Lang (1986) demonstrated that qualitatively different responses were conditioned to snakes (heart rate acceleration, indexing fear) than to flowers and mushrooms (heart rate deceleration, indexing attention to the eliciting stimulus). They also reported superior conditioning to snakes than to gun stimuli paired with loud noises. Such results suggest that the selective association between snakes and aversive USs reflects evolutionary history rather than cultural conditioning.

NONCONSCIOUS CONTROL OF RESPONSES TO SNAKES

If the prevalence and ease of learning snake fear represents a core mammalian heritage, its neural machinery must be found in brain structures that evolved in early mammals. Accordingly, the fear circuit of the mammalian brain relies heavily on limbic structures such as the amygdala, a collection of neural nuclei in the anterior temporal lobe. Limbic structures emerged in the evolutionary transition from reptiles to mammals and use preexisting structures in the "reptilian brain" to control emotional output such as flight/fight behavior and cardiovascular changes (see Öhman & Mineka, 2001).

From this neuroevolutionary perspective, one would expect the limbically controlled fear of snakes to be relatively independent of the most recently evolved control level in the brain, the neocortex, which is the site of advanced cognition. This hypothesis is consistent with the often strikingly irrational quality of snake phobia. For example, phobias may be activated by seeing mere pictures of snakes. Backward masking is a promising methodology for examining whether phobic responses can be activated without involvement of the cortex. In this method, a brief visual stimulus is blanked from conscious perception by an immediately following masking stimulus. Because backward masking disrupts visual processing in the primary visual cortex, responses to backward-masked stimuli reflect activation of pathways in the brain that may access the fear circuit without involving cortical areas mediating visual awareness of the stimulus.

In one study (Öhman & Soares, 1994), pictures of snakes, spiders, flowers, and mushrooms were presented very briefly (30 ms), each time immediately followed by a masking stimulus (a randomly cut and reassembled picture). Although the participants could not recognize the intact pictures, participants who were afraid of snakes showed enhanced SCRs only to masked snakes, whereas participants who were afraid of spiders responded only to spiders. Similar results were obtained (Öhman & Soares, 1993) when nonfearful participants, who had been conditioned to unmasked snake pictures by shock USs, were exposed to masked pictures without the US. Thus, responses to conditioned snake pictures survived backward masking; in contrast, masking eliminated conditioning effects in another group of participants conditioned to neutral stimuli such as flowers or mushrooms.

Furthermore, subsequent experiments (Öhman & Soares, 1998) also demonstrated conditioning to masked stimuli when masked snakes or spiders (but not masked flowers or mushrooms) were used as CSs followed by shock USs. Thus, these masking studies show that fear responses (as indexed by SCRs) can be learned and elicited when backward masking prevents visually presented

125

snake stimuli from accessing cortical processing. This is consistent with the notion that responses to snakes are organized by a specifically evolved primitive neural circuit that emerged with the first mammals long before the evolution of neocortex.

ILLUSORY CORRELATIONS BETWEEN SNAKES AND AVERSIVE STIMULI

If expression and learning of snake fear do not require cortical processing, are people's cognitions about snakes and their relationships to other events biased and irrational? One example of such biased processing occurred in experiments on illusory correlations: Participants (especially those who were afraid of snakes) were more likely to perceive that slides of fear-relevant stimuli (such as snakes) were paired with shock than to perceive that slides of control stimuli (flowers and mushrooms) were paired with shock. This occurred even though there were no such relationships in the extensive random sequence of slide stimuli and aversive and nonaversive outcomes (tones or nothing) participants had experienced (Tomarken, Sutton, & Mineka, 1995).

Similar illusory correlations were not observed for pictures of damaged electrical equipment and shock even though they were rated as belonging together better than snakes and shock (Tomarken et al., 1995). In another experiment, participants showed exaggerated expectancies for shock to follow both snakes and damaged electrical equipment before the experiment began (Kennedy, Rapee, & Mazurski, 1997), but reported only the illusory correlation between snakes and shock after experiencing the random stimulus series. Thus, it appears that snakes have a cognitive affinity with aversiveness and danger that is resistant to modification by experience.

AUTOMATIC CAPTURE OF ATTENTION BY SNAKE STIMULI

People who encounter snakes in the wild may report that they first froze in fear, only a split second later realizing that they were about to step on a snake. Thus, snakes may automatically capture attention. A study supporting this hypothesis (Öhman, Flykt, & Esteves, 2001) demonstrated shorter detection latencies for a discrepant snake picture among an array of many neutral distractor stimuli (e.g., flower pictures) than vice versa. Furthermore, "finding the snake in the grass" was not affected by the number of distractor stimuli, whereas it took longer to detect discrepant flowers and mushrooms among many than among few snakes when the latter served as distractor stimuli. This suggests that snakes, but not flowers and mushrooms, were located by an automatic perceptual routine that effortlessly found target stimuli that appeared to "pop out" from the matrix independently of the number of distractor stimuli. Participants who were highly fearful of snakes showed even superior performance in detecting snakes. Thus, when snakes elicited fear in participants, this fear state sensitized the perceptual apparatus to detect snakes even more efficiently.

THE CONCEPT OF A FEAR MODULE

The evidence we have reviewed shows that snake stimuli are strongly and widely associated with fear in humans and other primates and that fear of snakes is relatively independent of conscious cognition. We have proposed the concept of an evolved fear module to explain these and many related findings (Öhman & Mineka, 2001). The fear module is a relatively independent behavioral, mental, and neural system that has evolved to assist mammals in defending against threats such as snakes. The module is selectively sensitive to, and automatically activated by, stimuli related to recurrent survival threats, it is relatively encapsulated from more advanced human cognition, and it relies on specialized neural circuitry.

This specialized behavioral module did not evolve primarily from survival threats provided by snakes during human evolution, but rather from the threat that reptiles have provided through mammalian evolution. Because reptiles have been associated with danger throughout evolution, it is likely that snakes represent a prototypical stimulus for activating the fear module. However, we are not arguing that the human brain has a specialized module for automatically generating fear of snakes. Rather, we propose that the blueprint for the fear module was built around the deadly threat that ancestors of snakes provided to our distant ancestors, the early mammals. During further mammalian evolution, this blueprint was modified, elaborated, and specialized for the ecological niches occupied by different species. Some mammals may even prey on snakes, and new stimuli and stimulus features have been added to reptiles as preferential activators of the module. For example, facial threat is similar to snakes when it comes to activating the fear module in social primates (Öhman & Mineka, 2001). Through Pavlovian conditioning, the fear module may come under the control of a very wide range of stimuli signaling pain and danger. Nevertheless, evolutionarily derived constraints have afforded stimuli once related to recurrent survival threats easier access for gaining control of the module through fear conditioning (Öhman & Mineka, 2001).

ISSUES FOR FURTHER RESEARCH

The claim that the fear module can be conditioned without awareness is a bold one given that there is a relative consensus in the field of human conditioning that awareness of the CS-US contingency is required for acquiring conditioned responses. However, as we have extensively argued elsewhere (Öhman & Mineka, 2001; Wiens & Öhman, 2002), there is good evidence that conditioning to nonconsciously presented CSs is possible if they are evolutionarily fear relevant. Other factors that might promote such nonconscious learning include intense USs, short CS-US intervals, and perhaps temporal overlap between the CS and the US. However, little research on these factors has been reported, and there is a pressing need to elaborate their relative effectiveness in promoting conditioning of the fear module outside of awareness.

One of the appeals of the fear module concept is that it is consistent with the current understanding of the neurobiology of fear conditioning, which gives a central role to the amygdala (e.g., Öhman & Mineka, 2001). However, this understanding is primarily based on animal data. Even though the emerging brain-imaging literature on human fear conditioning is consistent with this database, systematic efforts are needed in order to tie the fear module more convincingly to human brain mechanisms. For example, a conspicuous gap in knowledge concerns whether the amygdala is indeed specially tuned to conditioning contingencies involving evolutionarily fear-relevant CSs such as snakes.

An interesting question that can be addressed both at a psychological and at a neurobiological level concerns the perceptual mechanisms that give snake stimuli privileged access to the fear module. For example, are snakes detected at a lower perceptual threshold relative to non-fear-relevant objects? Are they identified faster than other objects once detected? Are they quicker to activate the fear module and attract attention once identified? Regardless of the locus of perceptual privilege, what visual features of snakes make them such powerful fear elicitors and attention captors? Because the visual processing in pathways preceding the cortical level is crude, the hypothesis that masked presentations of snakes directly access the amygdala implies that the effect is mediated by simple features of snakes rather than by the complex configuration of features defining a snake. Delineating these features would allow the construction of a "super fear stimulus." It could be argued that such a stimulus would depict "the archetypical evil" as represented in the human brain.

Recommended Reading

Mineka, S. (1992). Evolutionary memories, emotional processing, and the emotional disorders. *The Psychology of Learning and Motivation, 28,* 161–206.

Öhman, A., Dimberg, U., & Öst, L.-G. (1985). Animal and social phobias: Biological constraints on learned fear responses. In S. Reiss & R.R. Bootzin (Eds.), *Theoretical issues in behavior therapy* (pp. 123–178). New York: Academic Press.

Öhman, A., & Mineka, S. (2001). (See References)

Note

1. Address correspondence to Arne Öhman, Psychology Section, Department of Clinical Neuroscience, Karolinska Institute and Hospital, Z6:6, S-171 76 Stockholm, Sweden; e-mail: arne. ohman@cns.ki.se.

References

Agras, S., Sylvester, D., & Oliveau, D. (1969). The epidemiology of common fears and phobias. *Comprehensive Psychiatry, 10,* 151–156.

Cook, E.W., Hodes, R.L., & Lang, P.J. (1986). Preparedness and phobia: Effects of stimulus content on human visceral conditioning. *Journal of Abnormal Psychology, 95,* 195–207.

Cook, M., & Mineka, S. (1990). Selective associations in the observational conditioning of fear in rhesus monkeys. *Journal of Experimental Psychology: Animal Behavior Processes, 16,* 372–389.

Cook, M., & Mineka, S. (1991). Selective associations in the origins of phobic fears and their implications for behavior therapy. In P. Martin (Ed.), *Handbook of behavior therapy and psychological science: An integrative approach* (pp. 413–434). Oxford, England: Pergamon Press.

Kennedy, S.J., Rapee, R.M., & Mazurski, E.J. (1997). Covariation bias for phylogenetic versus ontogenetic fear-relevant stimuli. *Behaviour Research and Therapy, 35,* 415–422.

King, G.E. (1997, June). *The attentional basis for primate responses to snakes.* Paper presented at the annual meeting of the American Society of Primatologists, San Diego, CA.

Mineka, S., Keir, R., & Price, V. (1980). Fear of snakes in wild- and laboratory-reared rhesus monkeys (*Macaca mulatta*). *Animal Learning and Behavior, 8,* 653–663.

Öhman, A., Flykt, A., & Esteves, F. (2001). Emotion drives attention: Detecting the snake in the grass. *Journal of Experimental Psychology: General, 131,* 466–478.

Öhman, A., & Mineka, S. (2001). Fear, phobias and preparedness: Toward an evolved module of fear and fear learning. *Psychological Review, 108,* 483–522.

Öhman, A., & Soares, J.J.F. (1993). On the automatic nature of phobic fear: Conditioned electrodermal responses to masked fear-relevant stimuli. *Journal of Abnormal Psychology, 102,* 121–132.

Öhman, A., & Soares, J.J.F. (1994). "Unconscious anxiety": Phobic responses to masked stimuli. *Journal of Abnormal Psychology, 103,* 231–240.

Öhman, A., & Soares, J.J.F. (1998). Emotional conditioning to masked stimuli: Expectancies for aversive outcomes following nonrecognized fear-irrelevant stimuli. *Journal of Experimental Psychology: General, 127,* 69–82.

Sagan, C. (1977). *The dragons of Eden: Speculations on the evolution of human intelligence.* London: Hodder and Stoughton.

Tomarken, A.J., Sutton, S.K., & Mineka, S. (1995). Fear-relevant illusory correlations: What types of associations promote judgmental bias? *Journal of Abnormal Psychology, 104,* 312–326.

Wiens, S., & Öhman, A. (2002). Unawareness is more than a chance event: Comment on Lovibond and Shanks (2002). *Journal of Experimental Psychology: Animal Behavior Processes, 28,* 27–31.

This article has been reprinted as it originally appeared in *Current Directions in Psychological Science*. Citation information for this article as originally published appears above.

Facilitation of Extinction of Conditioned Fear by D-Cycloserine: Implications for Psychotherapy

Michael Davis[1]

Departments of Psychology and Psychiatry & Behavioral Sciences Center for Behavioral Neuroscience, and Yerkes National Primate Research Center, Emory University

Karyn M. Myers

Department of Psychiatry & Behavioral Sciences, and Center for Behavioral Neuroscience, and Yerkes National Primate Research Center, Emory University

Kerry J. Ressler

Department of Psychiatry & Behavioral Sciences, and Center for Behavioral Neuroscience, and Yerkes National Primate Research Center, Emory University

Barbara O. Rothbaum

Department of Psychiatry & Behavioral Sciences, and Center for Behavioral Neuroscience

Abstract

Excessive fear and anxiety are characteristic of disorders such as post-traumatic stress disorder (PTSD) and phobias and are believed to reflect abnormalities in neural systems governing the development and reduction of conditioned fear. Conditioned fear can be suppressed through a process known as extinction, in which repeated exposure to a feared stimulus in the absence of an aversive event leads to a gradual reduction in the fear response to that stimulus. Like conditioned fear learning, extinction is dependent on a particular protein (the N-methyl-D-aspartate or NMDA receptor) in a part of the brain called the amygdala. Blockade of this receptor blocks extinction and improving the activity of this receptor with a drug called D-cycloserine speeds up extinction in rats. Because exposure-based psychotherapy for fear disorders in humans resembles extinction in several respects, we investigated whether D-cycloserine might facilitate the loss of fear in human patients. Consistent with findings from the animal laboratory, patients receiving D-cycloserine benefited more from exposure-based psychotherapy than did placebo-treated controls. Although very preliminary, these data provide initial support for the use of cognitive enhancers in psychotherapy and demonstrate that preclinical studies in rodents can have direct benefits to humans.

Keywords

amygdala; exposure therapy; fear; NMDA; post-traumatic stress disorder; phobias; extinction

I can't get the memories out of my mind! The images come flooding back in vivid detail, triggered by the most inconsequential things, like a door slamming or the smell

of stir-fried pork. Last night, I went to bed, was having a good sleep for a change. Then in the early morning a storm front passed through and there was a bolt of crackling thunder. I awoke instantly, frozen in fear. I am right back in Vietnam, in the middle of the monsoon season at my guard post. I am sure I'll get hit in the next volley and convinced I will die. My hands are freezing, yet sweat pours from my entire body. I feel each hair on the back of my neck standing on end. I can't catch my breath and my heart is pounding. I smell a damp sulfur smell. Suddenly I see what's left of my buddy Troy, his head on a bamboo platter, sent back to our camp by the Viet Cong. Propaganda messages are stuffed between his clenched teeth. The next bolt of lightning and clap of thunder makes me jump so much that I fall to the floor. [2]

Perhaps there are no more vivid memories than those stored in the brains of soldiers who have experienced combat situations. Witness the above account told by a 60-year-old Vietnam veteran who cannot hear a clap of thunder, see an Asian woman, or touch a bamboo placemat without re-experiencing the sight of his decapitated friend. Even though this traumatic event occurred in a faraway place and long ago, the memory is still vivid in every detail and continues to produce the same state of hyperarousal and fear as he experienced on that fateful day.

Once called combat fatigue, war neurosis, or shell shock, it is now clear that post-traumatic stress disorder (PTSD) results from intense trauma and produces vivid memories that last a lifetime. The memories can be triggered by stimuli associated with the original traumatic event (flashbacks), and in some individuals they are so intrusive that normal functioning is no longer possible. Particularly in light of the increased incidence of PTSD in the United States following the terrorist attacks on September 11, 2001 (Marshall and Galea, 2004), there has been increasing interest in the question of how to quiet these intense fears and help sufferers lead more normal lives.

It is now generally believed that PTSD is due at least in part to a learning process in which formerly neutral stimuli (e.g., a bamboo placemat) are paired with extremely aversive ones (e.g., the sight of a head without a body). This process is a classic example of Pavlovian fear conditioning, a form of learning that has been studied extensively by psychologists and about which a great deal of basic information has been gained. Patients suffering from PTSD seem not to benefit from the presence of safety signals (such as their spouses) that help those without the disorder cope with painful fear memories (Herman, 1992). An example might be a female rape victim who, before the rape, had an intimate, close relationship with her husband (a safety signal) but now feels unsafe with him and with other men as well. Likewise, despite the passage of many years and being in an environment very different from Vietnam, the war veteran's fear persists. Basic studies on the development and reduction of fear and anxiety are proving to have direct clinical relevance by increasing our understanding of these processes and the means by which they may become dysfunctional.

LEARNING TO BE AFRAID

Converging evidence from many different laboratories indicates that a brain structure called the amygdala, located in the temporal lobe, is critically involved in both the formation and expression of aversive memories (Aggleton, 2000). The amygdala receives highly processed information from all sensory modalities and it projects widely to parts of the brain involved in the autonomic and somatic aspects of fear and anxiety (cf. Davis and Whalen, 2001; Fendt and Fanselow, 1999; LeDoux, 1994). When the amygdala is removed or inactivated in animals, the acquisition and expression of conditioned fear is blocked. When people look at pictures of scary faces, remember traumatic events, or perceive cues previously paired with shocks, there is an increase in blood flow to the amygdala. Fear learning appears to involve movement of calcium into amygdala neurons followed by a complex pattern of intracellular changes that presumably leads to long-term structural changes, allowing conditioned fear to become more or less permanent.

The major problem in PTSD and certain other types of anxiety disorders is an inability to suppress or inhibit terrible memories. Hence, an important area of inquiry concerns the way in which unwanted memories are inhibited and the reasons they fail to be inhibited following traumatic fear conditioning.

LEARNING TO REDUCE FEAR

Inhibition of acquired fear is studied in the laboratory using a procedurally simple paradigm in which a rat or a human is conditioned to fear some neutral stimulus, such as a light or tone, by pairing it with some aversive stimulus, such as a mild shock. Following this, the fear stimulus is presented repeatedly in the absence of the shock. This procedure is known as *extinction training* and results in a gradual decline and ultimate disappearance of the fear response as the subject learns that the stimulus is no longer predictive of the aversive event (extinction).

Behavioral observations indicate that extinction is a form of learning in its own right, rather than an "unlearning" or forgetting of previous learning (cf. Myers & Davis, 2002). Thus, after extinction training, fear memories return over time (spontaneous recovery), when the fear stimulus is presented in a place different from the place where extinction training took place (renewal), or when there has been an intervening stress (reinstatement). The re-emergence of the fear response in these cases indicates that fear has not been lost through extinction, but rather has been actively suppressed through an additional learning process. Thus, extinction is considered to be a form of acquired inhibition that counteracts or suppresses fear responses that are no longer adaptive.

Much less is known about the neural underpinnings of extinction than about the underpinnings of fear learning. Significantly, however, it has been established that extinction shares with acquisition a dependence on the N-methyl-D-aspartate (NMDA) receptor within the amygdala. The NMDA receptor, a protein located at certain synapses that are innervated by the neurotransmitter glutamate, has been implicated in learning and memory in a variety of situations. Falls, Miserendino, and Davis (1992) reported that intra-amygdala infusions of a compound that interferes with activity of this receptor shortly before extinction training blocked extinction, with the degree of the blockade depending on the dose that was given. Importantly, extinction was measured the next day at a time when the NMDA blocker was no longer in the brain. Other experiments indicated that this impairment could not be attributed to an effect on NMDA receptors outside the amygdala, to damage to or destruction of the amygdala, or to an impairment of sensory transmission during extinction training. Additional studies using systemic administration of other compounds that block NMDA receptors have confirmed the extinction-blocking effect. Blocking NMDA receptors after extinction training also blocks extinction, suggesting that NMDA receptors are important for the consolidation of extinction (Santini, Muller, & Quirk, 2001).

In light of these findings, the question arose as to whether it would be possible to enhance extinction by enhancing the functioning of the NMDA receptor. It is known that a compound called D-cycloserine binds to the NMDA receptor and makes it work better. Thus, we predicted that giving D-cycloserine prior to extinction training would enhance extinction. In a series of experiments conducted very similarly to those of Falls et al. (1992), our laboratory (Walker, Ressler, Lu, & Davis, 2002) administered D-cycloserine either systemically or directly into the amygdala prior to extinction training and then tested retention of extinction the next day without administering any more of the drug. D-cycloserine dose-dependently enhanced extinction in rats exposed to lights in the absence of shock but not in control rats that did not receive extinction training (Fig. 1). This

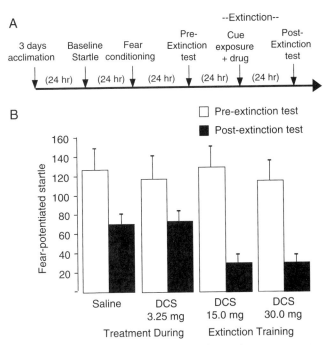

Fig. 1. Timeline for the experiment to test effects of D-cycloserine on extinction of conditioned fear in rats (A). Percent fear-potentiated startle measured 24 hours before (preextinction test) and 24 hours after (post-extinction test) extinction training (B). Saline (placebo) or D-cycloserine (DCS) in three different doses (3.25 mg/kg, 15 mg/kg, or 30 mg/kg) was administered 30 minutes prior to a single session of extinction training. Fear-potentiated startle was measured 24 hours later in the absence of the drug. From Walker et al. (2002) with permission from the Society for Neuroscience.

indicated that the drug's facilitatory effect was specific to extinction and did not result from a general dampening of fear expression.

Ledgerwood, Richardson, and Cranney (2003) found that D-cycloserine given either systemically or directly into the amygdala also facilitated extinction of conditioned freezing. Most interestingly, D-cycloserine could still facilitate extinction when given up to about 3 hours after extinction training, a finding consistent with the idea that D-cycloserine facilitates consolidation of extinction. More recently, the same researchers found that D-cycloserine reduced the ability of stress to disrupt extinction. Thus, control rats given shocks as a stressor after extinction training showed the typical return of conditioned fear (reinstatement), whereas experimental rats previously treated with D-cycloserine continued to express extinction (i.e., showed much less reinstated fear; Ledgerwood, Richardson, & Cranney, 2004).

Surprisingly, both our lab and the Richardson lab have found that D-cycloserine facilitates extinction only, not fear conditioning itself, although it is not clear why this is so. As mentioned earlier, D-cycloserine binds to the NMDA receptor to make it work better. D-cycloserine works similarly to D-serine, a chemical in the brain that, along with glycine, is believed to bind to the same site on the NMDA receptor. Hence, it is possible that NMDA receptors involved in fear conditioning are already saturated with D-serine or glycine, such that adding D-cycloserine cannot have any further effect; perhaps NMDA receptors involved in extinction are not saturated, such that their activity can be improved by giving D-cycloserine.

FROM LABORATORY TO CLINIC

Amygdala activation upon presentation of reminders of trauma is exaggerated greatly in people suffering from anxiety disorders such as PTSD, relative to equally traumatized individuals who did not go on to develop PTSD (cf. Rauch, Shin, & Wright, 2003). For this reason it has been hypothesized that inappropriate and excessive fear in humans results from abnormal fear learning processes and may reflect irregularities in the circuitry of the amygdala or related structures that play a role in either fear learning or fear inhibition (Quirk & Gehlert, 2003). Therapeutically, treatments for PTSD and other anxiety disorders typically involve a process similar to extinction. Techniques such as systematic desensitization, for example, involve exposure to feared stimuli in the absence of any aversive event or even the possibility that an aversive event might occur, with the result that the reflexive fear response of a person undergoing such treatment gradually subsides. Because this process is so similar to extinction, an understanding of the mechanisms of extinction should inform and refine the procedures of systematic desensitization.

An example of this translational approach from our own research is a preliminary study in which we evaluated the clinical utility of orally administered D-cycloserine in combination with exposure therapy for acrophobics (people suffering from an inordinate fear of heights). We could test this possibility immediately because the drug is known to be safe to use in humans: D-cycloserine at high doses has antibacterial effects and has been used to treat tuberculosis with very few side effects. The exposure therapy in these studies assumed a unique

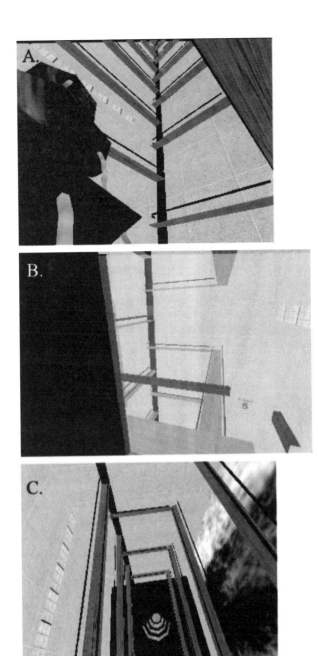

Fig. 2. Pictures from the virtual reality environment used to test fear in people suffering from acrophobia (fear of heights). Picture A is a view looking up from the bottom of the building as the subject gets onto the glass elevator. Note the catwalks where subjects will be asked to walk. Picture B is a view from inside the glass elevator on the fifth floor with the glass door closed. Subjects are asked to walk out onto the catwalk after the door opens. Picture C is a view looking down to the bottom of the building as subjects peer over the catwalk.

form: a virtual-reality situation developed by Rothbaum and colleagues in which patients rode in a virtual glass elevator to progressively higher floors (see Fig. 2; Ressler et al., 2004). This situation is very frightening to patients just entering treatment but becomes considerably more tolerable with increasing exposure to the virtual environment, typically over six to eight sessions.

In our study, 30 patients were rated for their initial fear of heights and divided into three groups that had comparable levels of fear, as well as being similar on other variables such as age, sex, etc. The participants received two sessions of virtual-reality exposure therapy. Single doses of placebo or D-cycloserine (50 or 500 mg) were taken 2 to 4 hours prior to each of the sessions. Neither the therapist nor the patient knew what medication was being taken. Self-reported levels of discomfort were rated at each floor in each session. Similar ratings were made both 1 week and 3 months following the initial exposure sessions. Spontaneous galvanic skin conductance fluctuations, a measure of overall anxiety, were measured during exposure and at the 1-week follow-up session. Finally, patients were asked to report the number of times they exposed themselves to real-life height encounters over the 3-month period.

Exposure therapy combined with D-cycloserine resulted in significantly larger reductions of acrophobia symptoms on all main outcome measures than the same amount of exposure in combination with a placebo (Fig. 3). Compared to subjects receiving the placebo, subjects receiving D-cycloserine had significantly more improvement within the virtual environment both 1 week and 3 months after treatment. Subjects receiving D-cycloserine also showed significantly greater decreases in post-treatment skin conductance fluctuations during the virtual exposure. Additionally, subjects receiving D-cycloserine had significantly greater improvement than those receiving a placebo on general measures of real-world acrophobia symptoms; this improvement was evident early in treatment and was maintained at 3 months, as indicated by a variety of scales such as acrophobia avoidance, acrophobia anxiety, attitudes towards heights, clinical global improvement, and number of self-exposures to real-world heights.

CONCLUSIONS AND FUTURE DIRECTIONS

Ours was a small clinical study and it needs to be replicated. In addition, it involved people with a specific phobia and it remains to be determined whether D-cycloserine will improve cognitive behavioral therapy for more complex disorders such as PTSD. Nonetheless, the finding that D-cycloserine facilitated exposure therapy for phobic patients in this study is important in a number of respects. First, combining D-cycloserine or similar medications with psychotherapy may offer patients suffering from phobias (and perhaps more complex anxiety disorders such as PTSD) a greater likelihood of overcoming their fears with as little stress as possible during therapy and a greater likelihood of maintaining that improvement over time. Second, the utility of the drug reaffirms basic research implicating NMDA receptors in extinction in rodents and extends the principle of their involvement to humans. Finally, this line of research is a good example of translational research that crosses the boundaries of behavior and biology and shows how basic knowledge of the physiological processes underlying fear and

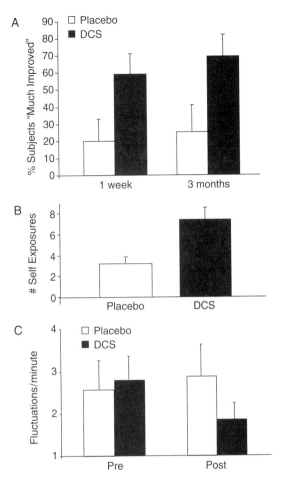

Fig. 3. Self-rated improvement (A), self-exposures to heights (B), and skin conductance levels (C) in acrophobics given D-cycloserine (DCS) or a placebo during exposure treatment. Subjects receiving DCS during treatment demonstrated significantly greater subjective improvement (i.e., by rating themselves as "Very Much Improved" or "Much Improved" on the Clinical Global Improvement Scale) compared to those receiving the placebo. Subjects receiving DCS during treatment demonstrated significantly more exposures to heights at 3 months than did subjects receiving the placebo, and subjects treated with DCS during exposure therapy showed significant decreases in post-treatment fluctuations in skin conductance compared to those treated with the placebo. From Ressler et al. (2004) with permission from the American Medical Association.

fear extinction in rodents can translate into improving existing therapies for psychiatric disorders.

Since the results of our clinical trial were presented for the first time in 2003, a number of groups have begun to combine D-cycloserine with exposure-based psychotherapy for the treatment of social phobia, obsessive-compulsive disorder, panic disorder, and PTSD. There are already encouraging reports of combining D-cycloserine with cognitive behavioral therapy in patients with social phobia (A. Goddard, M. Otto, personal communications). We plan to try D-cycloserine in people with fear of public speaking, using virtual reality that involves exposure to a "virtual audience." Thus, in a few years we may know whether this new methodology will be useful not only for treating simple phobias but also for treating more complex psychiatric disorders.

Recommended Reading

Myers, K.M., & Davis, M. (2002). (See References)
Ressler, K.J., Rothbaum, B.O., Tannenbaum, L., Anderson, P., Graap, K., Zimand, E., Hodges, L., & Davis, M. (2004). (See References)

Acknowledgments—This work was supported by National Institute of Mental Health Grant MH-047840 (MD), MH-069884 (KR), MH067314 (BR), a National Science Foundation Grant, IBN-987675 for the Science and Technology Center Program, Center for Behavioral Neuroscience and The Yerkes National Primate Center P-51 Base Grant. Barbara O. Rothbaum receives research funding and is entitled to sales royalties from Virtually Better, Inc., where the DCS therapy took place. Michael Davis and Kerry J. Ressler have submitted a patent for the use of D-cyloserine for the specific enhancement of learning during psychotherapy. The terms of these arrangements have been reviewed and approved by Emory University in accordance with their conflict of interest policies.

Notes

1. Address correspondence to Michael Davis, Yerkes National Primate Research Center, Emory University, 954 Gatewood Rd NE, Atlanta, GA 30329; e-mail: mdavis4@emory.edu.

2. Paraphrased from a war veteran's conversations with R.L. Gelman, Department of Psychiatry, Yale University School of Medicine (personal communication).

References

Aggleton, J.P. (Ed.). (2000). The Amygdala (Vol. 2). Oxford, England: Oxford University Press.

Davis, M., & Whalen, P. (2001). The amygdala: Vigilance and emotion. *Molecular Psychiatry, 6,* 13–34.

Falls, W.A., Miserendino, M.J., & Davis, M. (1992). Extinction of fear-potentiated startle: Blockade by infusion of an NMDA antagonist into the amygdala. *The Journal of Neuroscience, 12,* 854–63.

Fendt, M., & Fanselow, M.S. (1999). The neuroanatomical and neurochemical basis of conditioned fear. *Neuroscience and Biobehavioral Reviews, 23,* 743–760.

Herman, J.L. (1992). *Trauma and recovery.* New York: Basic Books.

Ledgerwood, L., Richardson, R., & Cranney, J. (2003). D-cycloserine facilitates extinction of conditioned fear as assessed by freezing in rats. *Behavioral Neuroscience, 117,* 341–349.

Ledgerwood, L., Richardson, R., & Cranney, J. (2004). D-cycloserine and the facilitation of conditioned fear: Consequences for reinstatement. *Behavioral Neuroscience, 118,* 505–513.

LeDoux, J.E. (1994). Emotion: Clues from the brain. *Annual Review of Psychology, 46,* 209–235.

Marshall, R.D., & Galea, S. (2004). Science for the community: Assessing mental health after 9/11. *Journal of Clinical Psychiatry, 65* (Suppl. 1), 37–43.

Myers, K.M., & Davis, M. (2002). Behavioral and neural analysis of extinction: A Review. *Neuron, 36,* 567–584.

Quirk, G.J., & Gehlert, D.R. (2003). Inhibition of the amygdala: Key to pathological states? *Annals of the New York Academy of Sciences, 985,* 263–72.

Rauch, S.L., Shin, L.M., & Wright, C.I. (2003). Neuroimaging studies of amygdala function in anxiety disorders. *Annals of the New York Academy of Sciences, 985,* 389–410.

Ressler, K.J., Rothbaum, B.O., Tannenbaum, L., Anderson, P., Graap, K., Zimand, E., Hodges, L., & Davis, M. (2004). Cognitive enhancers as adjuncts to psychotherapy: Use of D-cycloserine in phobic individuals to facilitate extinction of fear. *Archives of General Psychiatry, 61*, 1136–1144.

Santini, E., Muller, R.U., & Quirk, G.J. (2001). Consolidation of extinction learning involves transfer from NMDA-independent to NMDA-dependent memory. *The Journal of Neuroscience, 21*, 9009–9017.

Walker, D.L., Ressler, K.J., Lu, K.-T., & Davis, M. (2002). Facilitation of conditioned fear extinction by systemic administration or intra-amygdala infusions of D-cycloserine as assessed with fear-potentiated startle in rats. *The Journal of Neuroscience, 22*, 2343–2351.

This article has been reprinted as it originally appeared in *Current Directions in Psychological Science*. Citation information for this article as originally published appears above.

Who Develops Posttraumatic Stress Disorder?

Emily J. Ozer[1]
University of California-Berkeley School of Public Health

Daniel S. Weiss
Department of Psychiatry, University of California-San Francisco School of Medicine

Abstract

Nearly half of U.S. adults experience at least one traumatic event in their lifetimes, yet only 10% of women and 5% of men develop posttraumatic stress disorder (PTSD). Why this is so is among the most central questions in current PTSD research. This article reviews the current status of knowledge about who develops PTSD, discussing the strengths and weaknesses of the evidence. We describe the major models used to understand responses to traumatic events, as well as future research directions. We also propose that an exclusive focus on individual differences and individual intervention overlooks opportunities to reduce the prevalence of PTSD by modifying factors at the neighborhood, community, or national level.

Keywords

PTSD predictor; dissociation; traumatic event; prevention

The response to traumatic stress varies widely, ranging from transient disruption of functioning to the chronic clinical condition known as posttraumatic stress disorder (PTSD). Interest in and knowledge about PTSD increased dramatically after its diagnosis was formalized in 1980, but study of the effects of extreme stress has a long history, primarily focused on the effects of war (e.g., shell shock in World War I) and of sexual assault against women. According to generally accepted criteria, diagnosis of PTSD requires exposure to a traumatic event that causes feelings of extreme fear, horror, or helplessness. Traumatic events are defined as experiences that involve death, serious injury, or threat of death. The consequences of this exposure are manifested in three symptom clusters required for diagnosis: involuntary reexperiencing of the trauma (e.g., nightmares, intrusive thoughts), avoidance of reminders and numbing of responsivity (e.g., not being able to have loving feelings), and increased arousal (e.g., difficulty sleeping or concentrating, hypervigilance, exaggerated startle response).

Because PTSD requires the presence of an external event and symptoms linked to this event, it differs from virtually all other psychiatric disorders and raises intriguing issues regarding the definition of trauma, the role of individuals' appraisal of and responses to the event, the implications of a single versus repeated or ongoing exposure, and the role of community- and societal-level changes in attempting to prevent PTSD.

PREVALENCE

Results from a nationally representative study indicated that over the life course, 10% of women and 5% of men in the United States experience PTSD (Kessler, Sonnega, Bromet, Hughes, & Nelson, 1995). Moreover, approximately half of adults have experienced a traumatic event. In a national survey of Vietnam veterans conducted in the late 1980s, Kulka et al. (1990) estimated that 31% of males and 26% of females in this population had PTSD from their military service. Because PTSD symptoms wax and wane, especially in response to subsequent life events (not necessarily traumatic ones), many people experience *partial PTSD*, or clinically significant symptoms of PTSD that do not meet the diagnostic criteria for the disorder. Including individuals with partial PTSD resulted in an estimate of roughly 830,000 Vietnam veterans with significant posttraumatic distress or impairment approximately 20 years after service (Weiss et al., 1992).

The disparity between the 50% prevalence of exposure to trauma and the 7% lifetime prevalence of PTSD means that individual responses to trauma vary dramatically. This variability sparks what appears to be the key question in the field: Why do some people, and not others, develop PTSD? This issue has been of particular interest in recent years, leading to a search for systematic risk factors. Central questions have focused on the correlates or predictors of who develops the disorder and the strength of these effects. Current conceptualizations of PTSD symptoms provide potential explanatory frameworks for appreciating how predictors may influence the stress response and lead to differential risk for PTSD.

MODELS OF TRAUMA RESPONSE

Models Focused on Cognitive and Emotional Processes

The two most influential cognitively oriented formulations of trauma response and recovery highlight either the importance of beliefs and linked emotions about the self and the world (McCann & Pearlman, 1990) or the network of associations linking thinking about or reminders of a traumatic event to cognitive, emotional, physiological, and behavioral responses (Foa & Rothbaum, 1989). In the former formulation, a traumatic event is conceptualized as shattering the previously held assumption that though the world is not always safe, the lack of safety affects other people only. Thus, the trauma victim's thinking about the world must be adapted to assimilate this shattered assumption and make sense of and integrate the event. The PTSD symptoms of intrusion and avoidance arise from this process, which is generally experienced as painful because it requires remembering the trauma and the accompanying distress. Recovery gradually occurs when this iterative process can be tolerated without avoidance or being overwhelmed emotionally. Thus, factors that reduce the likelihood of effective integration and assimilation would theoretically increase the likelihood of chronic stress-related symptoms and PTSD. These factors include characteristics of the individual, his or her environment, and the event itself.

In the latter cognitive formulation, the metaphor of a memory network is invoked to describe linked information about the traumatic event and subsequent cognitive, affective, physiological, and behavioral responses. Activation of one element in the network activates other aspects—almost always including fear—and this uninterrupted repetition accounts for the continuing symptoms. Recovery occurs if the strength of the associations among network components is reduced by a combination of desensitization and substitution of more adaptive associations.

Biologically Focused Models

Research on the biology of PTSD initially focused on studying psychophysiological arousal in the presence of reminders (sounds, images, or scripts) of the traumatic event. Results indicated that individuals with PTSD demonstrated heightened arousal and prolonged duration of arousal compared with control subjects (e.g., Keane et al., 1998). Recently, researchers investigating the biological substrates of PTSD have focused on the processes and structures of the brain. Research has centered on the amygdala and hippocampus, key brain areas involved in the fear response and in the consolidation of memory (e.g., LeDoux, 2000), as well as on the hypothalamic-pituitary-adrenal (HPA) axis, the parts of the neuroendocrine system that control reactions to acute stress.

Examination of parts of the brain involved in the fear response has been extensive because traumatic events usually generate fear, and because fear initiates the "flight or fight" physiological arousal associated with the hyperarousal symptoms of PTSD. Fear has also been implicated in the mechanisms establishing and maintaining traumatic memories. Research in animals has generally examined brain circuitry; research in humans has included neuroimaging studies of brain structures (Schuff et al., 1997) and processes (Rauch et al., 1996). New findings from animal studies have established direct neural pathways from sensory input to areas of the amygdala. In light of the known reciprocal neuronal connections between the hippocampus and amygdala, these findings suggest a powerful explanation for the automaticity of the fear response and the manner in which emotional memories occur and are transmitted to the hippocampus.

Careful study of individuals with PTSD indicates that they are characterized by an oversensitivity of the HPA axis. The HPA axis is involved in generating, maintaining, and shutting down increases in stress-related hormones in the face of danger, a central aspect of traumatic events. Evidence suggests that individuals with PTSD exhibit dysregulation in the activity of cortisol, a hormone regulated by the HPA axis. The destructive effects of the excessive production of cortisol are believed to be responsible for the atrophy of the hippocampus frequently found among individuals with chronic PTSD. The dysregulation in the HPA axis involves the feedback loop that puts the brakes on the arousal generated by the perception of fear (Yehuda, 1998). These findings have generated research aimed at exploring the use of medications such as beta-blockers to dampen initial arousal. With initial arousal dampened, the consolidation of emotional memories may be attenuated. The hope, therefore, is that the reduction of physiological arousal immediately after the traumatic event will interfere with the processes that lead to the development of PTSD.

PREDICTORS OF PTSD

Two major meta-analyses (statistical analyses combining the results of many studies) of the predictors of PTSD have recently been published (Brewin, Andrews, & Valentine, 2000; Ozer, Best, Lipsey, & Weiss, 2003). These studies examined four categories of predictors: (a) historical or static characteristics such as family psychiatric history, intelligence, childhood trauma, and other previous trauma; (b) trauma severity; (c) psychological processes during and immediately after the trauma; and (d) social support and life stress after the traumatic event. Both meta-analyses showed that there were significant predictors of PTSD in all four categories, but that the strength of prediction varied across the categories. Those factors closer in time to the traumatic event (i.e., proximal factors) showed a stronger relationship to PTSD ($r \approx .40$) than did characteristics of the individual or his or her history that were more distant in time (i.e., distal factors; $r \approx .20$). The strongest predictor (included only in Ozer et al.) was peritraumatic dissociation. Peritraumatic dissociation refers to unusual experiences during and immediately after the traumatic event, such as a sense that things are not real, the experience of time stretching out, and an altered sense of self. Feeling that one is watching oneself in a movie or play as the event unfolds is a common description of the experience of dissociation. The strength of the relationship between such dissociation and likelihood of developing PTSD was in the moderate-to-large range.

Several important points regarding the predictors of PTSD should be highlighted. First, because largest correlations were about .40, peritraumatic dissociation and other predictors are neither necessary nor sufficient for developing PTSD. Second, the explanation for why peritraumatic dissociation is a predictor requires considering a host of differences in both the people exposed and the nature of the exposure. It may be that the severity of the traumatic event influences the likelihood of peritraumatic dissociation, either through the level of psychophysiological arousal the individual endures during the event or through more complicated relationships involving the effects of the individual's temperament, prior experience, prior psychological functioning, and other genetic or environmental factors that affect his or her capacity to regulate the emotional response. Third, level of social support following the trauma was also a strong predictor, with more social support associated with lower likelihood of later PTSD symptoms. An individual's level of social support likely relates to his or her history and functioning prior to the trauma, factors that this literature has generally not investigated and that meta-analytic approaches cannot easily summarize.

PROBLEMS AND POTENTIAL SOLUTIONS

The main limitation of the research on predictors of PTSD is the heavy reliance on self-report measures and retrospective designs. This naturalistic, retrospective approach makes sense considering the general unpredictability of exposure to trauma and the obvious ethical problems of exposing research participants to extreme stress in experimental or quasi-experimental designs. Prospective studies initiated prior to the occurrence of a major disaster or trauma, however, help address this limitation. For example, recent prospective research has assessed the psychological aftermath of the September 11 terrorist attacks in the United States (Silver, Holman, McIntosh, Poulin, & Gil-Rivas, 2002). Longitudinal research with individuals in high-risk jobs, such as jobs in the military, emergency services, and police force, also provides opportunities for prospective studies of possible predictors of PTSD.

Furthermore, the processes by which identified predictors may shape the development of PTSD remain largely unexamined. Systematic investigation of the ways in which these factors influence responses to trauma at multiple levels (e.g., behavioral, social, biological) could potentially inform interventions to attenuate or prevent PTSD. Future research should emphasize the more proximal mechanisms or processes—in psychological or physiological terms—that account for the relationship between PTSD symptoms and the more distal, static predictors such as prior trauma and family history of psychopathology. Evaluation of theory-based interventions with valid operationalization of critical variables could then provide data with which to evaluate current theory, an important area of study given the ethical prohibitions regarding experimental research in this field. Meta-analytic examination of the PTSD literature was useful in identifying simple, linear relationships between predictors and PTSD symptoms. It is likely, however, that some predictors influence each other in more complex ways; for example, a given predictor may strengthen the effects of another predictor on the development of PTSD (moderation) or may serve as the mechanism through which another predictor increases the likelihood of developing PTSD (mediation). Moreover, the unique meaning of exposure for a single individual may provide the most parsimonious explanation for why a person develops PTSD.

INTRIGUING ISSUES AND QUESTIONS

Definition of Traumatic Event

The definition of what constitutes a traumatic event is central to the diagnosis of PTSD and to all research regarding the disorder. Defining a traumatic event, however, is not simple; indeed, the diagnostic definition has changed over the past decade. Definitional issues raise interesting challenges for PTSD research as they call into question what kinds of experiences are traumatic and for whom. If two people experience the same event (e.g., encountering body parts) but only one reacts with fear, helplessness, or horror, has only one of them experienced a traumatic event?

Because traumatic events typically involve immediate horror and threat to survival (e.g., sexual assault at knifepoint, torture, combat), very high physiological arousal usually accompanies the experience. A broadening of the types of events that some people consider to be traumatic has led to inclusion in the PTSD literature of studies of highly distressing events (e.g., receiving a diagnosis of cancer) that may or may not invoke the same arousal that acute life-threatening situations do. The presence or absence of arousal may well become a key phenomenon that has implications for symptoms of PTSD and whether or not an event is deemed traumatic. If the subjective emotional and physiological response to the event is overlooked, research may not yield consistent findings that would perhaps emerge if arousal were required to identify an event as traumatic.

Ongoing Exposures and the Prototype of PTSD Symptoms

Early theories of trauma response and PTSD were largely based on individuals who lived in generally positive environments and experienced a discrete traumatic event or series of events within a discrete period of time (e.g., sexual assault, disaster, military service), so that the traumatic event or events signified a dramatic disruption of pre-trauma life. It is unclear how well this model fits the experience of individuals subjected to pervasive traumatic stress, for example, in the contexts of chronic physical or sexual abuse, deadly civilian conflicts and genocide, or severe community violence in low-income urban areas. The impairments of such individuals, including problems in interpersonal relationships and affect and impulse regulation, may be complicated and difficult to treat (Herman, 1992). The self-perceptions of people who have experienced ongoing trauma seem to be dramatically worse than those of individuals who have experienced discrete traumatic events in the context of otherwise normal development. Some researchers have suggested that a separate term, such as "complex PTSD" or "disorders of extreme stress—not otherwise specified," should be used in place of PTSD to better describe this disorder. Much prior research did not examine whether the predictors of disorder differ depending on whether trauma is experienced as a discrete event or as an ongoing condition of life. Future research that investigates this distinction may find clearer patterns of predictive relationships than have been uncovered so far.

Prevention of PTSD

What are the implications of the research on predictors of PTSD for the prevention of the disorder? Secondary-prevention efforts that seek to reduce the likelihood of PTSD among individuals who have recently been exposed to traumatic stress could utilize these findings by developing early-intervention models that target processes associated with PTSD risk in the meta-analyses reviewed here (e.g., social support, peritraumatic dissociation if the affected individuals could be seen immediately following the event). Strategies for the primary prevention of PTSD would entail reducing the incidence of traumatic events. The most frequent types of traumatic events studied in the research literature have been combat exposure, interpersonal assaults, accidents, and disasters. Although some traumatic stressors, such as earthquakes, are beyond human control, action at the individual and community levels could clearly reduce the risk of exposure to many forms of traumatic stress and also shape the impact of even uncontrollable traumatic stressors on populations. Indeed, such efforts form the backbone of diverse disciplines and public-health policy efforts in areas including building and transportation safety, community violence prevention, domestic violence prevention, and international diplomacy.

There have been numerous investigations of the prevalence of PTSD in diverse communities that have experienced armed civil conflict or war, political repression, or other chronic violence. In such settings of collective trauma, it is particularly critical to look beyond the individual when considering both the effects of trauma and strategies for intervention and prevention. For example, severe political repression affects not just individuals but also the social institutions and norms of a nation or community (Martin-Baro, 1994). Virtually all interventions for PTSD focus on the individual with symptoms and utilize medication or psychotherapy. Although these interventions may help alleviate individual symptoms, they are obviously inadequate for addressing the harm to social institutions or promoting long-term healing and mental health if the sources of persistent trauma are not addressed. When PTSD is a consequence of collective social and political conditions, primary prevention of this disorder involves social and political changes in the community or nation, as does repair of the social fabric. Thus, perhaps more than any other psychological disorder, PTSD forces consideration of advocacy and political action as primary (universal) prevention tools.

Recommended Reading

Brewin, C.R., Andrews, B., & Valentine, J.D. (2000). (See References)
McNally, R.J. (2003). Progress and controversy in the study of posttraumatic stress disorder. *Annual Review of Psychology, 54,* 229–252.
Ozer, E.J., Best, S.R., Lipsey, T.L., & Weiss, D.S. (2003). (See References)
Wilson, J.P., Friedman, M.J., & Lindy, J.D. (Eds.). (2001). *Treating psychological trauma and PTSD.* New York: Guilford Press.

Note

1. Address correspondence to Emily J. Ozer, UC-Berkeley School of Public Health, 140 Warren Hall, Berkeley, CA 94720-7360; e-mail: eozer@berkeley.edu.

References

Brewin, C.R., Andrews, B., & Valentine, J.D. (2000). Meta-analysis of risk factors for posttraumatic stress disorder in trauma-exposed adults. *Journal of Consulting and Clinical Psychology, 68,* 748–766.
Foa, E.B., & Rothbaum, B.O. (1989). Behavioral-cognitive conceptualizations of posttraumatic stress disorder. *Behavior Therapy, 20,* 155–176.
Herman, J. (1992). Complex PTSD. *Journal of Traumatic Stress, 5,* 377–391.
Keane, T.M., Kolb, L.C., Kaloupek, D.G., Orr, S.P., Blanchard, E.B., Thomas, R.G., Hsieh, F.Y., & Lavori, P.W. (1998). Utility of psychophysiological measurement in the diagnosis of posttraumatic stress disorder: Results from a Department of Veterans Affairs cooperative study. *Journal of Consulting and Clinical Psychology, 66,* 914–923.
Kessler, R.C., Sonnega, A., Bromet, E., Hughes, M., & Nelson, C.B. (1995). Posttraumatic stress disorder in the National Comorbidity Survey. *Archives of General Psychiatry, 52,* 1048–1060.
Kulka, R.A., Schlenger, W.E., Fairbank, J.A., Hough, R.L., Jordan, B.K., Marmar, C.R., & Weiss, D.S. (1990). *Trauma and the Vietnam war generation: Report of the findings from the National Vietnam Veterans Readjustment Study.* New York: Brunner/Mazel.
LeDoux, J.E. (2000). Emotion circuits in the brain. *Annual Review of Neuroscience, 23,* 155–184.
Martin-Baro, I. (1994). *Writings for a liberation psychology* (A. Aron & S. Corne, Eds.). Cambridge, MA: Harvard University Press.
McCann, I.L., & Pearlman, L.A. (1990). *Psychological trauma and the adult survivor.* New York: Brunner/Mazel.
Ozer, E.J., Best, S.R., Lipsey, T.L., & Weiss, D.S. (2003). Predictors of posttraumatic stress disorder and symptoms in adults: A meta-analysis. *Psychological Bulletin, 129,* 52–73.

Rauch, S.L., van der Kolk, B., Fisler, R.E., Alpert, N.M., Orr, S.P., Savage, C.R., Fischman, A.J., Jenike, M.A., & Pitman, R.K. (1996). A symptom provocation study of posttraumatic stress disorder using positron emission tomography and script-driven imagery. *Archives of General Psychiatry, 53*, 380–387.

Schuff, N., Marmar, C.R., Weiss, D.S., Neylan, T.C., Schoenfeld, F.B., Fein, G., & Weiner, M.W. (1997). Reduced hippocampal volume and n-acetyl aspartate in posttraumatic stress disorder. *Annals of the New York Academy of Sciences, 821*, 516–520.

Silver, R.C., Holman, E.A., McIntosh, D.N., Poulin, M., & Gil-Rivas, V. (2002). National Longitudinal Study of Psychological Responses to September 11. *Journal of the American Medical Association, 288*, 1235–1244.

Weiss, D.S., Marmar, C.R., Schlenger, W.E., Fairbank, J.A., Jordan, B.K., Hough, R.L., & Kulka, R.A. (1992). The prevalence of lifetime and partial post-traumatic stress disorder in Vietnam Theatre veterans. *Journal of Traumatic Stress, 5*, 365–376.

Yehuda, R. (1998). Psychoneuroendocrinology of post-traumatic stress disorder. *Psychiatric Clinics of North America, 21*, 359–379.

This article has been reprinted as it originally appeared in *Current Directions in Psychological Science*. Citation information for this article as originally published appears above.

Resilience in the Face of Potential Trauma

George A. Bonanno[1]

Teachers College, Columbia University

Abstract

Until recently, resilience among adults exposed to potentially traumatic events was thought to occur rarely and in either pathological or exceptionally healthy individuals. Recent research indicates, however, that the most common reaction among adults exposed to such events is a relatively stable pattern of healthy functioning coupled with the enduring capacity for positive emotion and generative experiences. A surprising finding is that there is no single resilient type. Rather, there appear to be multiple and sometimes unexpected ways to be resilient, and sometimes resilience is achieved by means that are not fully adaptive under normal circumstances. For example, people who characteristically use self-enhancing biases often incur social liabilities but show resilient outcomes when confronted with extreme adversity. Directions for further research are considered.

Keywords

loss; grief; trauma; resilience; coping

Life is filled with peril. During the normal course of their lives, most adults face one or more potentially traumatic events (e.g., violent or life-threatening occurrences or the death of close friends or relatives). Following such events, many people find it difficult to concentrate; they may feel anxious, confused, and depressed; and they may not eat or sleep properly. Some people have such strong and enduring reactions that they are unable to function normally for years afterward. It should come as no surprise that these dramatic reactions have dominated the literatures on loss and trauma. Until recently, the opposite reaction—the maintenance of a relative stable trajectory of healthy functioning following exposure to a potential trauma—has received scant attention. When theorists have considered such a pattern, they have typically viewed it either as an aberration resulting from extreme denial or as a sign of exceptional emotional strength (e.g., McFarlane & Yehuda, 1996).

RESILIENCE (NOT RECOVERY) IS THE MOST COMMON RESPONSE TO POTENTIALTRAUMA

Over a decade ago, my colleagues and I began an ongoing investigation of this supposedly rare response, and the means by which people might achieve such presumably superficial (or exemplary) functioning in the aftermath of a potentially traumatic event. The results of our research have consistently challenged the prevailing view on the subject. We took as our starting point the burgeoning developmental literature on resilience. Developmental researchers and theorists had for several decades highlighted various protective factors (e.g., ego-resiliency, the presence of supportive relationships) that promote healthy trajectories among children exposed to unfavorable life circumstances such as poverty (e.g., Garmezy, 1991; Rutter, 1987). We sought to adapt this body of research to the study of resilient outcomes among adults in otherwise normal circumstances who are exposed to isolated and potentially highly disruptive events.

Our research led to three primary conclusions, each mirroring but also extending the insights gained from developmental research. First, resilience following potentially traumatic events represents a distinct outcome trajectory from that typically associated with recovery from trauma. Historically, there have been few attempts to distinguish subgroups within the broad category of individuals exposed to potential trauma who do not develop post-traumatic stress disorder (PTSD). When resilience had been considered, it was often in terms of factors that "favor a path to recovery" (McFarlane & Yehuda, 1996, p. 158). However, studies have now demonstrated that resilience and recovery are discrete and empirically separable outcome trajectories following a dramatic event such as the death of a spouse (e.g., Bonanno, Wortman, et al., 2002) or direct exposure to terrorist attack (e.g., Bonanno, Rennicke, & Dekel, in press). Figure 1 depicts the prototypical resilience and recovery trajectories, as well as trajectories representing chronic and delayed symptom elevations (discussed later).

In this framework, recovery is defined by moderate to severe initial elevations in psychological symptoms that significantly disrupt normal functioning and that decline only gradually over the course of many months before returning to pretrauma levels. In contrast, resilience is characterized by relatively mild and short-lived disruptions and a stable trajectory of healthy functioning across time. A key point is that even though resilient individuals may experience an initial, brief spike in distress (Bonanno, Moskowitz, Papa, & Folkman, 2005) or may struggle for a short period to maintain psychological equilibrium (e.g., several weeks of sporadic difficulty concentrating, intermittent sleeplessness, or daily variability in

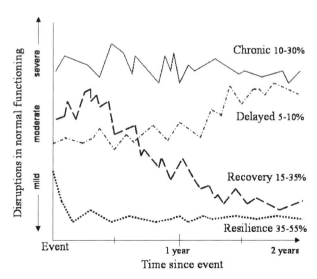

Fig. 1. Prototypical trajectories of disruption in normal functioning during the 2-year period following a loss or potential trauma.

levels of well-being; Bisconti et al., in press), they nonetheless manage to keep functioning effectively at or near their normal levels. For example, resilience has been linked to the continued fulfillment of personal and social responsibilities and the capacity for positive emotions and generative experiences (e.g., engaging in new creative activities or new relationships), both immediately and in the months following exposure to a potentially traumatic event (Bonanno & Keltner, 1997; Bonanno, Wortman, et al., 2002; Bonanno, Rennicke, & Dekel, in press; Fredrickson et al., 2003).

A second conclusion that emerges from our research is that resilience is typically the most common outcome following exposure to a potentially traumatic event. It has been widely assumed in the literature that the most common response to such an occurrence is an initial but sizeable elevation in trauma symptoms followed by gradual resolution and recovery (McFarlane & Yehuda, 1996). However, although symptom levels tend to vary for different potentially traumatic events, resilience has consistently emerged as the most common outcome trajectory. In one study, for example, over half of the people in a sample of middle-aged individuals who had lost their spouses showed a stable, low level of symptoms; and stable low symptoms were observed in more than a third of a group of gay men who were bereaved after providing care for a partner dying of AIDS, a considerably more stressful context (Bonanno, Moskowitz, et al., 2005). Resilience was also readily observed in a random phone-dialing survey of Manhattan residents following the September 11 terrorist attack (Bonanno, Galea, Bucciarelli, & Vlahov, 2005). Following conventions established in the study of subthreshold depression, we defined a mild to moderate trauma reaction as two or more PTSD symptoms and resilience as one or no PTSD symptoms in the first 6 months following the attack. Over 65% in the New York metropolitan area were resilient. Among people with more concentrated exposure (e.g., those who had either witnessed the attack in person or who were in the World Trade Center during the attack), the proportion showing resilience was still over 50%. Finally, even among people who were physically injured in the attack, a group for whom the estimated proportion of PTSD was extremely high (26.1%), one third (32.8%) of the individuals were resilient.

In establishing the validity of the resilient trajectory it is imperative to distinguish stable, healthy functioning from denial or other forms of superficial adjustment. To this end, several studies have now documented links between resilience and generally high functioning prior to a potentially traumatic event (Bonanno, Wortman, et al., 2002; Bonanno, Moskowitz, et al., 2005). Several studies have also documented resilient outcomes using relatively objective measures that go beyond participant self-report, including structured clinical interviews and anonymous ratings of functioning from participants' friends or relatives (e.g., Bonanno, Rennicke, & Dekel, in press; Bonanno, Moskowitz, et al., 2005). For example, we (Bonanno, Rennicke, & Dekel, in press) recruited the friends and relatives of high-exposure survivors of the World Trade Center terrorist attack and asked them to assign the survivors to either the resilience trajectory or one of the other outcome trajectories depicted in Figure 1. The assignments of friends and relatives closely matched the survivors' actual symptom levels over time, and thus provided important validation for the resilient trajectory.

THE HETEROGENEITY OF RESILIENCE: FLEXIBLE AND PRAGMATIC COPING

A third conclusion to emerge from our research, again extending the conclusions of developmental researchers, is that there are multiple and sometimes unexpected factors that might promote a resilient outcome. At the most general level, many of the same characteristics that promote healthy development should also foster adult resilience. These would include both situational factors, such as supportive relationships, and individual factors, such as the capacity to adapt flexibly to challenges (Block & Block, 1980). The capacity for adaptive flexibility was mirrored in a recent study associating resilience among New York City college students in the aftermath of September 11 with flexibility in emotion regulation, defined as the ability to effectively enhance or suppress emotional expression when instructed to do so (Bonanno, Papa, Lalande, Westphal, & Coifman, 2004).

In addition to these general health-promoting factors, however, our research also underscores a crucial point of departure from the developmental literature. Childhood resilience is typically understood in response to corrosive environments, such as poverty or enduring abuse. By contrast, adult resilience is more often a matter of coping with an isolated and usually (but not always) brief potentially traumatic event. The key point is that whereas corrosive environments require longer-term adaptive solutions, isolated events often oblige a more pragmatic form of coping, a "whatever it takes" approach, which may involve behaviors and strategies that are less effective or even maladaptive in other contexts. For instance, considerable research attests to the health benefits of expressing negative emotions. Although most resilient bereaved individuals express at least some negative emotion while talking about their loss, they nonetheless express relatively less negative emotion and greater positive emotion than other bereaved individuals (e.g., Bonanno & Keltner, 1997), thereby minimizing the impact of the loss while "increasing continued contact with and support from important people in the social environment" (p. 134).

Another example of pragmatic coping is illustrated by trait self-enhancement, the tendency toward self-serving biases in perception and attribution (e.g., overestimating one's own positive qualities). People given to self-serving biases tend to be narcissistic and to evoke negative reactions in other people. However, they also have high self-esteem and cope well with isolated potential traumas. Our research team examined self-enhancement among people dealing with two powerful stressor events, the premature death of a spouse and exposure to urban combat during the recent civil war in Bosnia (Bonanno, Field, Kovacevic, & Kaltman, 2002). In both samples, trait self-enhancement was positively associated with ratings of functioning made by mental health experts. In the bereavement study, however, untrained observers rated self-enhancers relatively unfavorably (lower on positive traits, e.g., honest; and higher on negative traits, e.g., self-centered). Yet, these negative impressions did not appear to interfere with self-enhancers' ability to maintain a high level of functioning after the loss.

This same pattern of findings was observed among high-exposure survivors of the September 11 attack (Bonanno et al., in press). Trait self-enhancement was more prevalent among individuals exhibiting the resilient trajectory, whether established by self-reported symptoms or ratings from friends or relatives. Self-enhancers also had greater positive affect and were rated by their friends and relatives as having consistently higher levels of mental and physical health, goal accomplishment, and coping ability. However, self-enhancers' friends and relatives also rated them as decreasing in social adjustment over the 18 months after September 11 and, among those with the highest levels of exposure, as less honest. This mixed pattern of findings suggests again that self-enhancers are able to maintain generally high levels of functioning in most areas except their social relations. Interestingly, however, self-enhancers themselves perceived their social relationships in relatively more positive terms than other participants, and this factor fully mediated their low levels of PTSD symptoms. In other words, self-enhancers appear to be blissfully unaware of the critical reactions they can evoke in others, and this type of self-serving bias evidently plays a crucial role in their ability to maintain stable levels of healthy functioning in other areas following a potentially traumatic event.

DIRECTIONS FOR FUTURE RESEARCH

The study of adult resilience is nascent and there are myriad questions for future research. An obvious imperative is to learn how the various costs and benefits of resilience vary across different types and durations of potentially traumatic events. Is there a point, for example, when the long-term costs of a particular type of coping might outweigh whatever crucial short-term advantages it provides? Might such trade-offs vary by gender or culture? Western, independence-oriented societies, for example, tend to focus more heavily than collectivist societies on the personal experience of trauma. However, little is known about the extent that loss and trauma reactions vary across cultures. A recent comparative study showed that bereaved people in China recovered more quickly from loss than did bereaved Americans (Bonanno, Papa, et al., 2005). However, as is typical of Chinese culture, Chinese bereaved also reported more physical symptoms than Americans. These data raise the intriguing questions of whether resilience has different meanings in different cultural contexts and, perhaps even more important, whether different cultures may learn from each other about effective and not-so-effective ways of coping with extreme adversity.

These questions in turn raise multiple practical and philosophical uncertainties about whether resilience can or should be learned. On the one hand, the observed link between resilient outcomes and personality variables suggests that resilient traits may be relatively fixed and not easily inculcated in others. And, given the social costs associated with some of the traits found in resilient people (e.g., self-enhancement), the advantage of simply imitating resilient individuals is questionable. On the other hand, a more promising avenue for training people to cope resiliently with trauma is suggested by the evidence linking resilience to flexible adaptation (Block & Block, 1980; Bonanno et al., 2004). Because adaptive flexibility can be manipulated experimentally (e.g., people's ability to engage in various cognitive or emotional processes can be measured under different stressor conditions; Bonanno et al., 2004), it should be possible to systematically examine the stability of such a trait over time and the conditions under which it might be learned or enhanced.

A related question pertains to how resilient individuals might view their own effectiveness at coping with potential trauma. Although at least some resilient individuals are surprised at how well they cope (Bonanno, Wortman, et al., 2002), it seems likely that others (e.g., self-enhancers) might overestimate their own resilience. This issue is particularly intriguing in relation to the distinction between stable resilience and delayed reactions. Although delayed reactions are not typically observed during bereavement (e.g., Bonanno, Wortman, et al., 2002), a small subset of individuals exposed to potentially traumatic events (5–10%) typically exhibit delayed PTSD. Preliminary evidence indicates that delayed-PTSD responders have higher initial symptom levels than do resilient individuals (e.g., Bonanno et al., in press). Further evidence of this distinction would hold potentially important diagnostic implications for early intervention.

Finally, another question pertains to how resilient individuals experience the crucial early weeks after an extreme stressor event. A recent study by Bisconti, Bergeman, and Boker (in press) shed some welcome light on this issue by examining daily well-being ratings in the early months after the death of a spouse. Although resilient bereaved typically show only mild and relatively short-lived overall decreases in well-being, examination of their daily ratings indicated marked variability across the first 3 weeks and then a more stable but still variable period that endured through the second month of bereavement. Perhaps similar research using larger samples and Internet methods might illuminate how resilient individuals manage to continue functioning and meeting the ongoing demands of their lives while nonetheless struggling, at least for a short period, to maintain self-regulatory equilibrium.

Recommended Readings

Bonanno, G.A. (2004). Loss, trauma, and human resilience: Have we underestimated the human capacity to thrive after extremely aversive events. *American Psychologist, 59*, 20–28.

Bonanno, G.A., & Kaltman, S. (2001). The varieties of grief experience. *Clinical Psychology Review, 21*, 705–734.

Gilbert, D.T., Pinel, E.C., Wilson, T.D., Blumberg, S.J., & Wheatley, T. (1998). Immune neglect: A source of durability bias in affective forecasting. *Journal of Personality and Social Psychology, 75*, 617–638.

Luthar, S.S. (in press). Resilient adaptation. In D. Cicchetti & D.J. Cohen (Eds.), *Developmental psychopathology: Risk, disorder, and adaptation*. New York: Wiley.

Acknowledgments—This research was supported by grants from the National Institutes of Health (R29-MH57274) and the National Science Foundation (BCS-0202772 and BCS-0337643).

Note

1. Address correspondence to George A. Bonanno, Clinical Psychology Program, 525 West 120th St., Box 218, Teachers College, Columbia University, New York, NY 10027; e-mail: gab38@columbia.edu.

References

Bisconti, T.L., Bergeman, C.S., & Boker, S.M. (in press). Social support as a predictor of variability: An examination of recent widows' adjustment trajectories. *Psychology and Aging.*

Block, J.H., & Block, J. (1980). The role of ego-control and ego-resiliency in the organization of behavior. In W.A. Collins (Ed.), *The Minnesota Symposia on Child Psychology* (Vol. 13, pp. 39–101). Hillsdale, NJ: Erlbaum.

Bonanno, G.A., Field, N.P., Kovacevic, A., & Kaltman, S. (2002). Self-enhancement as a buffer against extreme adversity: Civil war in Bosnia and traumatic loss in the United States. *Personality and Social Psychology Bulletin, 28*, 184–196.

Bonanno, G.A., Galea, S., Bucciarelli, A., & Vlahov, D. (2005). Psychological resilience after disaster: New York City in the aftermath of the September 11th terrorist attack. Manuscript submitted for publication.

Bonanno, G.A., & Keltner, D. (1997). Facial expressions of emotion and the course of conjugal bereavement. *Journal of Abnormal Psychology, 106*, 126–137.

Bonanno, G.A., Moskowitz, J.T., Papa, A., & Folkman, S. (2005). Resilience to loss in bereaved spouses, bereaved parents, and bereaved gay men. *Journal of Personality and Social Psychology, 88*, 827–843.

Bonanno, G.A., Papa, A., Lalande, K., Nanping, Z., & Noll, J.G. (2005). Grief processing and deliberate grief avoidance: A prospective comparison of bereaved spouses and parents in the United States and China. *Journal of Consulting and Clinical Psychology, 73*, 86–98.

Bonanno, G.A., Papa, A., Lalande, K., Westphal, M., & Coifman, K. (2004). The importance of being flexible: The ability to both enhance and suppress emotional expression predicts long-term adjustment. *Psychological Science, 15*, 482–487.

Bonanno, G.A., Rennicke, C., & Dekel, S. (in press). Self-enhancement among high-exposure survivors of the September 11th terrorist attack: Resilience or social maladjustment? *Journal of Personality and Social Psychology.*

Bonanno, G.A., Wortman, C.B., Lehman, D.R., Tweed, R.G., Haring, M., Sonnega, J., Carr, D., & Neese, R.M. (2002). Resilience to loss and chronic grief: A prospective study from pre-loss to 18 months post-loss. *Journal of Personality and Social Psychology, 83*, 1150–1164.

Fredrickson, B.L., Tugade, M.M., Waugh, C.E., & Larkin, G.R. (2003). What good are positive emotions in crisis? A prospective study of resilience and emotion following the terrorist attacks on the United States on September 11th, 2001. *Journal of Personality and Social Psychology, 84*, 365–376.

Garmezy, N. (1991). Resilience and vulnerability to adverse developmental outcomes associated with poverty. *American Behavioral Scientist, 34*, 416–430.

McFarlane, A.C., & Yehuda, R. (1996). Resilience, vulnerability, and the course of posttraumatic reactions. In B.A. van der Kolk, A.C. McFarlane, & L. Weisaeth (Eds.), *Traumatic stress* (pp. 155–181). New York: Guilford.

Rutter, M. (1987). Psychosocial resilience and protective mechanisms. *American Journal of Orthopsychiatry, 57*, 316–331.

This article has been reprinted as it originally appeared in *Current Directions in Psychological Science*. Citation information for this article as originally published appears above.

Recovering Memories of Trauma: A View from the Laboratory

Richard J. McNally[1]
Department of Psychology, Harvard University,
Cambridge, Massachusetts

Abstract

The controversy over the validity of repressed and recovered memories of childhood sexual abuse (CSA) has been extraordinarily bitter. Yet data on cognitive functioning in people reporting repressed and recovered memories of trauma have been strikingly scarce. Recent laboratory studies have been designed to test hypotheses about cognitive mechanisms that ought to be operative if people can repress and recover memories of trauma or if they can form false memories of trauma. Contrary to clinical lore, these studies have shown that people reporting CSA histories are not characterized by a superior ability to forget trauma-related material. Other studies have shown that individuals reporting recovered memories of either CSA or abduction by space aliens are characterized by heightened proneness to form false memories in certain laboratory tasks. Although cognitive psychology methods cannot distinguish true memories from false ones, these methods can illuminate mechanisms for remembering and forgetting among people reporting histories of trauma.

Keywords

recovered memories; trauma; repression; sexual abuse; dissociation

How victims remember trauma is among the most explosive issues facing psychology today. Most experts agree that combat, rape, and other horrific experiences are unforgettably engraved on the mind (Pope, Oliva, & Hudson, 1999). But some also believe that the mind can defend itself by banishing traumatic memories from awareness, making it difficult for victims to remember them until many years later (Brown, Scheflin, & Hammond, 1998).

This controversy has spilled out of the clinics and cognitive psychology laboratories, fracturing families, triggering legislative change, and determining outcomes in civil suits and criminal trials. Most contentious has been the claim that victims of childhood sexual abuse (CSA) often repress and then recover memories of their trauma in adulthood.[2] Some psychologists believe that at least some of these memories may be false—inadvertently created by risky therapeutic methods (e.g., hypnosis, guided imagery; Ceci & Loftus, 1994).

One striking aspect of this controversy has been the paucity of data on cognitive functioning in people reporting repressed and recovered memories of CSA. Accordingly, my colleagues and I have been conducting studies designed to test hypotheses about mechanisms that might enable people either to repress and recover memories of trauma or to develop false memories of trauma.

For several of our studies, we recruited four groups of women from the community. Subjects in the *repressed-memory group* suspected they had been sexually abused as children, but they had no explicit memories of abuse. Rather, they inferred their hidden abuse history from diverse indicators, such as depressed mood, interpersonal problems with men, dreams, and brief, recurrent visual images (e.g., of a penis), which they interpreted as "flashbacks" of early trauma. Subjects in the *recovered-memory group* reported having remembered their abuse after long periods of not having thought about it.[3] Unable to corroborate their reports, we cannot say whether the memories were true or false. Lack of corroboration, of course, does not mean that a memory is false. Subjects in the *continuous-memory group* said that they had never forgotten their abuse, and subjects in the *control group* reported never having been sexually abused.

PERSONALITY TRAITS AND PSYCHIATRIC SYMPTOMS

To characterize our subjects in terms of personality traits and psychiatric symptoms, we asked them to complete a battery of questionnaires measuring normal personality variation (e.g., differences in absorption, which includes the tendency to fantasize and to become emotionally engaged in movies and literature), depressive symptoms, posttraumatic stress disorder (PTSD) symptoms, and dissociative symptoms (alterations in consciousness, such as memory lapses, feeling disconnected with one's body, or episodes of "spacing out"; McNally, Clancy, Schacter, & Pitman, 2000b).

There were striking similarities and differences among the groups in terms of personality profiles and psychiatric symptoms. Subjects who had always remembered their abuse were indistinguishable from those who said they had never been abused on all personality measures. Moreover, the continuous-memory and control groups did not differ in their symptoms of depression, posttraumatic stress, or dissociation. However, on the measure of negative affectivity—proneness to experience sadness, anxiety, anger, and guilt—the repressed-memory group scored higher than did either the continuous-memory or the control group, whereas the recovered-memory group scored midway between the repressed-memory group on the one hand and the continuous-memory and control groups on the other.

The repressed-memory subjects reported more depressive, dissociative, and PTSD symptoms than did continuous-memory and control subjects. Repressed-memory subjects also reported more depressive and PTSD symptoms than did recovered-memory subjects, who, in turn, reported more dissociative and PTSD symptoms than did control subjects. Finally, the repressed- and recovered-memory groups scored higher than the control group on the measure of fantasy proneness, and the repressed-memory group scored higher than the continuous-memory group on this measure.

This psychometric study shows that people who believe they harbor repressed memories of sexual abuse are more psychologically distressed than those who say they have never forgotten their abuse.

FORGETTING TRAUMA-RELATED MATERIAL

Some clinical theorists believe that sexually molested children learn to disengage their attention during episodes of abuse and allocate it elsewhere (e.g., Terr, 1991). If CSA survivors possess a heightened ability to disengage attention from threatening cues, impairing their subsequent memory for them, then this ability ought to be evident in the laboratory. In our first experiment, we used directed-forgetting methods to test this hypothesis (McNally, Metzger, Lasko, Clancy, & Pitman, 1998). Our subjects were three groups of adult females: CSA survivors with PTSD, psychiatrically healthy CSA survivors, and nonabused control subjects. Each subject was shown, on a computer screen, a series of words that were either trauma related (e.g., *molested*), positive (e.g., *charming*), or neutral (e.g., *mailbox*). Immediately after each word was presented, the subject received instructions telling her either to remember the word or to forget it. After this encoding phase, she was asked to write down all the words she could remember, irrespective of the original instructions that followed each word.

If CSA survivors, especially those with PTSD, are characterized by heightened ability to disengage attention from threat cues, thereby attenuating memory for them, then the CSA survivors with PTSD in this experiment should have recalled few trauma words, especially those they had been told to forget. Contrary to this hypothesis, this group exhibited memory deficits for positive and neutral words they had been told to remember, while demonstrating excellent memory for trauma words, including those they had been told to forget. Healthy CSA survivors and control subjects recalled remember-words more often than forget-words regardless of the type of word. Rather than possessing a superior ability to forget trauma-related material, the most distressed survivors exhibited difficulty banishing this material from awareness.

In our next experiment, we used this directed-forgetting approach to test whether repressed- and recovered-memory subjects, relative to nonabused control subjects, would exhibit the hypothesized superior ability to forget material related to trauma (McNally, Clancy, & Schacter, 2001). If anyone possesses this ability, it ought to be such individuals. However, the memory performance of the repressed- and recovered-memory groups was entirely normal: They recalled remember-words better than forget-words, regardless of whether the words were positive, neutral, or trauma related.

INTRUSION OF TRAUMATIC MATERIAL

The hallmark of PTSD is involuntary, intrusive recollection of traumatic experiences. Clinicians have typically relied on introspective self-reports as confirming the presence of this symptom. The emotional Stroop color-naming task provides a quantitative, non-introspective measure of intrusive cognition. In this paradigm, subjects are shown words varying in emotional significance, and are asked to name the colors the words are printed in while ignoring the meanings of the words. When the meaning of a word intrusively captures the subject's attention despite the subject's efforts to attend to its color, Stroop interference—delay in color naming—occurs. Trauma survivors with PTSD take longer to name the colors of words related to trauma than do survivors without the disorder, and also take longer to name the colors of trauma words than to name the colors of positive and neutral words or negative words unrelated to their trauma (for a review, see McNally, 1998).

Using the emotional Stroop task, we tested whether subjects reporting either continuous, repressed, or recovered memories of CSA would exhibit interference for trauma words, relative to nonabused control subjects (McNally, Clancy, Schacter, & Pitman, 2000a). If severity of trauma motivates repression of traumatic memories, then subjects who cannot recall their presumably repressed memories may nevertheless exhibit interference for trauma words. We presented a series of trauma-related, positive, and neutral words on a computer screen, and subjects named the colors of the words as quickly as possible. Unlike patients with PTSD, including children with documented abuse histories (Dubner & Motta, 1999), none of the groups exhibited delayed color naming of trauma words relative to neutral or positive ones.

MEMORY DISTORTION AND FALSE MEMORIES IN THE LABORATORY

Some psychotherapists who believe their patients suffer from repressed memories of abuse will ask them to visualize hypothetical abuse scenarios, hoping that this guided-imagery technique will unblock the presumably repressed memories. Unfortunately, this procedure may foster false memories.

Using Garry, Manning, Loftus, and Sherman's (1996) methods, we tested whether subjects who have recovered memories of abuse are more susceptible than control subjects to this kind of memory distortion (Clancy, McNally, & Schacter, 1999). During an early visit to the laboratory, subjects rated their confidence regarding whether they had experienced a series of unusual, but nontraumatic, childhood events (e.g., getting stuck in a tree). During a later visit, they performed a guided-imagery task requiring them to visualize certain of these events, but not others. They later rerated their confidence that they had experienced each of the childhood events. Nonsignificant trends revealed an inflation in confidence for imagined versus non-imagined events. But the magnitude of this memory distortion was more than twice as large in the control group as in the recovered-memory group, contrary to the hypothesis that people who have recovered memories of CSA would be especially vulnerable to the memory-distorting effects of guided imagery.

To use a less-transparent paradigm for assessing proneness to develop false memories, we adapted the procedure of Roediger and McDermott (1995). During the encoding phase in this paradigm, subjects hear word lists, each consisting of semantically related items (e.g., *sour*, *bitter*, *candy*, *sugar*) that converge on a non-presented word—the *false target*—that captures the gist of the list (e.g., *sweet*). On a subsequent recognition test, subjects are given a list of words and asked to indicate which ones they heard during the previous phase. The false memory effect occurs when subjects "remember" having heard the false target. We found that recovered-memory subjects exhibited greater proneness to this false memory effect than did subjects reporting either repressed memories of CSA, continuous memories of CSA, or no abuse (Clancy, Schacter, McNally, & Pitman, 2000). None of the lists was trauma related, and so we cannot say whether the effect would have been more or less pronounced for words directly related to sexual abuse.

In our next experiment, we tested people whose memories were probably false: individuals reporting having been abducted by space aliens (Clancy, McNally, Schacter, Lenzenweger, & Pitman, 2002). In addition to testing these individuals (and control subjects who denied having been abducted by aliens), we tested individuals who believed they had been abducted, but who had no memories of encountering aliens. Like the repressed-memory subjects in our previous studies, they inferred their histories of trauma from various "indicators" (e.g., a passion for reading science fiction, unexplained marks on their bodies). Like subjects with recovered memories of CSA, those reporting recovered memories of alien abduction exhibited pronounced false memory effects in the laboratory. Subjects who only believed they had been abducted likewise exhibited robust false memory effects.

CONCLUSIONS

The aforementioned experiments illustrate one way of approaching the recovered-memory controversy. Cognitive psychology methods cannot ascertain whether the memories reported by our subjects were true or false, but these methods can enable testing of hypotheses about mechanisms that ought to be operative if people can repress and recover memories of trauma or if they can develop false memories of trauma.

Pressing issues remain unresolved. For example, experimentalists assume that directed forgetting and other laboratory methods engage the same cognitive mechanisms that generate the signs and symptoms of emotional disorder in the real world. Some therapists question the validity of this assumption. Surely, they claim, remembering or forgetting the word *incest* in a laboratory task fails to capture the sensory and narrative complexity of autobiographical memories of abuse. On the one hand, the differences between remembering the word *incest* in a directed-forgetting experiment, for example, and recollecting an episode of molestation do, indeed, seem to outweigh the similarities. On the other hand, laboratory studies may underestimate clinical relevance. For example, if someone cannot expel the word *incest* from awareness during a directed-forgetting experiment, then it seems unlikely that this person would be able to banish autobiographical memories of trauma from consciousness. This intuition notwithstanding, an important empirical issue concerns whether these tasks do, indeed, engage the same mechanisms that figure in the cognitive processing of traumatic memories outside the laboratory.

A second issue concerns attempts to distinguish subjects with genuine memories of abuse from those with false memories of abuse. Our group is currently exploring whether this might be done by classifying trauma narratives in terms of how subjects describe their memory-recovery experience. For example, some of the subjects in our current research describe their recovered memories of abuse by saying, "I had forgotten about that. I hadn't thought about the abuse in years until I was reminded of it recently." The narratives of other recovered-memory subjects differ in their experiential quality. These subjects, as they describe it, suddenly realize that they are abuse survivors, sometimes attributing current life difficulties to these long-repressed memories. That is, they do not say that they have remembered forgotten events they once knew, but rather indicate that they have learned (e.g., through hypnosis) the abuse occurred. It will be important to determine whether these two groups of recovered-memory subjects differ cognitively. For example, are subjects exemplifying the second type of recovered-memory experience more prone to develop false memories in the laboratory than are subjects exemplifying the first type of experience?

Recommended Reading

Lindsay, D.S., & Read, J.D. (1994). Psychotherapy and memories of childhood sexual abuse: A cognitive perspective. *Applied Cognitive Psychology, 8*, 281–338.
McNally, R.J. (2001). The cognitive psychology of repressed and recovered memories of childhood sexual abuse: Clinical implications. *Psychiatric Annals, 31*, 509–514.
McNally, R.J. (2003). Progress and controversy in the study of posttraumatic stress disorder. *Annual Review of Psychology, 54*, 229–252.
McNally, R.J. (2003). *Remembering trauma.* Cambridge, MA: Belknap Press/Harvard University Press.
Piper, A., Jr., Pope, G., Jr., & Borowiecki, J., III. (2000). Custer's last stand: Brown, Scheflin, and Whitfield's latest attempt to salvage "dissociative amnesia." *Journal of Psychiatry and Law, 28*, 149–213.

Acknowledgments—Preparation of this article was supported in part by National Institute of Mental Health Grant MH61268.

Notes

1. Address correspondence to Richard J. McNally, Department of Psychology, Harvard University, 1230 William James Hall, 33 Kirkland St., Cambridge, MA 02138; e-mail: rjm@wjh.harvard.edu.

2. Some authors prefer the term *dissociation* (or *dissociative amnesia*) to *repression.* Although these terms signify different proposed mechanisms, for practical purposes these variations make little difference in the recovered-memory debate. Each term implies a defensive process that blocks access to disturbing memories.

3. However, not thinking about a disturbing experience for a long period of time must not be equated with an inability to remember it. Amnesia denotes an inability to recall information that has been encoded.

References

Brown, D., Scheflin, A.W., & Hammond, D.C. (1998). *Memory, trauma treatment, and the law.* New York: Norton.
Ceci, S.J., & Loftus, E.F. (1994). 'Memory work': A royal road to false memories? *Applied Cognitive Psychology, 8*, 351–364.
Clancy, S.A., McNally, R.J., & Schacter, D.L. (1999). Effects of guided imagery on memory distortion in women reporting recovered memories of childhood sexual abuse. *Journal of Traumatic Stress, 12*, 559–569.
Clancy, S.A., McNally, R.J., Schacter, D.L., Lenzenweger, M.F., & Pitman, R.K. (2002). Memory distortion in people reporting abduction by aliens. *Journal of Abnormal Psychology, 111*, 455–461.
Clancy, S.A., Schacter, D.L., McNally, R.J., & Pitman, R.K. (2000). False recognition in women reporting recovered memories of sexual abuse. *Psychological Science, 11*, 26–31.
Dubner, A.E., & Motta, R.W. (1999). Sexually and physically abused foster care children and post-traumatic stress disorder. *Journal of Consulting and Clinical Psychology, 67*, 367–373.
Garry, M., Manning, C.G., Loftus, E.F., & Sherman, S.J. (1996). Imagination inflation: Imagining a childhood event inflates confidence that it occurred. *Psychonomic Bulletin & Review, 3*, 208–214.
McNally, R.J. (1998). Experimental approaches to cognitive abnormality in posttraumatic stress disorder. *Clinical Psychology Review, 18*, 971–982.

McNally, R.J., Clancy, S.A., & Schacter, D.L. (2001). Directed forgetting of trauma cues in adults reporting repressed or recovered memories of childhood sexual abuse. *Journal of Abnormal Psychology, 110*, 151–156.

McNally, R.J., Clancy, S.A., Schacter, D.L., & Pitman, R.K. (2000a). Cognitive processing of trauma cues in adults reporting repressed, recovered, or continuous memories of childhood sexual abuse. *Journal of Abnormal Psychology, 109*, 355–359.

McNally, R.J., Clancy, S.A., Schacter, D.L., & Pitman, R.K. (2000b). Personality profiles, dissociation, and absorption in women reporting repressed, recovered, or continuous memories of childhood sexual abuse. *Journal of Consulting and Clinical Psychology, 68*, 1033–1037.

McNally, R.J., Metzger, L.J., Lasko, N.B., Clancy, S.A., & Pitman, R.K. (1998). Directed forgetting of trauma cues in adult survivors of childhood sexual abuse with and without posttraumatic stress disorder. *Journal of Abnormal Psychology, 107*, 596–601.

Pope, H.G., Jr., Oliva, P.S., & Hudson, J.I. (1999). Repressed memories: The scientific status. In D.L. Faigman, D.H. Kaye, M.J. Saks, & J. Sanders (Eds.), *Modern scientific evidence: The law and science of expert testimony* (Vol. 1, pocket part, pp. 115–155). St. Paul, MN: West Publishing.

Roediger, H.L., III, & McDermott, K.B. (1995). Creating false memories: Remembering words not presented in lists. *Journal of Experimental Psychology: Learning, Memory, and Cognition, 21*, 803–814.

Terr, L.C. (1991). Childhood traumas: An outline and overview. *American Journal of Psychiatry, 148*, 10–20.

This article has been reprinted as it originally appeared in *Current Directions in Psychological Science*. Citation information for this article as originally published appears above.

Mood and Emotion in Major Depression

Jonathan Rottenberg[1]

University of South Florida

Abstract

Nothing is more familiar to people than their moods and emotions. Oddly, however, it is not clear how these two kinds of affective processes are related. Intuitively, it makes sense that emotional reactions are stronger when they are congruent with a preexisting mood, an idea reinforced by contemporary emotion theory. Yet empirically, it is uncertain whether moods actually facilitate emotional reactivity to mood-congruent stimuli. One approach to the question of how moods affect emotions is to study mood-disturbed individuals. This review describes recent experimental studies of emotional reactivity conducted with individuals suffering from major depression. Counter to intuitions, major depression is associated with reduced emotional reactivity to sad contexts. A novel account of emotions in depression is advanced to assimilate these findings. Implications for the study of depression and normal mood variation are considered.

Keywords

depression; emotion; mood; affect; reactivity

Isn't it a common experience that moods make people more emotionally volatile? For example, don't irritable moods make it easier for even a minor slight to trigger outbursts of rage? Don't anxious moods make people so jumpy that a few strange noises in the night will provoke full panic and terror? This article considers the interplay of moods and emotions, by focusing on studies that examine one mood (depressed mood) and one emotion (sadness) in one population (clinically depressed persons). I first consider the intuitive hypothesis that major depression facilitates sad emotional reactions. Second, I describe a series of experiments that yielded results largely inconsistent with this idea. Third, I assimilate these novel findings into an alternative framework for understanding emotions in major depression. Finally, I highlight three directions for future research on the interaction between mood and emotion.

DOES DEPRESSED MOOD FACILITATE SAD EMOTIONAL REACTIONS?

One approach to studying mood–emotion interaction is to examine mood-disturbed individuals. People who suffer from major depressive disorder, commonly known as major depression, have a markedly severe type of mood disturbance. Major depression is the leading cause of psychiatric hospitalization; it is estimated to affect nearly one out of seven people and is associated with several adverse consequences, including increased risk of suicide. Major depression is defined as a 2-week period of persistent sad mood and/or a loss of interest or pleasure in daily activities, as well as four or more additional symptoms, such as marked changes in weight or appetite, sleep disturbance, pervasive guilt, fatigue, and difficulty concentrating. Although major depression is a complex package of symptoms, a profound change in mood is its most characteristic feature. Major depression thus provides a rich context for exploring the ways that mood alters emotional reactivity.

In considering mood–emotion interaction in depression, the first problem arises from the very slipperiness of the core terms, *mood* and *emotion*. Indeed, some researchers, clinicians, and laypeople have used these terms in confusing and incommensurate ways. For clarity and to follow current practices in affective science (Watson, 2000; Rottenberg & Gross, 2003), I here use moods to mean diffuse, slow-moving feeling states that are weakly tied to specific objects or situations. By contrast, emotions are quick-moving reactions that occur when organisms encounter meaningful stimuli that call for adaptive responses. Emotional reactions typically involve coordinated changes in feeling state, behavior, and physiology, and last seconds or minutes. Moods, by contrast, exert their clearest effects on feeling states and cognitions (as opposed to behavior and physiology) and last hours or days. When mood and emotion are distinguished in this way, it becomes apparent that depression, by definition, involves changes in moods but does not necessarily involve changes in emotional reactions.

Emotion theorists have posited that moods facilitate emotional reactions when the mood and the emotion are similar in nature (e.g., Rosenberg, 1998). Does depressed mood facilitate sad emotional reactions? Circumstantial evidence suggests it does. From early psychoanalytic formulations of depression to contemporary cognitive conceptualizations, depression scholars have noted an increased expression of negative thoughts and feelings in this disorder. Depressed persons' increased report and display of negative feelings is apparent in several settings. For example, depressed persons typically report (in interviews and on questionnaires) strong sadness behaviors such as crying spells. These self-reports of increased tearfulness are corroborated by the observations of mental health professionals, who note that depressed persons are prone to cry in therapeutic settings.

Although these clinical observations are consistent with the mood-facilitation hypothesis, they do not in themselves establish that depressed persons react more strongly than other people to sad stimuli. For example, observations of notable crying in clinical contexts could reflect changes in depressed persons' social behavior, such as a tendency to seek comfort from potentially sympathetic others (Coyne, 1976). Likewise, increased crying could reflect that depressed persons are exposed to more sad stimuli in their everyday environments than are healthy individuals. Indeed, depressed persons are almost certainly faced with a different world of emotion-generative stimuli than healthy individuals are. For these reasons, a better way to test the mood-facilitation hypothesis is to assess depressed and healthy individuals' emotional reactivity to controlled sadness-eliciting stimuli in the laboratory.

Testing the Mood-Facilitation Hypothesis

To test the mood-facilitation hypothesis, my colleagues and I created short films, using material taken from commercially available movies; our films were designed to elicit specific emotional states, and we pretested them in healthy populations. Of particular interest were responses to films that were edited either to elicit sadness or a neutral state (i.e., few reports or displays of emotion in healthy participants; Rottenberg, Kasch, Gross, & Gotlib, 2002). The sad film dramatized a death scene and revolved around themes of loss and grief; the neutral film depicted relatively innocuous landscape scenery. We recorded depressed and nondepressed participants' self-reported emotional experience and their observed expressive behavioral reactions and physiological reactions to the films. Surprisingly, the results from this study did not support the mood-facilitation hypothesis. First, depressed individuals' experiential, behavioral, and physiological reactions to the sad film were of similar magnitude to those of healthy people. Second, depressed participants reported greater sadness than healthy participants in response to the neutral film. Third, and most strikingly, when responses to the neutral film were used as a reference point, a typical practice in studies of emotional reactivity, depressed subjects actually reported smaller increases in sad feelings in response to the sad film than healthy controls did. Finally, this group difference did not appear to be a ceiling effect—that is, a consequence of depressed persons' sadness already being at an upper limit of measure while watching the neutral film. The difference remained significant even after depressed participants who had reported very high levels of sadness to the neutral film were removed from the analysis.

Further Violations of the Mood-Facilitation Hypothesis in Depression

Although a single violation of the mood-facilitation hypothesis is not decisive in itself, the lack of any support for the hypothesis in our first analysis gave us pause. Were our results an anomaly? To find out, we sought to test the mood-facilitation hypothesis under conditions that we expected to favor its confirmation.

Crying Responses   One alternative explanation for why depressed individuals originally reported relatively little change in their feeling state in response to our sad film is that the film simply failed to engage the depressed participants. It is easy to imagine, for example, that the concentration difficulties experienced by depressed persons, or their lack of motivation to watch films, could curtail the impact of a sad film. To address the possibility that our results were a consequence of low engagement, we reanalyzed our data, focusing only on those depressed and healthy participants who responded to the sad film with verifiable crying behavior (visible tears in the eyes); we assumed that participants who visibly cried during the film were fully engaged with it. Indeed, given the popular belief that depressed persons cry readily and intensely, it seemed reasonable to expect that these analyses of criers would favor the facilitation hypothesis.

Despite this expectation, when criers in the two diagnostic groups were compared directly, depressed criers did not exhibit a greater response to the sad film in their emotional experience, expressive behavior (e.g., tearful eyes, furrowed brow, downturned mouth), or physiological responses such as heart rate and skin conductance (a measure of sweat gland activity). In fact, as displayed in Figure 1, when reactivity was computed from a neutral reference, depressed criers actually

164

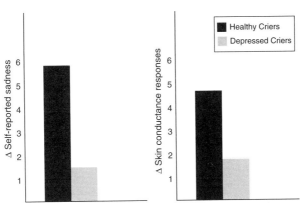

Fig. 1. Differences in self-reported sadness (left) and skin-conductance response rate (right) between healthy and depressed individuals who cried in response to a sad film. Adapted from "Crying threshold and intensity in major depressive disorder," by J. Rottenberg, J.J. Gross, F.H. Wilhelm, S. Najmi, and I.H. Gotlib, 2002, *Journal of Abnormal Psychology, 111*, p. 307. Copyright 2002 by the American Psychological Association. Adapted with permission.

showed smaller changes in their emotional experience and physiology than healthy criers did (Rottenberg, Gross, Wilhelm, Najmi, & Gotlib, 2002). Therefore, restriction of the analysis to criers did not yield support for the mood-facilitation hypothesis. In fact, our results suggested that depression might actually blunt the distress and arousal that is typically associated with crying (Gross, Frederickson, & Levenson, 1994).

Personally Tailored Sad Stimuli   Analysis of criers suggested that depressed persons' reduced response to sad material was unlikely to be an artifact of low engagement. Still, the possibility remained that our sad film was not an ideal stimulus for eliciting sadness in a depressed individual, in part because it was not relevant to the concerns of someone suffering from a serious disorder such as major depression. After all, the sad film had been drawn from a commercial entertainment, and it dramatized the misfortunes of other people using a fairly generic theme of loss. Would the mood-facilitation hypothesis hold if a more personally relevant sad stimulus were employed?

To answer this question, we repeated our experiment with a new sample of participants (again, depressed people and a healthy control group). This time, we included personally tailored emotional films alongside the standardized emotional films previously used. The personally tailored films, drawn from videotaped interviews, were videotapes of the participants themselves talking about the saddest and happiest events from their own lives. (Segments of videotape of participants answering demographic questions about themselves were used as a neutral reference.) Remarkably, results indicated that even when they were responding to emotional films depicting themselves relating sad events that had happened to them personally, depressed persons still did not show greater sensitivity to sad stimuli than healthy controls did. The results instead confirmed our earlier result: Depressed individuals reported considerable sadness to neutral emotional material and reported little differential response to acutely sad material (Rottenberg, Gross, & Gotlib, 2004).

IMPLICATIONS OF THESE FINDINGS

In summary, none of our work conducted with individuals with major depression has adduced evidence for the mood-facilitation hypothesis. In fact, our data indicate that major depression actually impedes reactivity to sad stimuli. Thus, contrary to both common intuition and emotion theory (Rosenberg, 1998), strong moods may not always facilitate strong emotional reactions to a mood-relevant stimulus. These findings have implications for how we understand major depression and the broader relationship between mood and emotion.

Rethinking Emotional Functioning in Depression

It has long been known that depressed individuals exhibit relatively little reactivity to positive emotional contexts (e.g., less smiling at jokes). The data presented here are novel in suggesting that this lack of reactivity extends to negative emotional contexts. To be clear, in these studies, depressed persons do respond to sad stimuli with reports of sadness and behavioral signs of sadness. But, remarkably, they appear to show essentially the same pattern of response to sad stimuli as they do to emotionally innocuous stimuli. In other words, depression flattens the emotional landscape, greatly constricting the range of emotional reactions to differing emotional contexts. My colleagues and I label this emotionally constricted pattern *emotion context insensitivity* (ECI; Rottenberg et al., 2004).

Converging Evidence for ECI in Major Depression

ECI—though a novel label—accords with several previous observations of depression. First, ECI accords with naturalistic observations of depressed persons' behavior. Depressed patients often exhibit few changes in expressive behavior to environmental events and display monotonous sad expressions. Second, ECI accords with depressed patients' personal descriptions of their disorder, which often feature emotional constriction: Patients describe their world as being flat, dull, and empty, and they remark that "everything is the same" (Healy, 1993). Third, ECI accords with the findings of recent investigations of emotion in major depression. For example, a recent naturalistic study found that, relative to healthy persons, depressed persons reported less emotional sensitivity to negative events (Peeters, Nicolson, Berkhof, Delespaul, & deVries, 2003).

The Clinical Significance of ECI

What are the clinical implications of ECI? Although ECI is a generally observable feature in depressed patients, patients also vary in the extent to which they show ECI. Early data suggests that depressed patients with the most pronounced ECI may face a relatively worse prognosis. For example, we found that those depressed persons who reported the most similar reactions to sad and neutral contexts (the constricted pattern expected by ECI) evidenced the most impaired functioning—specifically, the most severe depression, the longest episodes of depression, and the poorest overall psychosocial functioning (Rottenberg, Kasch, et al., 2002). Also underscoring the potential clinical importance of ECI, we recently found that depressed individuals who disclosed the least sad emotion when discussing memories of sad life events showed the least improvement of their symptoms 1 year later (Rottenberg, Joormann, Brozovich, & Gotlib, in press).

Does Depressed Mood Have a Purpose?

Depressed mood is painful, is associated with terrible human costs, and is remarkably prevalent. Scholars and sufferers alike have wondered whether depressed mood has any purpose. That severe depressed-mood states impede emotional reactions may speak to the possible functions of depressed mood. Nesse (2000) postulated that depressed mood evolved originally as an internal signal designed to bias an organism against action, particularly in adverse situations in which continued activity might prove to be futile or dangerous (e.g., famine). Depressed mood may drive several features associated with depression—such as pessimism, self-absorption, and loss of interest in the environment—that hold a person in place and prevent ill-considered actions. In this way, severe depressed-mood states may constitute a broad defensive response that "shuts down" motivated activity.

When Might Mood Facilitation Hold?

Strong moods may not always facilitate emotional reactions to mood-relevant stimuli, but how general is the exception? Should the intuition that irritable moods predispose people to angry outbursts and tense moods to anxiety attacks be abandoned? Although more compelling empirical demonstration of mood facilitation is needed, considerable indirect evidence for mood facilitation does exist, particularly for anxiety. In fact, most characterizations of anxiety disorders refer to prevailing anxious mood and to strong emotional reactions to mood-relevant stimuli (e.g., panic attacks, phobic reactions; see Barlow, 2002). Clinical anxiety and depression often co-occur; if it can be shown that anxious and depressed moods affect emotion differently, this fact may help better distinguish the two conditions (Watson, 2000).

FUTURE DIRECTIONS

This review suggests that studying emotional disorders such as major depression can yield surprising insights about the interactions of mood and emotion. As we learn more about mood–emotion interaction, surely other surprising findings will follow. I close by highlighting three important questions for future research.

Do mild depressed moods affect emotion differently than clinical depression does? Careful assessment of emotional reactivity across the range of depressed mood may reveal that mild depression facilitates emotional reactions, whereas clinical depression impedes them. Such nonlinearity would further enrich the debate about whether depression is best conceived as a continuum or a discrete category (Beach & Amir, 2003). Such nonlinearity would also raise intriguing questions about research on neuroticism (a personality trait, involving unstable affect, that is a risk factor for depression), which has demonstrated that neurotic individuals react more strongly than non-neurotic individuals to negative stimuli (Larsen & Ketalaar, 1991).

How do the consequences of depressed moods differ from that of other moods? Parallel investigations using other mood states (e.g., irritable, anxious, and positive) will be critical for examining the boundary conditions for mood facilitation. Likewise, to determine whether depressed persons' diminished response to stimuli designed to elicit sadness is generalizable, other negative emotions (e.g., anger) should be examined with equal care.

How does mood influence other aspects of emotion besides the magnitude of emotional responses? Affective science is increasingly highlighting the payoffs of studying the timing and orchestration of emotion, for instance the speed at which emotional responses rise and fall (e.g., Rottenberg & Gross, 2003). Thus, future work on mood–emotion interaction should study not only mood's effects on emotion magnitude but on these other aspects of the unfolding emotion waveform.

Recommended Reading

Nesse, R.M. (2000). (See References)
Rottenberg, J., Gross, J.J., Wilhelm, F.H., Najmi, S., & Gotlib, I.H. (2002). (See References)
Rottenberg, J., Kasch, K.L., Gross, J.J., & Gotlib, I.H. (2002). (See References)

Note

1. Address correspondence to Jonathan Rottenberg, Department of Psychology, University of South Florida, 4202 E. Fowler Ave., PCD 4118G, Tampa, FL 33620-7200; e-mail: jrottenb@cas.usf.edu.

References

Barlow, D. (2002). *Anxiety and its disorders*. New York: Guilford Press.
Beach, S.R.H., & Amir, N. (2003). Is depression taxonic, dimensional, or both? *Journal of Abnormal Psychology, 112*, 228–236.
Coyne, J.C. (1976). Toward an interactional description of depression. *Psychiatry, 39*, 28–40.
Gross, J.J., Frederickson, B.L., & Levenson, R.W. (1994). The psychophysiology of crying. *Psychophysiology, 31*, 460–468.
Healy, D. (1993). Dysphoria. In C.G. Costello (ed.) *Symptoms of Depression* (pp. 23–42). New York: John Wiley.
Larsen, R.J., & Ketelaar, T. (1991). Personality and susceptibility to positive and negative emotional states. *Journal of Personality and Social Psychology, 61*, 132–140.
Nesse, R.M. (2000). Is depression an adaptation? *Archives of General Psychiatry, 57*, 14–20.
Peeters, F., Nicolson, N.A., Berkhof, J., Delespaul, P., & deVries, M. (2003). Effects of daily events on mood states in Major Depressive Disorder. *Journal of Abnormal Psychology, 112*, 203–211.
Rosenberg, E.L. (1998). Levels of analysis and the organization of affect. *Review of General Psychology, 2*, 247–270.
Rottenberg, J., Gross, J.J., & Gotlib, I.H. (2004). Emotion context insensitivity in major depression. Manuscript submitted for publication.

Rottenberg, J., Gross, J.J., Wilhelm, F.H., Najmi, S., & Gotlib, I.H. (2002). Crying threshold and intensity in major depressive disorder. *Journal of Abnormal Psychology, 111*, 302–312.

Rottenberg, J., Joormann, J., Brozovich, F., & Gotlib, I.H. (in press). Emotional intensity of idiographic sad memories in depression predicts symptom levels one year later. *Emotion.*

Rottenberg, J., Kasch, K.L., Gross, J.J., & Gotlib, I.H. (2002). Sadness and amusement reactivity differentially predict concurrent and prospective functioning in major depressive disorder. *Emotion, 2*, 135–146.

Rottenberg, J., & Gross, J.J. (2003). When emotion goes wrong: Realizing the promise of affective science. *Clinical Psychology: Science and Practice, 10*, 227–232.

Watson, D. (2000). *Mood and temperament.* New York: Guilford Press.

This article has been reprinted as it originally appeared in *Current Directions in Psychological Science*. Citation information for this article as originally published appears above.

Molecular Genetic Studies of Eating Disorders: Current Status and Future Directions

Kelly L. Klump[1] and Kristen M. Culbert
Michigan State University

Abstract

We review association studies that have examined the genetic basis of eating disorders. Overall, findings suggest that serotonin, brain-derived neurotrophic factor, and estrogen genes may be important for the development of the disorders. These neuronal systems influence behavioral and personality characteristics (e.g., anxiety, food intake) that are disrupted in eating disorders. Future studies would benefit from larger sample sizes and inclusion of behavioral and personality covariates in analyses. Consideration of the mechanisms of genetic effects and interactions between genes and environment is also needed to extend conceptualizations of the genetic basis of these disorders.

Keywords

anorexia nervosa; bulimia nervosa; genetic; gene

Eating disorders have traditionally been viewed as having psychosocial origins. However, twin studies suggest the importance of genetic factors, as over half (58–83%) of the variation in risk for eating disorders may be accounted for by genes. Given this substantial heritability, it is important to identify the specific genes that contribute to the disorders. Genetic information can then be combined with information on environmental and psychosocial risk factors to develop a more comprehensive bio-psychosocial model of eating disorder development.

This article reviews genetic studies that have attempted to identify susceptibility genes for anorexia nervosa and bulimia nervosa and describes promising directions for future research. Because most genetic data for eating disorders come from association studies, this review will focus on association studies and their attempts to identify the genes contributing to eating disorders.

ASSOCIATION STUDIES

Association studies identify genes that contribute to disorders. These designs are conceptually equivalent to case-control studies in which individuals with eating disorders are compared to controls in terms of their allele (alternate form of a gene) and genotype (the combination of alleles) frequencies. A higher frequency of a particular allele or genotype in individuals with eating disorders suggests that that gene may be associated with the disorder.

Association studies of eating disorders have taken a two-pronged approach to selecting genes for analysis. In a manner similar to association studies of other disorders, eating disorder researchers early on examined genes as they were identified within the genome, without knowing the possible relevance of the gene or the biological system for eating disorders. This atheoretical approach was largely

170

due to the scarcity of identified genes and the lack of knowledge of their functional significance (i.e., their specific biological effect or product).

Although this approach is still used today, it is more common for researchers to choose genes based on biological systems that are relevant for eating disorders. For example, researchers have focused on genes within neurotransmitter (e.g., serotonin), neuropeptide (e.g., neuropeptide Y), and hormone (e.g., estrogen) systems that are known to affect food intake and/or mood states (e.g., anxiety) that are disrupted in eating disorders. Unfortunately, whether and how particular genes within these systems contribute to disrupted food intake and mood remains largely unknown, as the specific functional significance of most genes has not been explicated. An important direction for future research is to further elucidate these functions so that the neurobiological mechanisms by which genes lead to eating disorders can be identified.

Table 1 illustrates these points by depicting all of the genes that have been shown to be associated with eating disorders. Again, the specific functional significance of most of these genes is unknown, although many are within biological systems that influence food intake, metabolism, and/or mood. Nonetheless, only a handful of studies per gene exist, small sample sizes predominate, and non-replication of results has been the norm. Conclusions about the role of candidate genes in the development of eating disorders therefore await additional research. Promising exceptions include genes involved in the serotonin, brain-derived

Table 1. *Summary of Genes Associated with Eating Disorders*

Genes	Anorexia nervosa			Bulimia nervosa		
	No. of studies conducted	No. of studies reporting significant results	Sample size range	No. of studies conducted	No. of studies reporting significant results	Sample size range
Systems involved in food intake and mood						
Serotonin						
5-HT2a (serotonin 2a receptor)	16	7	$n = 43–316$	8	2	$n = 22–110$
5-HT2c(serotonin 2c receptor)	4	2	$n = 45–118$	2	0	$n = 40–59$
5-HTT (serotonin transporter)	7	2	$n = 55–138$	4	3	$n = 50–125$
HTR1D (serotonin 1D receptor)	1	1	$n = 191$	0	–	–
BDNF (brain-derived neuro-trophic factor)						
BDNF	6	4	$n = 26–510$	4	1	$n = 70–403$
Estrogens						
ER b (estrogen receptor beta)	2	2	$n = 50–170$	2	1	$n = 28–76$
Systems involved in food intake and/or energy balance						
Neuropeptides						
AgRP (agouti-related protein)	1	1	$n = 145$	0	–	–

(Continued)

Table 1. *(Continued)*

Genes	Anorexia nervosa			Bulimia nervosa		
	No. of studies conducted	No. of studies reporting significant results	Sample size range	No. of studies conducted	No. of studies reporting significant results	Sample size range
UCP (uncoupling protein)						
UCP-2/UCP-3 (uncoupling protein 2/3 gene cluster)	2	1	$n = 139–170$	0	–	–
		Systems involved in pleasure and reward				
Dopamine						
DAT1 (dopamine transporter)	0	–	–	1a	1	$n = 90$
DRD2 (dopamine D2 receptor)	1	1	$n = 191$ & 253	0	–	–
DRD3 (dopamine D3 receptor)	1	1	$n = 39$	0	–	–
Opioids						
OPRD1 (opioid delta receptor)	1	1	$n = 191$	0	–	–
Catecholamines						
COMT (catechol-O-methyltransferase)	3	2	$n = 45–66$	0	–	–
		Miscellaneous systems				
Small Conductance Ca+2 activated K+						
KCNN3 (calcium-activated potassium channel)	2	2	$n = 40–90$	0	–	–
NMDA (N-methyl-D-aspartate)						
NR2B (NMDA receptor 2B)	1	1	$n = 90$	0	–	–

Note. Genes are arranged by the biological system in which they reside. Only genes that show significant associations with eating disorders in at least one study are included in the table. Association study results were considered significant and included in the "No. of Studies Reporting Significant Results" column if the association was significant at $p < .05$. Some studies report results from two samples; the "Sample size range" column for these studies includes both sample sizes separated by an "&".

[a]This study examined a combined sample of women with bulimia nervosa and anorexia nervosa binge-purge subtype.

neurotrophic factor (BDNF), and ovarian hormone systems, as sufficient data exist for an evaluation of these genes.

Serotonin

Serotonin is a neurotransmitter that functions in the brain to control appetite, mood, sleep, memory, and learning. Serotonin genes have been studied more extensively than other genes for eating disorders, likely because of extant data showing serotonergic disturbances in eating disorders that may reflect serotonin's role in food intake and mood. The most promising serotonin genes are the serotonin 2a receptor ($5\text{-}HT_{2a}$) and serotonin transporter (5-HTT) genes. The A allele of the $5\text{-}HT_{2a}$–1438 gene has been associated with anorexia nervosa in several studies (see Klump & Gobrogge, 2005). The functional significance of this allele versus the G allele is unknown, as some studies show associations with increased $5\text{-}HT_{2a}$ receptor binding while others do not (Norton & Owen, 2005). Future studies should clarify the specific function of the A allele and the extent to which it influences the disruptions in food intake (i.e., decreased food intake) and mood (i.e., increased anxiety) observed in anorexia nervosa.

Findings for the $5\text{-}HT_{2a}$ receptor gene in bulimia nervosa are more equivocal. Studies show associations with both A and G alleles. Importantly, the G allele has been associated with increased impulsivity and decreased postsynaptic serotonin activity in bulimic subjects (Bruce et al., 2005). Thus, the association of the G allele with traits (i.e., impulsivity and decreased serotonin levels) that are common in bulimia nervosa but not anorexia nervosa may explain its preferential association with bulimia nervosa. Moreover, differences in impulsivity across bulimia nervosa samples may explain why the G allele is associated with the disorder in some but not all studies. These findings highlight the need to continue utilizing quantitative traits to determine if differential associations between $5\text{-}HT_{2a}$ receptor alleles and eating disorders reflect differences between subjects. Allelic variations may contribute to the development of eating pathology in only a subgroup of individuals with eating disorders (e.g., those with impulsive traits).

Another serotonin-receptor gene that may prove important for bulimia nervosa is the 5-HTT gene-linked polymorphism region (5-HTTLPR). The short ("s") version of 5-HTTLPR has been associated with both bulimia and higher levels of serotonin in brain synapses (as a result of reduced reuptake into axon terminals). Increased serotonin has been associated with anxiety, exaggerated stress responses, and, to a lesser extent, neuroticism and harm avoidance. All of these characteristics have been linked to the development of eating disorders. An interesting picture is therefore emerging, in which 5-HTTLPR may increase vulnerability to anxiety that then contributes to the development of bulimia nervosa. Notably, one study found the s allele to be associated with impulsivity rather than anxiety in women with bulimia nervosa (Steiger et al., 2005). Thus, a more fine-tuned analysis of this allele is warranted as it may be related to affective instability rather than to single affective states in women with bulimia nervosa.

BDNF

BDNF is a protein that acts within the brain to support the growth, differentiation, and survival of new and existing neurons. BDNF also influences food intake, making it a promising candidate for genetic studies of eating disorders. Increased BDNF causes appetite suppression and weight loss, whereas decreased levels cause weight gain (Hashimoto, Koizumi, Nakazato, Shimizu, & Iyo, 2005).

The Met66 variant of a BDNF gene (i.e., the Val66Met single nucleotide polymorphism) has been associated with anorexia nervosa, particularly restricting-type anorexia nervosa (anorexia nervosa without binge eating or purging). Findings for bulimia nervosa and binge/purge anorexia nervosa are mixed, suggesting that the gene may be specifically linked both to the low weight and sustained dietary restriction characteristic of restricting-type anorexia nervosa. The functional significance of the Met66 variant remains unknown; however, it may be involved in the regulated secretion of the BNDF protein (Hashimoto et al., 2005). Additional research into this candidate gene is warranted given associations between BDNF functioning, anxiety, and increased levels of extracellular serotonin (Hashimoto et al., 2005).

Estrogens

Several lines of evidence highlight the potential importance of estrogen in the genetic underpinnings of eating pathology. Estrogen directly influences food intake and has been linked to eating pathology in women (Edler, Lipson, & Keel, 2007). Moreover, genetic effects on disordered eating are present only after puberty (Klump, McGue, & Iacono, 2003), a developmental stage dominated by ovarian hormone activation in girls.

Variants of the estrogen receptor beta gene have been associated with both anorexia nervosa and bulimia nervosa (see Klump & Gobrogge, 2005, for a review). The functional significance of these variants is unknown, although estrogen receptor beta plays a key role in estrogen's effects on food intake and is associated with depressive and anxiety states (Walf & Frye, 2006).

DISCUSSION

Twin data indicate that genes play an important role in the etiology of eating disorders. Although definitive support for any candidate gene is lacking, association studies offer at least speculative hypotheses about the role of serotonin, BDNF, and estrogen genes. These candidate systems are all involved in affect regulation in general, and anxiety in particular. Anxiety-related traits are prospective risk factors for the development of eating pathology and have been shown to co-occur with eating disorders in families (Keel, Klump, Miller, McGue, & Iacono, 2005). Thus, the genetic influences on eating pathology may be linked to genes that contribute to anxiety.

As noted earlier, serotonin, BDNF, and estrogen also strongly influence food intake. All three systems could influence feeding behaviors independently, although they may also interact, with estrogen acting as a regulator. Estrogen influences the expression of genes within the serotonin and BDNF systems by regulating gene transcription (i.e., the process by which a gene's DNA sequence is copied into messenger RNA). Estrogen's mediation of gene transcription is particularly strong for tryptophan hydroxylase (the enzyme influencing the conversion of tryptophan to serotonin; Shively & Bethea, 2004) and 5-HT$_{2a}$ receptors (Norton & Owen, 2005), although it also influences 5-HTT transcription (Shively & Bethea, 2004). Interestingly, the serotonin system and BDNF show differences in function between males and females, and genetic effects on disordered eating are only present after puberty (Klump et al., 2003). Thus, estrogen, which is prominent in females after puberty, is an interesting candidate in the search for mechanisms underlying neurobiological and genetic influences on eating disorders.

The aforementioned hypotheses are tentative, given limitations of past research. Small sample sizes make findings difficult to interpret. Multisite collaborations with aggregated data are needed to ensure adequate power. In addition, studies have generally relied on categorical phenotypes of the *Diagnostic and Statistical Manual of Mental Disorders*. This reliance ignores the substantial heterogeneity in symptom and personality profiles for eating disorders. For example, research has shown that individuals with the same eating disorder diagnosis (e.g., bulimia nervosa) can exhibit very different personality characteristics that have significant implications for disorder course and outcome (Westen & Harnden-Fischer, 2001).

The recognition that this heterogeneity may also have significant implications for understanding the causes of eating disorders has already enhanced genetic research. Association studies have identified relationships between temperament dimensions (e.g., impulsivity) and gene variants (e.g., 5-HTTLPRs allele) that strengthen evidence for association in women with bulimia nervosa. Moreover, studies utilizing narrow categorical definitions of eating disorders (e.g., using restricting-type anorexia nervosa instead of all anorexia nervosa subtypes) have enhanced efforts to identify susceptibility genes. These findings highlight the need for future genetic studies to explore alternative continuous and categorical definitions of eating disorders.

FUTURE DIRECTIONS

In addition to these broad recommendations, there are several novel directions for future research. Genetic research on eating disorders has been hampered by a limited understanding of the biological mechanisms underlying the illnesses. Although general biological mechanisms have been identified (e.g., alterations in serotonin functioning, BDNF), knowledge of specific biological risk factors (as opposed to correlates) is lacking. This knowledge gap is partially due to the nature of eating pathology: Because eating disorders cause physiological changes, it is difficult to examine whether biological alterations are causes or consequences of the disorders. For example, although decreased BDNF levels characterize patients with anorexia nervosa, increased levels are associated with low body weight and decreased food intake in animal studies. Thus, decreased BDNF levels may be a correlate rather than a cause of anorexia nervosa.

Despite the strong need for prospective studies to disentangle biological causes from effects, the low base rate of eating disorders (.5–3% of females) has resulted in lower funding priorities for this type of research. The currently tight funding climate has exacerbated this problem, as biological data tend to be expensive to collect and analyze, particularly for prospective studies in which multiple biological samples are collected per subject. Nonetheless, until funding priorities and levels change, alternative designs could be used to identify important candidate systems. For example, twin studies can examine whether two phenotypes, such as eating disorder symptoms (e.g., binge eating) and neurobiological functioning (e.g., estrogen), share genetic transmission in twins from the general population. Although such twins may not have clinical eating disorders, knowledge regarding shared genetic factors for disordered eating symptoms and biological alterations could significantly inform genetic models of eating disorders. This approach has provided evidence for shared genetic effects between eating disorders and anxiety-related phenotypes (Keel et al., 2005).

Another approach entails examining endophenotypes. Endophenotypes are heritable neurophysiological, biochemical, endocrinological, neuroanatomical, cognitive, or neuropsychological traits that are correlates (but not symptoms) of the disorder. Because endophenotypes are purportedly influenced by a fewer number of genes than influence the disorder, identifying the genetic basis of endophenotypes is thought to be more straightforward and could lead to insights regarding the disorder's genetic basis. An ideal strategy for investigating endophenotypes is to examine biological disturbances in unaffected relatives of individuals with the disorder. If unaffected relatives show the biological dysfunction, then the alterations are not consequences of the disorder but are instead familial (and likely genetic) traits. This set of findings would suggest that (a) the genes contributing to the biological alteration directly contribute to the disorder (although the disorder's expression also depends upon other genetic and environmental risk factors); or (b) the genes for the biological dysfunction lie close to the genes for the disorder and, thus, are transmitted together.

Generally, eating disorder researchers have not used the endo-phenotype approach. One exception is Steiger and colleagues (Steiger et al., 2006), who found that unaffected female relatives of women with bulimia nervosa exhibited reduced 5-HTT activity that was similar to that of bulimia nervosa patients. These findings attest to the potential role of serotonergic dysfunction in the genetic diathesis of bulimia nervosa and highlight the utility of endophenotypes for identifying genetic risk factors for eating disorders.

A final approach for elucidating biological mechanisms is to combine genetic and neurobiological methods to identify the functional significance of genes. Studies by Steiger and colleagues (e.g., Steiger et al., 2005) exemplify this approach, as they have found associations between genetic variants (e.g., the 5-HTTLPRs allele) and serotonergic functioning in women with bulimia nervosa. A potential problem is noted earlier—namely, that neurobiological alterations may be consequences of the disorder rather than characteristics that were present before the illness onset (i.e., traits). This possibility highlights the need to determine which neurobiological indices are "trait" disturbances that may map onto genetic variations. Careful consideration of the nutritional state of participants, and the sampling of populations at different stages of illness (e.g., recovered subjects), will help with this determination.

In addition to further elucidating biological mechanisms, there is a need to understand how the environment interacts with genetic factors to lead to eating pathology. Moffitt, Caspi, and Rutter (2005) argue that failure to examine these interactions may be the reason for nonreplications in genetic research. If genes only increase risk in individuals exposed to putative environmental risk factors, then genetic studies that include exposed and unexposed individuals will fail to find significant genetic effects. These authors argue that psychiatric disorders may not be due to several genes of small effect, but may instead be due to fewer genes of large effect that are conditional upon exposure to environmental risk.

An important putative risk factor to investigate for eating disorders is dieting. Dieting is not a sufficient risk factor for eating disorders, as most women diet but only a small proportion develop eating disorders. However, dieting may lead to eating disorders in individuals with genetic risk for eating pathology. Moffitt et al. (2005) argue that examining "exposed samples" (e.g., studying the genotypes of dieting individuals) is a powerful strategy for confirming the role of gene–environment interactions, as well as for identifying candidate genes for the disorder. Given the link between food intake and serotonin, BDNF, and estrogen, future research should examine gene–environment interactions for dieting.

Recommended Reading

Gottesman, I.I., & Gould, T.D. (2003). The endophenotype concept in psychiatry: Etymology and strategic intentions. *American Journal of Psychiatry, 160,* 1–10.
Hashimoto, K., Koizumi, H., Nakazato, M., Shimizu, E., & Iyo, M. (2005). (See References)
Moffitt, T.E., Caspi, A., & Rutter, M. (2005). (See References)

Note

1. Address correspondence to Kelly L. Klump, Department of Psychology, Michigan State University, 107B Psychology Building, East Lansing, MI 48824-1116; e-mail: klump@msu.edu.

References

Bruce, K.R., Steiger, H., Joober, R., Ng Yink Kin, N.M.K., Israel, M., & Young, S.N. (2005). Association of the promoter polymorphism -1438G/A of the 5-HT2A receptor gene with behavioral impulsiveness and serotonin function in women with bulimia nervosa. *American Journal of Medical Genetics Part B: Neuropsychiatric Genetics, 37B,* 40–44.
Edler, C., Lipson, S.F., & Keel, P.K. (2007). Ovarian hormones and binge eating in bulimia nervosa. *Psychological Medicine, 37,* 131–141.
Hashimoto, K., Koizumi, H., Nakazato, M., Shimizu, E., & Iyo, M. (2005). Role of brain-derived neurotrophic factor in eating disorders: Recent findings and its pathophysiological implications. *Progress in Neuro-Psychopharmacology & Biological Psychiatry, 29,* 499–504.
Keel, P.K., Klump, K.L., Miller, K.B., McGue, M., & Iacono, W.G. (2005). Shared transmission of eating disorders and anxiety disorders. *International Journal of Eating Disorders, 38,* 99–105.
Klump, K.L., & Gobrogge, K.L. (2005). A review and primer of molecular genetic studies of anorexia nervosa. *International Journal of Eating Disorders, 37,* S43–S48.
Klump, K.L., McGue, M., & Iacono, W.G. (2003). Differential heritability of eating pathology in prepubertal versus pubertal twins. *International Journal of Eating Disorders, 33,* 287–292.
Moffitt, T.E., Caspi, A., & Rutter, M. (2005). Strategy for investigating interactions between measured genes and measured environments. *Archives of General Psychiatry, 62,* 473–481.
Norton, N., & Owen, M.J. (2005). 5HTR2A Association and expression studies in neuropsychiatric genetics. *Annals of Medicine, 37,* 121–129.
Shively, C.A., & Bethea, C.L. (2004). Cognition, mood disorders, and sex hormones. Institute of *Laboratory Animal Resources Journal, 45,* 189–199.
Steiger, H., Gauvin, L., Joober, R., Israel, M., Ng Yin Kin, N.M.K., Bruce, K.R., Richardson, J., Young, S.N., & Hakim, J. (2006). Intrafamilial correspondences on platelet [³H-] paroxetine-

binding indices in bulimic probands and their unaffected first-degree relatives. *Neuropsychopharmacology, 31,* 1785–1792.

Steiger, H., Joober, R., Israel, M., Young, S.N., Ng Yin Kin, N.M.K., Gauvin, L., Bruce, K.R., Joncas, J., & Torkaman-Zehi, A. (2005). The 5HTTLPR polymorphism, psychopathologic symptoms, and platelet [^{3}H-] paroxetine binding in bulimic syndromes. *International Journal of Eating Disorders, 37,* 57–60.

Walf, A.A., & Frye, C.A. (2006). A review of mechanisms of estrogen in the hippocampus and amygdala for anxiety and depression behavior. *Neuropsychopharmacology, 31,* 1097–1111.

Westen, D., & Harnden-Fischer, J. (2001). Personality profiles in eating disorders: Rethinking the distinction between axis I and axis II. *American Journal of Psychiatry, 158,* 547–562.

Section 4: Critical Thinking Questions

1. Ohman and Mineka describe the evolutionary history of snake phobias. Might other forms of psychopathology also have emerged out of mechanisms that evolved as adaptations to recurrent environmental challenges?

2. What kinds of factors prior to exposure to a traumatic event may influence responses to those events, and why?

3. Rottenberg describes findings indicating reduced emotional reactivity to negative emotion eliciting stimuli in depressed individuals. What function might this reduced reactivity or insensitivity to emotional context serve? How does this model converge with Barlow's view of depression as being characterized by an avoidance of emotion?

4. If genes that contribute to eating disorders are also implicated in anxiety disorders, what does this suggest about functional relationships between anxiety and disordered eating?

This article has been reprinted as it originally appeared in *Current Directions in Psychological Science*. Citation information for this article as originally published appears above.

Section 5: Externalizing Disorders (Substance and Conduct Disorder)

The final section of this reader addresses issues related to externalizing forms of psychopathology, include substance use disorders and conduct/behavioral problems. These reviews concern the normal development of processes related to externalizing problems (risk taking and decision making) and a variety of components of substance use problems, such as tolerance and withdrawal.

First, Steinberg provides an authoritative review of the developmental trajectory of risk taking behavior. This paper is a compelling account of why externalizing problems tend to increase in severity and diversity during adolescence. Steinberg explains this developmental phenomenon as the result of differential maturation of a cognitive/effortful system and an emotional system. This dual process system is also used as an organizing framework by other authors in this for understanding processes involved in the abuse of addictive substances. Wiers and Stacy argue that the continued use of substances despite explicit knowledge of the resultant harm they produce results from implicit cognitions governed by emotional/impulsive cognitive systems that becomes sensitized to the effects of drugs of abuse, which in turn weaken the slower, effortful cognitive system.

Papers by Siegel and by Baker and colleagues describe current theories guiding research on addiction and withdrawal processes. The former describes mechanisms that may link the processes of tolerance and of withdrawal, specifically compensatory physiological responses that emerge as conditioned responses to cues for drug use. These compensatory mechanisms contribute to the development of tolerance and to the symptoms of withdrawal that emerge when drug use cues are not followed by administration of the substance. Baker et al.'s paper provides a model for explaining the causal role of withdrawal symptoms in relapse to substance use. This model emphasizes the central role of drug use as a means of regulating negative affect, and the loss of this coping method during abstinence as a setting factor for relapse. Finally, Goders describes biological mechanisms that explain how stress (which likely increases negative affect) may facilitate the use of substances via increased sensitivity to the physiological effects of substances. This model provides a useful framework for understanding the high rates of comorbidity between substance use disorders and other forms of psychopathology.

Risk Taking in Adolescence: New Perspectives from Brain and Behavioral Science

Laurence Steinberg

Temple University

Abstract

Trying to understand why adolescents and young adults take more risks than younger or older individuals do has challenged psychologists for decades. Adolescents' inclination to engage in risky behavior does not appear to be due to irrationality, delusions of invulnerability, or ignorance. This paper presents a perspective on adolescent risk taking grounded in developmental neuroscience. According to this view, the temporal gap between puberty, which impels adolescents toward thrill seeking, and the slow maturation of the cognitive-control system, which regulates these impulses, makes adolescence a time of heightened vulnerability for risky behavior. This view of adolescent risk taking helps to explain why educational interventions designed to change adolescents' knowledge, beliefs, or attitudes have been largely ineffective, and suggests that changing the contexts in which risky behavior occurs may be more successful than changing the way adolescents think about risk.

Keywords

adolescence; decision making; risk taking; brain development

Adolescents and college-age individuals take more risks than children or adults do, as indicated by statistics on automobile crashes, binge drinking, contraceptive use, and crime; but trying to understand why risk taking is more common during adolescence than during other periods of development has challenged psychologists for decades (Steinberg, 2004). Numerous theories to account for adolescents' greater involvement in risky behavior have been advanced, but few have withstood empirical scrutiny (but see Reyna & Farley, 2006, for a discussion of some promising approaches).

FALSE LEADS IN RISK-TAKING RESEARCH

Systematic research does not support the stereotype of adolescents as irrational individuals who believe they are invulnerable and who are unaware, inattentive to, or unconcerned about the potential harms of risky behavior. In fact, the logical-reasoning abilities of 15-year-olds are comparable to those of adults, adolescents are no worse than adults at perceiving risk or estimating their vulnerability to it (Reyna & Farley, 2006), and increasing the salience of the risks associated with making a potentially dangerous decision has comparable effects on adolescents and adults (Millstein & Halpern-Felsher, 2002). Most studies find few age differences in individuals' evaluations of the risks inherent in a wide range of dangerous behaviors, in judgments about the seriousness of the consequences that might result from risky behavior, or in the ways that the relative costs and benefits

181

of risky activities are evaluated (Beyth-Marom, Austin, Fischoff, Palmgren, & Jacobs-Quadrel, 1993).

Because adolescents and adults reason about risk in similar ways, many researchers have posited that age differences in actual risk taking are due to differences in the information that adolescents and adults use when making decisions. Attempts to reduce adolescent risk taking through interventions designed to alter knowledge, attitudes, or beliefs have proven remarkably disappointing, however (Steinberg, 2004). Efforts to provide adolescents with information about the risks of substance use, reckless driving, and unprotected sex typically result in improvements in young people's thinking about these phenomena but seldom change their actual behavior. Generally speaking, reductions in adolescents' health-compromising behavior are more strongly linked to changes in the contexts in which those risks are taken (e.g., increases in the price of cigarettes, enforcement of graduated licensing programs, more vigorously implemented policies to interdict drugs, or condom distribution programs) than to changes in what adolescents know or believe.

The failure to account for age differences in risk taking through studies of reasoning and knowledge stymied researchers for some time. Health educators, however, have been undaunted, and they have continued to design and offer interventions qof unproven effectiveness, such as Drug Abuse Resistance Education (DARE), driver's education, or abstinence-only sex education.

A NEW PERSPECTIVE ON RISK TAKING

In recent years, owing to advances in the developmental neuro-science of adolescence and the recognition that the conventional decision-making framework may not be the best way to think about adolescent risk taking, a new perspective on the subject has emerged (Steinberg, 2004). This new view begins from the premise that risk taking in the real world is the product of both logical reasoning and psychosocial factors. However, unlike logical-reasoning abilities, which appear to be more or less fully developed by age 15, psychosocial capacities that improve decision making and moderate risk taking—such as impulse control, emotion regulation, delay of gratification, and resistance to peer influence—continue to mature well into young adulthood (Steinberg, 2004; see Fig. 1). Accordingly, psychosocial immaturity in these respects during adolescence may undermine what otherwise might be competent decision making. The conclusion drawn by many researchers, that adolescents are as competent decision makers as adults are, may hold true only under conditions where the influence of psychosocial factors is minimized.

Evidence from Developmental Neuroscience

Advances in developmental neuroscience provide support for this new way of thinking about adolescent decision making. It appears that heightened risk taking in adolescence is the product of the interaction between two brain networks. The first is a socioemotional network that is especially sensitive to social and emotional stimuli, that is particularly important for reward processing, and that

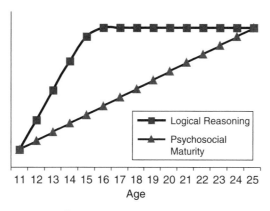

Fig. 1. Hypothetical graph of development of logical reasoning abilities versus psychosocial maturation. Although logical reasoning abilities reach adult levels by age 16, psychosocial capacities, such as impulse control, future orientation, or resistance to peer influence, continue to develop into young adulthood.

is remodeled in early adolescence by the hormonal changes of puberty. It is localized in limbic and paralimbic areas of the brain, an interior region that includes the amygdala, ventral striatum, orbitofrontal cortex, medial prefrontal cortex, and superior temporal sulcus. The second network is a cognitive-control network that subserves executive functions such as planning, thinking ahead, and self-regulation, and that matures gradually over the course of adolescence and young adulthood largely independently of puberty (Steinberg, 2004). The cognitive-control network mainly consists of outer regions of the brain, including the lateral prefrontal and parietal cortices and those parts of the anterior cingulate cortex to which they are connected.

In many respects, risk taking is the product of a competition between the socioemotional and cognitive-control networks (Drevets & Raichle, 1998), and adolescence is a period in which the former abruptly becomes more assertive (i.e., at puberty) while the latter gains strength only gradually, over a longer period of time. The socioemotional network is not in a state of constantly high activation during adolescence, though. Indeed, when the socioemotional network is not highly activated (for example, when individuals are not emotionally excited or are alone), the cognitive-control network is strong enough to impose regulatory control over impulsive and risky behavior, even in early adolescence. In the presence of peers or under conditions of emotional arousal, however, the socioemotional network becomes sufficiently activated to diminish the regulatory effectiveness of the cognitive-control network. Over the course of adolescence, the cognitive-control network matures, so that by adulthood, even under conditions of heightened arousal in the socioemotional network, inclinations toward risk taking can be modulated.

It is important to note that mechanisms underlying the processing of emotional information, social information, and reward are closely interconnected. Among adolescents, the regions that are activated during exposure to social and emotional stimuli overlap considerably with regions also shown to be sensitive to variations in reward magnitude (cf. Galvan, et al., 2005; Nelson, Leibenluft,

McClure, & Pine, 2005). This finding may be relevant to understanding why so much adolescent risk taking—like drinking, reckless driving, or delinquency— occurs in groups (Steinberg, 2004). Risk taking may be heightened in adolescence because teenagers spend so much time with their peers, and the mere presence of peers makes the rewarding aspects of risky situations more salient by activating the same circuitry that is activated by exposure to nonsocial rewards when individuals are alone.

The competitive interaction between the socioemotional and cognitive-control networks has been implicated in a wide range of decision-making contexts, including drug use, social-decision processing, moral judgments, and the valuation of alternative rewards/costs (e.g., Chambers, Taylor, & Potenza, 2003). In all of these contexts, risk taking is associated with relatively greater activation of the socioemotional network. For example, individuals' preference for smaller immediate rewards over larger delayed rewards is associated with relatively increased activation of the ventral striatum, orbitofrontal cortex, and medial prefrontal cortex—all regions linked to the socioemotional network—presumably because immediate rewards are especially emotionally arousing (consider the difference between how you might feel if a crisp $100 bill were held in front of you versus being told that you will receive $150 in 2 months). In contrast, regions implicated in cognitive control are engaged equivalently across decision conditions (McClure, Laibson, Loewenstein, & Cohen, 2004). Similarly, studies show that increased activity in regions of the socioemotional network is associated with the selection of comparatively risky (but potentially highly rewarding) choices over more conservative ones (Ernst et al., 2005).

Evidence from Behavioral Science

Three lines of behavioral evidence are consistent with this account. First, studies of susceptibility to antisocial peer influence show that vulnerability to peer pressure increases between preadolescence and mid-adolescence, peaks in mid-adolescence—presumably when the imbalance between the sensitivity to socioemotional arousal (which has increased at puberty) and capacity for cognitive control (which is still immature) is greatest—and gradually declines thereafter (Steinberg, 2004). Second, as noted earlier, studies of decision making generally show no age differences in risk processing between older adolescents and adults when decision making is assessed under conditions likely associated with relatively lower activation of brain systems responsible for emotion, reward, and social processing (e.g., the presentation of hypothetical decision-making dilemmas to individuals tested alone under conditions of low emotional arousal; Millstein, & Halpern-Felsher, 2002). Third, the presence of peers increases risk taking substantially among teenagers, moderately among college-age individuals, and not at all among adults, consistent with the notion that the development of the cognitive-control network is gradual and extends beyond the teen years. In one of our lab's studies, for instance, the presence of peers more than doubled the number of risks teenagers took in a video driving game and increased risk taking by 50% among college undergraduates but had no effect at all among adults (Gardner & Steinberg, 2005; see Fig. 2). In adolescence, then, not only is more merrier—it is also riskier.

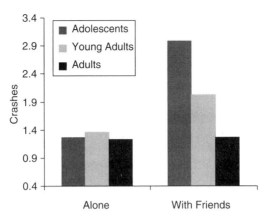

Fig. 2. Risk taking of adolescents, young adults, and adults during a video driving game, when playing alone and when playing with friends. Adapted from Gardner & Steinberg (2004).

What Changes During Adolescence?

Studies of rodents indicate an especially significant increase in reward salience (i.e., how much attention individuals pay to the magnitude of potential rewards) around the time of puberty (Spear, 2000), consistent with human studies showing that increases in sensation seeking occur relatively early in adolescence and are correlated with pubertal maturation but not chronological age (Steinberg, 2004). Given behavioral findings indicating relatively greater reward salience among adolescents than adults in decision-making tasks, there is reason to speculate that, when presented with risky situations that have both potential rewards and potential costs, adolescents may be more sensitive than adults to variation in rewards but comparably sensitive (or perhaps even less sensitive) to variation in costs (Ernst et al., 2005).

It thus appears that the brain system that regulates the processing of rewards, social information, and emotions is becoming more sensitive and more easily aroused around the time of puberty. What about its sibling, the cognitive-control system? Regions making up the cognitive-control network, especially prefrontal regions, continue to exhibit gradual changes in structure and function during adolescence and early adulthood (Casey, Tottenham, Liston, & Durston, 2005). Much publicity has been given to the finding that synaptic pruning (the selective elimination of seldom-used synapses) and myelination (the development of the fatty sheaths that "insulate" neuronal circuitry)—both of which increase the efficiency of information processing—continue to occur in the prefrontal cortex well into the early 20s. But frontal regions also become more integrated with other brain regions during adolescence and early adulthood, leading to gradual improvements in many aspects of cognitive control such as response inhibition; this integration may be an even more important change than changes within the frontal region itself. Imaging studies using tasks in which individuals are asked to inhibit a "prepotent" response–like trying to look away from, rather than toward, a point of light—have shown that adolescents tend to recruit the cognitive-control network less broadly than do adults, perhaps overtaxing the capacity of the more limited number of regions they activate (Luna et al., 2001).

In essence, one of the reasons the cognitive-control system of adults is more effective than that of adolescents is that adults' brains distribute its regulatory responsibilities across a wider network of linked components. This lack of cross-talk across brain regions in adolescence results not only in individuals acting on gut feelings without fully thinking (the stereotypic portrayal of teenagers) but also in thinking too much when gut feelings ought to be attended to (which teenagers also do from time to time). In one recent study, when asked whether some obviously dangerous activities (e.g., setting one's hair on fire) were "good ideas," adolescents took significantly longer than adults to respond to the questions and activated a less narrowly distributed set of cognitive-control regions (Baird, Fugelsang, & Bennett, 2005). This was not the case when the queried activities were not dangerous ones, however (e.g., eating salad).

The fact that maturation of the socioemotional network appears to be driven by puberty, whereas the maturation of the cognitive-control network does not, raises interesting questions about the impact—at the individual and at the societal levels—of early pubertal maturation on risk-taking. We know that there is wide variability among individuals in the timing of puberty, due to both genetic and environmental factors. We also know that there has been a significant drop in the age of pubertal maturation over the past 200 years. To the extent that the temporal disjunction between the maturation of the socioemotional system and that of the cognitive-control system contributes to adolescent risk taking, we would expect to see higher rates of risk taking among early maturers and a drop over time in the age of initial experimentation with risky behaviors such as sexual intercourse or drug use. There is evidence for both of these patterns (Collins & Steinberg, 2006; Johnson & Gerstein, 1998).

IMPLICATIONS FOR PREVENTION

What does this mean for the prevention of unhealthy risk taking in adolescence? Given extant research suggesting that it is not the way adolescents think or what they don't know or understand that is the problem, a more profitable strategy than attempting to change how adolescents view risky activities might be to focus on limiting opportunities for immature judgment to have harmful consequences. More than 90% of all American high-school students have had sex, drug, and driver education in their schools, yet large proportions of them still have unsafe sex, binge drink, smoke cigarettes, and drive recklessly (often more than one of these at the same time; Steinberg, 2004). Strategies such as raising the price of cigarettes, more vigilantly enforcing laws governing the sale of alcohol, expanding adolescents' access to mental-health and contraceptive services, and raising the driving age would likely be more effective in limiting adolescent smoking, substance abuse, pregnancy, and automobile fatalities than strategies aimed at making adolescents wiser, less impulsive, or less shortsighted. Some things just take time to develop, and, like it or not, mature judgment is probably one of them.

The research reviewed here suggests that heightened risk taking during adolescence is likely to be normative, biologically driven, and, to some extent, inevitable. There is probably very little that can or ought to be done to either attenuate or delay the shift in reward sensitivity that takes place at puberty. It may be possible to accelerate the maturation of self-regulatory competence, but no research has examined whether this is possible. In light of studies showing familial influences on psychosocial maturity in adolescence, understanding how contextual factors influence the development of self-regulation and knowing the neural underpinnings of these processes should be a high priority for those interested in the well-being of young people.

Recommended Reading

Casey, B.J., Tottenham, N., Liston, C., & Durston, S. (2005). (See References)
Johnson, R., & Gerstein, D. (1998). (See References)
Nelson, E., Leibenluft, E., McClure, E., & Pine, D. (2005). (See References)
Spear, P. (2000). (See References)
Steinberg, L. (2004). (See References)

Acknowledgments—Thanks to Nora Newcombe for comments on an earlier draft and to Jason Chein for his expertise in developmental neuroscience.

Note

1. Address correspondence to Laurence Steinberg, Department of Psychology, Temple University, Philadelphia, PA 19122; lds@temple.edu.

References

Baird, A., Fugelsang, J., & Bennett, C. (2005, April). *"What were you thinking?": An fMRI study of adolescent decision making.* Poster presented at the annual meeting of the Cognitive Neuroscience Society, New York.

Beyth-Marom, R., Austin, L., Fischoff, B., Palmgren, C., & Jacobs-Quadrel, M. (1993). Perceived consequences of risky behaviors: Adults and adolescents. *Developmental Psychology, 29,* 549–563.

Casey, B.J., Tottenham, N., Liston, C., & Durston, S. (2005). Imaging the developing brain: What have we learned about cognitive development? *Trends in Cognitive Science, 9,* 104–110.

Chambers, R.A., Taylor, J.R., & Potenza, M.N. (2003). Developmental neurocircuitry of motivation in adolescence: A critical period of addiction vulnerability. *American Journal of Psychiatry, 160,* 1041–1052.

Collins, W.A., & Steinberg, L. (2006). Adolescent development in interpersonal context. In W. Damon & R. Lerner (Series Eds.) & N. Eisenberg (Vol. Ed.), *Handbook of Child Psychology: Social,* emotional, and personality development (Vol. 3, pp. 1003–1067). New York: Wiley.

Drevets, W.C., & Raichle, M.E. (1998). Reciprocal suppression of regional cerebral blood flow during emotional versus higher cognitive processes: Implications for interactions between emotion and cognition. *Cognition and Emotion, 12,* 353–385.

Ernst, M., Jazbec, S., McClure, E.B., Monk, C.S., Blair, R.J.R., Leibenluft, E., & Pine, D.S. (2005). Amygdala and nucleus accumbens activation in response to receipt and omission of gains in adults and adolescents. *Neuroimage, 25,* 1279–1291.

Galvan, A., Hare, T., Davidson, M., Spicer, J., Glover, G., & Casey, B.J. (2005). The role of ventral frontostriatal circuitry in reward-based learning in humans. *Journal of Neuroscience, 25,* 8650–8656.

Gardner, M., & Steinberg, L. (2005). Peer influence on risk-taking, risk preference, and risky decision-making in adolescence and adulthood: An experimental study. *Developmental Psychology, 41*, 625–635.

Johnson, R., & Gerstein, D. (1998). Initiation of use of alcohol, cigarettes, marijuana, cocaine, and other substances in US birth cohorts since 1919. *American Journal of Public Health, 88*, 27–33.

Luna, B., Thulborn, K.R., Munoz, D.P., Merriam, E.P., Garver, K.E., Minshew, N.J., et al. (2001). Maturation of widely distributed brain function subserves cognitive development. *Neuroimage, 13*, 786–793.

McClure, S.M., Laibson, D.I., Loewenstein, G., & Cohen, J.D. (2004). Separate neural systems value immediate and delayed monetary rewards. *Science, 306*, 503–507.

Millstein, S.G., & Halpern-Felsher, B.L. (2002). Perceptions of risk and vulnerability. *Journal of Adolescent Health, 31S*, 10–27.

Nelson, E., Leibenluft, E., McClure, E., & Pine, D. (2005). The social re-orientation of adolescence: A neuroscience perspective on the process and its relation to psychopathology. *Psychological Medicine, 35*, 163–174.

Reyna, V., & Farley, F. (2006). Risk and rationality in adolescent decision-making: Implications for theory, practice, and public policy. *Psychological Science in the Public Interest, 7*, 1–44.

Spear, P. (2000). The adolescent brain and age-related behavioral manifestations. *Neuroscience and Biobehavioral Reviews, 24*, 417–463.

Steinberg, L. (2004). Risk-taking in adolescence: What changes, and why? *Annals of the New York Academy of Sciences, 1021*, 51–58.

This article has been reprinted as it originally appeared in *Current Directions in Psychological Science*. Citation information for this article as originally published appears above.

Implicit Cognition and Addiction

Reinout W. Wiers[1]

Maastricht University, Maastricht, Radboud University, Nijmegen, The Netherlands, and IVO Addiction Research Institute, Rotterdam, The Netherlands

Alan W. Stacy[2]

University of Southern California, Los Angeles

Abstract

Extensive recent research has begun to unravel the more implicit or automatic cognitive mechanisms in addiction. This effort has increased our understanding of some of the perplexing characteristics of addictive behaviors. The problem, often, is not that substance abusers do not understand that the disadvantages of continued use outweigh the advantages; rather, they have difficulty resisting their automatically triggered impulses to use their substance of abuse. Existing interventions may help to moderate these impulses. In addition, new techniques aimed at directly modifying implicit cognitive processes in substance abuse are being developed.

Keywords

implicit cognition; addiction; attentional bias; associations

Until recently, most cognitive research on addictive behaviors was grounded in theories of rational decision making. The logic behind this approach was that people generally do things expected to yield good outcomes and refrain from actions likely to harm them. Applied to addiction, this approach suggested a central role of expected benefits versus costs of continued drug use. However, the typical problem in addiction is not that drug abusers do not realize that the disadvantages of continued drug use outweigh the advantages. The central paradox in addictive behaviors is that people continue to use drugs even though they know the harm. Recent research on implicit or automatic processes provides clues to understanding this paradox. The essential idea is that behavior is partly governed through automatic processes that often exert their influence outside conscious control. The growing focus on these processes does not imply that explicit or deliberate processes are unimportant, but rather that implicit processes must be acknowledged if addictive behaviors are to be understood and treated.

The term *implicit cognition* is used in relation both to implicit processes and to their assessment. Fazio and Olson (2003) defined implicit measures as indirect measures, procedures in which constructs (e.g., attitudes) are indirectly inferred from behavior (e.g., reaction times). These measures are implicit in the sense that they capture the to-be-measured construct in a relatively uncontrolled or unintentional manner. As such, they may uniquely capture processes that are important in real-life behaviors including addictions (De Houwer, 2006). An example illustrates this. Upon arriving at a colleague's farewell reception, John, a heavy drinker, is shown a tray of alcoholic and non-alcoholic drinks. The beer catches his eye

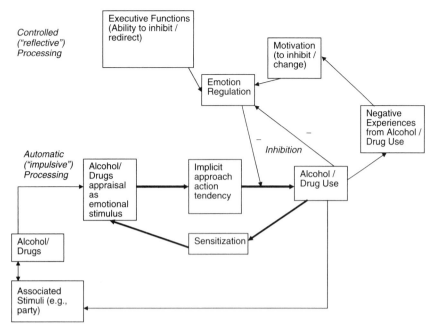

Fig. 1. A schematic overview of different processes involved in the development of addictive behaviors. As an addictive behavior develops, automatic affective (or "impulsive"; Strack & Deutsch, 2004) processing of alcohol- or drug-related stimuli increases in strength, through adaptations at the neural level called sensitization (i.e., a stronger neural response after repeated exposure to a stimulus). The automatically triggered impulse to engage in an addictive behavior can be moderated or inhibited (emotion regulation), provided that there are sufficient motivation and cognitive resources available to do so (controlled or "reflective" processes). As the addictive behavior develops, the modulation of these impulses becomes more difficult through two processes: stronger automatic approach tendencies and weaker abilities to moderate (both as a direct effect of acute intoxication and as the long-term result of heavy alcohol or drug use).

(attentional bias) and he feels inclined to reach for it (action tendency). This inclination may be suppressed (conscious control) when John is motivated to do so, perhaps because he must drive home later. When there is little room for conscious control at the moment of this drinking decision (for example because John is talking with a colleague), the automatic action tendency may drive the behavior without conscious deliberation or control (see Fig. 1). For each process in this example, researchers have developed assessment tools, described later in this article.

DUAL-PROCESS MODELS

Acknowledgment and assessment of implicit processes have been accompanied by new dual-process models of addictive behaviors (for examples, see Wiers & Stacy, 2006). Although the models proposed differ in their levels of description (from neurobiology to social cognition) and the number of systems proposed, the general picture is that of at least two semi-independent systems: a fast associative "impulsive" system, which includes automatic appraisal of stimuli in terms of their emotional and motivational significance; and a slower "reflective" system, which includes controlled processes related to conscious deliberations, emotion regulation, and expected outcomes (Strack & Deutsch, 2004). Different neural structures underlie these processes (see Berridge, 2001; Bechara, Noel, & Crone, 2006; Yin & Knowlton, 2006).

Neurobiological research reveals that the brain changes as a result of continued substance use (e.g., Berridge, 2001). Importantly, some of these changes involve the neural substrates related to emotion and motivation. With repeated drug use, the impulsive system becomes sensitized to the drug and to cues that predict use (note that some neurobiologists suggest this neuro-adaptation is characteristic only of early stages of addiction). As a result, drug-related cues automatically capture attention (e.g., the sight of a bottle of beer). This may foster automatic onset of approach action tendencies toward the drug. This action tendency can still be inhibited if the person has enough ability and motivation to do so (see Fig. 1; cf., Fazio & Olson, 2003). Importantly, long-term effects of many drugs are impairments of the ability to inhibit and regulate impulsive action tendencies (Bechara et al., 2006). Moreover, impulsive individuals are at enhanced risk to develop addictive behaviors (Bechara et al., 2006; Strack & Deutsch, 2004). To make things worse, an acute effect of alcohol and many other drugs of abuse is to affect controlled cognitive processes while leaving the automatic associative processes intact (Fillmore & Vogel-Sprott, 2006). Taken together, the changes in the balance between these systems make the addictive behavior more "stimulus driven" and outside conscious control as an addiction develops.

EVIDENCE THROUGH NEW ASSESSMENT METHODS

Although some earlier theorizing addressed automatic processes in addiction (e.g., Tiffany, 1990), systematic research gained substantial momentum only recently. New assessment strategies that measure automatic or implicit processes involved in addiction are applied. There are two general classes of implicit-cognition tests used: tests of attentional bias and tests of memory associations. The best-known test of attentional bias is the drug-Stroop task. The participants' task is to name the color of words (i.e., name the color of the ink, irrespective of the meaning of the word). Substance abusers do this more slowly for words related to their addiction (e.g., alcohol abusers are slower to say "red" to the word beer printed in red letters than to the word barn). This drug-Stroop interference effect is a robust phenomenon that has been demonstrated for many addictions. A recent meta-analysis including dozens of drug-Stroop studies (primarily on smoking and drinking) found that as participants have a stronger urge to use a drug, their drug-Stroop-interference effect is larger (i.e., slower color naming of drug words; Cox, Fadardi, & Pothos, 2006). A second often-used test of attentional bias is the visual-probe test. In this test, two pictures are shown simultaneously on a computer screen, one drug related, the other not. After a brief interval, these pictures disappear and the target cue appears in place of either the drug-related picture or the neutral one (Fig. 2). Drug abusers more

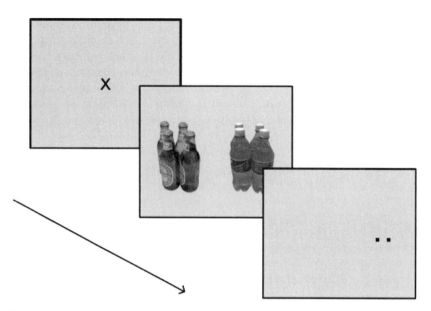

Fig. 2. Schematic overview of a visual probe test, here used to assess an attentional bias for alcohol. Participants ignore the primes (two pictures, one alcohol, one soft drink) and respond to the target (one or two dots, here two dots). Normally, the target replaces alcoholic drinks 50% of the time and soft drinks 50% of the time. In a retraining version, the target replaces soft drinks 90% of the time. The result is that heavy drinkers implicitly learn to direct their attention to the soft drink rather than to the alcoholic drink.

rapidly detect a target stimulus when it replaces a drug-related picture than when it replaces a neutral picture (see Field, Mogg, & Bradley, 2006). This test is thought to reflect an early component of attention (orienting), while the drug-Stroop test is thought to assess problems in disengaging attention from drug-related cues. Recently, researchers have begun to use eye movements to further investigate these attentional subprocesses (Field et al., 2006).

The second class of implicit measures assesses memory associations. Stacy and colleagues have developed a variety of memory-association tasks, modeled after tests used in basic memory research. Importantly, in these tests, the target behavior (alcohol or drug use) is not mentioned. Participants give their first association to a cue, which is either drug related or not (e.g., "Friday night" vs. "Thursday morning"). Another associative-memory test presents participants with affective phrases that can be alcohol or drug related (e.g., "having fun"). In these tests, the dependent variable is the number of substance-related associations. Stacy (1997) demonstrated that this variable was the best cognitive predictor of alcohol and marijuana use in the month following the assessment, after controlling for previous use, background variables, and sensation seeking. Changes in alcohol use were predicted both by memory associations and by explicit outcome expectancies, while for marijuana use only memory associations predicted prospective use after controlling for previous use. This finding illustrates that spontaneous associations, which we believe reflect impulsive, automatic processes in addictive behaviors, assess unique information beyond more explicit expected outcomes.

Wiers and colleagues assessed memory associations through various reaction-time measures, mostly using adapted versions of the Implicit Association Test (IAT). The IAT is a timed classification test in which participants use two response keys to sort two times two opposing categories (hence two categories per response key). Two opposite concepts are the target categories (in our case usually alcoholic drinks vs. soft drinks) and the other two opposite concepts are the attributes (e.g., positive vs. negative valence). These target and attribute categories are combined in two different ways (i.e., the combination alcohol or positive press left, negative or soft drink press right, is compared with the combination soft drink or positive press left, negative or alcoholic drink press right). The IAT effect is the difference in reaction times between these two sorting conditions, based on the idea that when two concepts are associated, sorting is easier (faster and fewer errors). For many examples of the IAT, see www.implicit.harvard.edu.

Wiers et al. combined alcoholic drinks and soft drinks with two different emotional dimensions: positive–negative (valence) and arousal–sedation (Wiers, Van Woerden, Smulders, & De Jong, 2002). Perhaps surprisingly, faster reaction times were found for the combination alcohol–negative than for alcohol–positive, suggesting that both heavy and light drinkers have negative associations with alcohol. This reliable finding contrasted with the explicit positive attitudes of the same participants. Recent research suggests that heavy drinkers hold both positive and negative associations and that the strong negative associations found in the IAT are partly but not fully due to the fact that both alcoholic drinks and negative words are salient (Houben & Wiers, 2006). Does this mean that heavy and light drinkers do not differ in their implicit associations? No, it does not. On the arousal dimension, it was found that heavy but not light drinkers associated alcohol with arousal, and this was related to their alcohol use and problems (Houben & Wiers, 2006; Wiers et al., 2002). We hypothesized that this reflects sensitization, an important concept in current animal models of addiction (Berridge, 2001). The same has been hypothesized for other implicit measures of appetitive motivation, such as automatic alcohol–approach associations (Palfai & Ostafin, 2003) and attentional bias. Overall, the rapidly growing literature on new assessments reveals the potential importance of implicit processes and suggests many applications to addiction research (see Wiers & Stacy, 2006).

IMPLICATIONS FOR INTERVENTIONS

The work reviewed reveals that we are beginning to develop a better understanding of implicit processes that play a role in addictive behaviors. The next important question is whether these findings are helpful for interventions. First, implicit cognition may help by increasing our understanding of current interventions. Wiers, Van de Luitgaarden, Van den Wildenberg, and Smulders (2005) tested the effects of a cognitive-behavioral intervention in problem drinkers. They found a significant decrease in explicit arousal expectancies as a result of the intervention (not found in the control group), whereas the implicit arousal associations were hardly affected. Interestingly, changes in implicit and explicit cognitions were entirely uncorrelated. The change in explicit cognitions predicted a short-lived reduction in problem drinking in men. This finding suggests that this cognitive intervention is better suited to change explicit cognitive processes than to change implicit ones. Another application in interventions is a study showing that the increase of alcohol abusers' attentional bias during treatment predicted their later dropout (Cox, Hogan, Kristian, & Race, 2002). This suggests that implicit processes play an important role in relapse.

Second, researchers are beginning to develop new interventions, aimed at directly influencing implicit cognitive processes. One approach uses "attentional retraining." In this approach, tests used to assess an attentional bias (e.g., drug-Stroop or visual-probe task) are modified so that attention is trained away from the drug-related stimulus. For example, in a normal visual-probe task, the target replaces the alcohol and neutral pictures equally often. In a retraining version, the target replaces the neutral picture 90% of the time. This way, the alcohol abuser implicitly learns to turn attention away from alcohol, toward the neutral stimulus (see Fig. 2). Initial findings from three different labs are quite promising: Heavy drinkers implicitly learn to direct their attention away from alcohol. A study by Field and Eastwood found significant effects on subsequent craving and alcohol consumption (see Wiers et al., 2006). An initial finding by Cox and colleagues suggests that repeated retraining may help heavy drinkers to learn to control their drinking (see Wiers et al., 2006).

Another approach aimed at changing automatic processes in addiction takes a different perspective: Rather than trying to unlearn maladaptive associations, one tries to automatize action plans that lead to alternative behaviors. When stated in simple "if-then" formulations (implementation intentions), these action plans can lead to action without the need for controlled processes. An example could be: "If I drive, then I drink soft drinks." Given the negative effects of many drugs on controlled processes, automatic action plans may be particularly beneficial in curtailing or reducing use of alcohol and other drugs (for examples, see chapters by Palfai and by Prestwich and colleagues in Wiers & Stacy, 2006).

How do these interventions relate to existing treatments? We see the newly developed interventions as potentially helpful supplements to existing treatments rather than as replacements. It has been well documented that motivation to change addictive behavior plays an important role in the change process. One way to increase motivation to change is through motivational interviewing. Moreover, sufficient motivation to change is a prerequisite for participation in any intervention, and often severe negative drug-related consequences need to be experienced before this point is reached (Fig. 1). Existing interventions may help to moderate the influence of appetitive processes on behavior. This can be done by increasing motivation to change or by training control over the impulse to use drugs. Perhaps newly developed tools such as attentional retraining can add to current treatments. However, we stress that this work is currently in an early, developmental phase; the first clinical trials are now being conducted.

FUTURE DIRECTIONS

The first future challenge in research on implicit cognition and addiction concerns theory and assessment. The newly developed assessment tools are not yet optimal and much effort is currently being devoted to improving them and to developing new ones. A related issue concerns the relationship between different measures of implicit cognition and the processes they assess. A second issue concerns the relationship between implicit measures and neurobiological processes. Many authors (see Wiers & Stacy, 2006) have expressed the idea that implicit measures may better reflect "deeper" affective mechanisms that operate outside awareness than may explicit measures, and thus may provide a unique window on these processes in the development of human addiction. However, this idea largely awaits empirical confirmation. If validated, it would imply that the current gap between neurobiological models of addiction (largely based on animal research) and psychological addiction research might be bridged. Additionally, few studies have addressed the development of implicit versus explicit cognitive processes in relation to the development of addictive behaviors. Recent evidence indicates that long-term effects of alcohol and drugs on systems of emotion and motivation are particularly pronounced during adolescence, probably because these systems are still developing then. Unfortunately, this is also the period in which alcohol and drug use peak, making this an important issue for further study. Finally, the research on new ways to change implicit cognitive processes and on helping substance abusers regain executive control over implicit processes is an exciting avenue for future research. These efforts may eventually lead to better prevention and treatment of this widespread problem.

Recommended Reading

Berridge, K.C. (2001). (See References)
Stacy, A.W. (1997). (See References)
Strack, F., & Deutsch, R. (2004). (See References)
Wiers, R.W., & Stacy, A.W. (Eds.). (2006). (See References)
Wiers R.W., van Woerden, N., Smulders, F.T.Y., & De Jong, P.J. (2002). (See References)

Acknowledgments—Reinout Wiers is supported by "VIDI" Grant 452.02.005 from the Netherlands Science Foundation and Alan Stacy by Grant DA16094 from the National Institute on Drug Abuse. We thank Jan de Houwer, Nico Metaal, Tim Schoen-makers, and Ken Sher for comments.

Note

1. Address correspondence to Reinout W. Wiers, Experimental Psychology, UNS 40, Universiteit Maastricht, 6200 MD, Maastricht, The Netherlands; e-mail: r.wiers@psychology.unimaas.nl.

References

Bechara, A., Noel, X., & Crone, E.A. (2006). Loss of Willpower: Abnormal neural mechanisms of impulse control and decision making in addiction. In R.W. Wiers & A.W. Stacy (Eds.), *Handbook of implicit cognition and addiction* (pp. 215–232). Thousand Oaks, CA: SAGE.

Berridge, K.C. (2001). Reward learning: Reinforcement, incentives, and expectations. In D.L. Medin (Ed.), *The psychology of learning and motivation: Advances in research and theory* (Vol. 40, pp. 223–278). San Diego, CA: Academic Press.

Cox, W.M., Hogan, L.M., Kristian, M.R., & Race, J.H. (2002). Alcohol attentional bias as predictor of alcohol abusers' treatment outcome. *Drug and Alcohol Dependence, 68,* 237–243.

Cox, W.M., Fadardi, J.S., & Pothos, E.M. (2006). The addiction-Stroop test: Theoretical considera-tions and procedural recommendations. *Psychological Bulletin, 132,* 443–476.

De Houwer, J. (2006). What are implicit measures and why are we using them? In R.W. Wiers & A.W. Stacy (Eds.), *Handbook of implicit cognition and addiction* (pp. 11–28). Thousand Oaks, CA: SAGE.

Fazio, R.H., & Olson, M.A. (2003). Implicit measures in social cognition research: Their meaning and use. *Annual Review of Psychology, 54,* 297–327.

Field M., Mogg, K., & Bradley, B.P. (2006). Attention to drug-related cues in drug abuse and addic-tion: Component processes. In R.W. Wiers & A.W. Stacy (Eds.), *Handbook of implicit cognition and addiction* (pp. 45–57). Thousand Oaks, CA: SAGE.

Fillmore, M.T. & Vogel-Sprott, M. (2006). Acute effects of alcohol and other drugs on automatic and intentional control. In R.W. Wiers & A.W. Stacy (Eds.), *Handbook of implicit cognition and addiction* (pp. 293–306). Thousand Oaks, CA: SAGE.

Houben, K., & Wiers, R.W. (2006). Assessing implicit alcohol associations with the IAT: Fact or arti-fact? *Addictive Behaviors, 31,* 1346–1362.

Palfai, T.P., & Ostafin, B.D. (2003). Alcohol-related motivational tendencies in hazardous drinkers: Assessing implicit response tendencies using the modified IAT. *Behaviour Research and Ther-apy, 41,* 1149–1162.

Stacy, A.W. (1997). Memory activation and expectancy as prospective predictors of alcohol and mari-juana use. *Journal of Abnormal Psychology, 106,* 61–73.

Strack, F., & Deutsch, R. (2004). Reflective and impulsive determinants of social behavior. *Personality and Social Psychology Review, 3,* 220–247.

Tiffany, S.T. (1990). A cognitive model of drug urges and drug-use behavior: Role of automatic and nonautomatic processes. *Psychological Review,* 97, 147–168.

Wiers, R.W., Cox, W.M., Field, M., Fadardi, J.S., Palfai, T.P., Schoen-makers, T., & Stacy, A.W. (2006). The search for new ways to change implicit alcohol-related cognitions in heavy drinkers. *Alcoholism, Clinical and Experimental Research, 30,* 320–331.

Wiers, R.W., & Stacy, A.W. (Eds.). (2006). *Handbook of implicit cognition and addiction.* Thousand Oaks, CA: SAGE Publishers.

Wiers R.W., Van de Luitgaarden, J., Van den Wildenberg, E., & Smulders, F.T.Y. (2005). Challenging implicit and explicit alcohol-related cognitions in young heavy drinkers. *Addiction, 100,* 806–819.

Wiers W., Van Woerden, N., Smulders, F.T.Y., & De Jong, P.J. (2002). Implicit and explicit alcohol-related cognitions in heavy and light drinkers. *Journal of Abnormal Psychology, 111,* 648–658.

Yin, H.R., & Knowlton, B.J. (2006). Addiction and learning in the brain. In R.W. Wiers & A.W. Stacy (Eds.), *Handbook of implicit cognition and addiction.* (pp. 185–199). Thousand Oaks, CA: SAGE.

This article has been reprinted as it originally appeared in *Current Directions in Psychological Science*. Citation information for this article as originally published appears above.

Pharmacologic and Behavioral Withdrawal from Addictive Drugs

Timothy B. Baker[1], Sandra J. Japuntich, Joanne M. Hogle,
Danielle E. McCarthy, and John J. Curtin
University of Wisconsin-Madison

Abstract

Recent theories suggest that drug withdrawal does not motivate drug use and relapse. However, data now show that withdrawal produces complex changes over time in at least two symptoms (i.e., negative affect and urges) that are highly predictive of relapse. Evidence suggests that falling levels of the drug in the blood and interruption of the drug self-administration ritual both affect these symptoms. Both of these forms of withdrawal motivate renewed drug use in addicted individuals.

Keywords

smoking; tobacco dependence; tobacco withdrawal; drug withdrawal

Addicts have written powerfully about the "abstinence agony" that occurs when they stop using a drug. For instance, Sigmund Freud described quitting smoking as an "agony beyond human power to bear." One would assume from such accounts that drug withdrawal produces a powerful motive to resume or continue drug use. Indeed, movies and other popular accounts of addiction typically emphasize the role of withdrawal. However, current theoretical models of addiction downplay the role of drug withdrawal in the maintenance of addictive behaviors (Robinson & Berridge, 1993). Such models hold that withdrawal symptoms do not motivate relapse; for example, measures of withdrawal severity do not predict who is likely to relapse. Also, these models assert that withdrawal is brief and, therefore, cannot account for relapse that occurs long after drug use. Finally, these models assert that effective addiction treatments do not work via the suppression of withdrawal symptoms. These theoretical views of drug motivation emphasize incentive or reward processes rather than withdrawal.

In contrast to the claims of recent theories, addicted individuals typically report that withdrawal symptoms motivate them to relapse and that fear of withdrawal causes them to maintain drug use. There is now mounting evidence that the addicted individuals are correct—that withdrawal is a crucial motivator of their drug use. While drug use is no doubt determined by multiple factors, there is compelling evidence that, in the addicted individual, withdrawal potently influences the fluctuating course of drug motivation.

We believe that the motivational impact of withdrawal has been obscured by a failure to assess it sensitively and comprehensively. There are two reasons for this failure. One is that withdrawal is multidimensional, and only some elements, such as urges and negative affect, have motivational relevance. Unless studies focus on these symptoms, the motivational impact of withdrawal may be lost. The second reason is that most previous assessments of withdrawal have not adequately captured its dynamic symptom patterns, which may be both highly complex and persistent. These complex symptom patterns provide important clues regarding the nature and determinants of withdrawal. Withdrawal symptoms appear to reflect the effects of two distinct types of deprivation: deprivation of the drug molecule and deprivation of the drug-use instrumental response (such as injecting a drug or lighting and smoking a cigarette). A reduced level of the drug in the body, or *pharmacologic withdrawal,* results in the escalation of symptoms that has traditionally been labeled withdrawal. However, ceasing drug use also deprives the individual of a behavioral means of regulating or coping with escalating symptoms such as negative affect—in other words, it also causes *behavioral withdrawal.* At the heart of this model is the notion that the self-administration ritual per se quells withdrawal symptoms and that the absence of the ritual will actually exacerbate symptoms because of a disruption in symptom-regulatory processes. In theory, this disruption leads to very persistent and complex symptom profiles because symptoms may arise in response to cues that occur months after discontinuing drug use. This symptom dysregulation will persist until drug cues lose their associative strength (e.g., via extinction) and/or until the individual acquires a coping response that replaces use of the drug.

COMPONENTS OF WITHDRAWAL

Physical Signs

Previous views of withdrawal have been unduly influenced by characteristics of the physical symptoms of withdrawal. Each class of addictive drug produces a withdrawal syndrome that comprises different sorts of physical signs. For instance, ethanol withdrawal produces tremors, exaggerated reflexive behavior, and sometimes convulsions. Opiate withdrawal produces hypothermia, piloerection (gooseflesh), rhinnorhea (nasal discharge), and diarrhea. These signs all tend to follow the same rise-and-fall pattern after the discontinuation of drug use, with symptoms being largely absent within a couple of weeks after cessation.

Research has shown that these physical signs are not consistently related to drug motivation (e.g., Baker, Piper, McCarthy, Majeskie, & Fiore, 2004), supporting the idea that withdrawal is motivationally inert. However, the motivational irrelevance of these physical signs should not be surprising as they are so dissimilar across different types of drugs. If withdrawal has a motivational influence that is common to all addictive drugs, it seems sensible to look for this influence among the symptoms that are themselves common across drugs. Negative affect and drug urges are such symptoms.

Negative Affect

Many of the symptoms used to characterize withdrawal are, in fact, affective terms such as "irritable," "stressed," "anxious," and "depressed." Robust correlations are observed between measures of withdrawal and mood, and factor-analytic studies have demonstrated that affective items capture much of the reliable variance in withdrawal measures (Piasecki et al., 2000). Experimental manipulations of tobacco withdrawal in the laboratory prompt increases in self-reported and physiological indicators of negative affect (Hogle & Curtin, in press).

A listing of negative mood adjectives does not do justice to the affective consequences of withdrawal. Addicted individuals commonly report that giving up a drug seems like losing a dear friend or experiencing a death of a family member. We believe that this reflects a crucial part of the withdrawal syndrome: a feeling akin to social loss or separation distress. Indeed, at the neuropharmacologic and experiential levels, withdrawal produces effects similar to intense social loss (Panksepp, Herman, Connor, Bishop, & Scott, 1978). However, the relationship with the drug, once lost, can be reinstated at any time.

There is evidence that the emotional distress of withdrawal differs from other withdrawal elements in terms of both its motivational significance and its physiological substrata. For instance, researchers have shown that brain structures associated with the motivational components of the withdrawal syndrome (e.g., negative affect) show different sensitivity to the opioid antagonist, naloxone, than do brain structures associated with the somatic components (Frenois, Cador, Caille, Stinus, & Le Moine, 2002). In addition, research shows that it is the affective and not the somatic signs of withdrawal that are responsible for its motivational effects (Mucha, 1987; Piasecki et al., 2000). In sum, assessment strategies should target the affective elements of the withdrawal syndrome if the intent is to assess drug motivation or relapse vulnerability.

Urge/Craving

An urge may be viewed as the conscious recognition of the desire to use a drug. Since a variety of influences may stimulate such desire and make it available to consciousness, urges are not uniquely related to withdrawal (as negative affect is not uniquely related). However, urge measures appear to be sensitive indices of withdrawal and rise precipitously in response to abstinence (Baker et al., 2004).

There exist both biological and theoretical reasons to distinguish urges from the emotional components of withdrawal. First, urges and withdrawal-related affectivity appear to be associated with different physiologic substrata (e.g., Curtin, McCarthy, Piper, & Baker, 2006). Moreover, urges show different trajectories in response to drug removal and environmental events (McCarthy, Piasecki, Fiore, & Baker, in press). Finally, as we shall review momentarily, urges appear to exert their own distinct motivational influences.

EXTRACTING MEANING FROM COMPLEX WITHDRAWAL PROFILES

As noted earlier, most studies of withdrawal have assumed a standard pattern across time (waveform) for all symptoms and signs. This was used, either implicitly or explicitly, to justify simplistic measurement strategies. Researchers often used only a single measure of peak or average withdrawal, collapsing all symptoms together, to reflect the potentially meaningful information. Interviews with

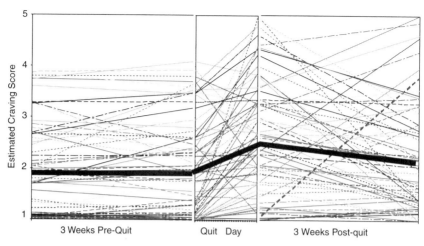

Fig. 1. Estimated cigarette-craving growth curves for 70 adult smokers. Craving ratings were collected multiple times per day for 3 weeks before and after the target quit date. The central panel labeled "Quit Day" reflects the change in craving ratings from just before to just after midnight on the quit day. The heavy black line represents the mean trend in craving ratings across individuals (from McCarthy, Piasecki, Fiore, & Baker, in press).

addicted individuals, however, indicate that they experience strong urges and negative affect many weeks after discontinuing drug use. This suggests that withdrawal patterns should be assessed in a more comprehensive manner. Therefore, we measured profiles of withdrawal symptoms, especially urges and negative affect, so as to capture their average elevation, trajectories (e.g., whether symptoms are worsening or improving), rise times (how quickly symptoms increase following abstinence), durations, and reactivity to stressors and environmental events.

Waveforms of urges and affective symptoms show dramatic differences from one person to the next and possess motivational relevance (see Fig. 1; McCarthy, Piasecki et al., in press). When researchers measure withdrawal in a way that captures this variability, strong relations with smoking relapse are obtained. For instance, relapse to smoking is consistently and powerfully predicted by such measures as the rise time of craving, the average levels of craving and negative affect, and the duration of high levels of craving and negative affect (Baker et al., 2004). Moreover, such measurement strategies show that withdrawal symptoms are very persistent and predict the occurrence of relapses long after the initiation of the attempt to quit. Finally, these strategies have shown that suppression of withdrawal can indeed account for the therapeutic effects of drug treatments for addiction. For instance, recent studies show that smoking-cessation pharmacotherapies reduce relapse risk, at least in part, by suppressing negative affect and craving (McCarthy, Bolt, & Baker, in press). In sum, when researchers measure the temporal dynamics of urges and affective withdrawal symptoms, the resulting profiles provide insights into why addicted individuals persist in drug use and how treatments can help them quit.

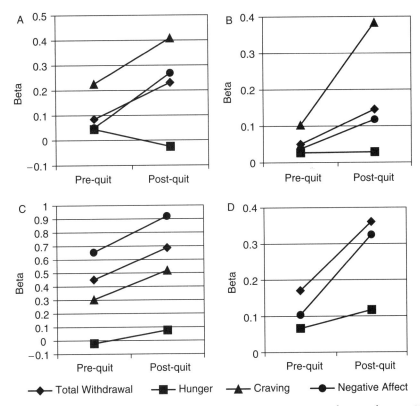

Fig. 2. The degree of association between four episodic events—smoking in the past 15 minutes (A), exposure to others' smoking since the last report (B), occurrence of stressful events since the last report (C), and occurrence of a strong urge or temptation to smoke since the last report (D)—and withdrawal symptoms. Episodic event coefficients (beta values) reflect changes in overall withdrawal summary scores (collapsed across specific symptoms) and hunger, smoking-urge (craving), and negative-affect (sadness, worry, and irritability) ratings associated with each of the events; these were estimated separately in the pre-quit and post-quit periods.

WITHDRAWAL AS CONTROL-SYSTEM DYSREGULATION

The preceding discussion raises several questions. For instance, what could cause the highly variable and prolonged symptoms that are observed, and should these be considered withdrawal?

Dependent drug users cite affect regulation as a major reason for drug use, and research supports their claims. Addicted individuals have learned through repeated pairings of drug use with withdrawal relief that addictive drugs are extremely effective at quelling the affective distress and urges occasioned by withdrawal (Baker et al., 2004). It is not surprising, then, that when addicts stop using a drug they show evidence of symptom dysregulation. Evidence of symptom dysregulation is found in the prolonged and variable affective and urge symptoms noted earlier (e.g., Piasecki et al., 2000) and in smokers' amplified emotional and urge responses to environmental events (see Fig. 2; McCarthy, Piasecki et al., in press). In addition, laboratory research using both psychophysiological and neuroendocrine responses finds that smokers in withdrawal show disturbed patterns of emotion regulation in response to stressors (Hogle & Curtin, in press).

Thus, both self-report and physiological measures point to withdrawal-induced dysregulation of negative affect (Hogle & Curtin, in press; McCarthy, Piasecki et al., in press). If withdrawal varies in intensity, trajectory, and duration across individuals, is there a common mechanism that accounts for this variability? We believe that prolonged symptom dysregulation following withdrawal occurs because addicted individuals are withdrawn from both the self-administration ritual and from the drug molecule. That is, such individuals experience behavioral withdrawal as well as pharmacologic withdrawal. Pharmacologic withdrawal may be largely responsible for the characteristic rise and fall in withdrawal symptoms that occurs in the 1 to 2 weeks after initial drug abstinence, but we assert that behavioral withdrawal accounts for prolonged symptom persistence, the volatility and variability of symptoms, and exaggerated symptomatic reactivity to environmental events. In theory, the loss of a highly practiced and effective symptomatic control strategy should exert effects that occur again and again over a lengthy post-cessation period: Effects that persist until the organism has acquired new regulatory strategies or until once-evocative stimuli (e.g., drug cues) no longer elicit withdrawal responses. The organism may attempt to use nondrug coping strategies in response to symptomatic distress, but lack of practice may lead to inadequate affect regulation as compared to drug use.

The absence of a self-administration coping response leads to dysregulated symptomatic expression for several reasons. First, the lack of the drug per se leaves pharmacologic withdrawal untreated. Second, failure to use the self-administration ritual produces intense response conflict resulting in strong urges, frustration, and feelings of helplessness as the individual fights the urge to use the tried-and-true self-administration ritual (Curtin et al., 2006). Conflict between the well-learned drug-use response and a substitute response should elicit intrusive and effortful cognitive-control processes as well as frustration. Finally, the individual does not benefit from the positive conditioned associations (including anticipatory and placebo effects) that are activated by the ritual (Sayette et al., 2003).

If there is a behavioral withdrawal, there should be evidence that the self-administration ritual per se can suppress withdrawal symptoms in addicted individuals. Indeed, there is evidence that mere practice of the self-administration ritual, without any actual drug delivery, effectively suppresses withdrawal symptoms. For instance, heroin withdrawal is suppressed by injections of saline, and nicotine withdrawal is suppressed by smoking nicotine-free cigarettes (Butschky, Bailey, Henningfield, & Pickworth, 1995). Such effects are remarkably persistent and resistant to extinction. This is consistent with observations that organisms persist in the drug self-administration response long after the response ceases to deliver the drug (Caggiula et al., 2001). We believe this occurs because the self-administration ritual quells distress via learned associations. Consistent with this hypothesis, there is evidence that the self-administration ritual itself activates brain reward and incentive systems (Balfour, 2004). This hypothesis also accounts for the finding that drug replacement (e.g., nicotine patch and methadone) without the self-administration ritual only partially suppresses the drug withdrawal syndrome even with very high drug-replacement doses. The behavioral-withdrawal hypothesis suggests some novel predictions: For example, if the drug is administered without the self-administration ritual (e.g., via passive infusion), withdrawal will be less prolonged, persistent, and variable than it will be if the self-administration ritual is routinely reinforced. This explains the observation that the passive receipt of opiates by hospital patients tends not to lead to intense withdrawal or addiction: Such patients are withdrawn only from the drug, not from a highly ingrained self-administration ritual.

Viewing withdrawal as dysregulation helps to explain the apparently anomalous finding that withdrawal symptoms persist as long as they do: The addicted individual undergoes behavioral withdrawal each time he or she experiences spikes in negative affect or urges (regardless of the cause) and does not or cannot revert to drug use to cope. This perspective has implications for treatment. For instance, it suggests that pairing drug replacement with the self-administration ritual (e.g., using the nicotine patch and smoking nicotine-free cigarettes) will effectively quell withdrawal distress and promote successful cessation of drug use. In addition, it suggests that addicted individuals might be helped by practicing symptomatic regulation strategies well before they attempt to quit, in order to reduce the intense response conflict that occurs upon cessation.

SUMMARY

Modern theories of addiction motivation suggest that withdrawal is not a potent motivator of drug use and relapse. However, addicted individuals routinely attribute relapse to withdrawal distress. We believe that the motivational role of withdrawal is clear once withdrawal is conceptualized appropriately and accordingly analyzed. First, researchers should focus on a subset of withdrawal symptoms that possess motivational relevance: negative affect and urges. Second, when addicted individuals stop using drugs, they withdraw from both the drug molecule and from the self-administration ritual. Falling levels of the drug in the body certainly produce a rise-and-fall pattern in withdrawal symptoms. However, the absence of the drug self-administration ritual exacerbates negative affect and urges, making such symptoms especially prolonged, volatile, and intense. Research shows that when assessments focus on the motivationally relevant elements of withdrawal and capture the complex patterns of withdrawal over time, withdrawal is indeed an important influence on drug motivation and relapse. Therefore, according to the present model, withdrawal may be defined as response dysregulation that occurs due to decreased levels of the drug in the body and discontinuation of the self-administration response.

Recommended Reading

Baker, T., Piper, M., McCarthy, D., Majeskie, M., & Fiore, M. (2004). (See References)
Curtin, J., McCarthy, D., Piper, M., & Baker, T. (2006). (See References)
Robinson, T., & Berridge, K. (1993). (See References)

Note

1. Address correspondence to Timothy B. Baker, Center for Tobacco Research and Intervention, University of Wisconsin School of Medicine and Public Health, 1930 Monroe St. Suite 200, Madison, WI 53711; e-mail: tbb@ctri.medicine.wisc.edu.

References

Baker, T., Piper, M., McCarthy, D., Majeskie, M., & Fiore, M. (2004). Addiction motivation reformulated: An affective processing model of negative reinforcement. *Psychological Review, 111*, 33–51.

Balfour, D. (2004). The neurobiology of tobacco dependence: A preclinical perspective on the role of dopamine projections to the nucleus. *Nicotine and Tobacco Research, 6*, 899–912.

Butschky, M., Bailey, D., Henningfield, J., & Pickworth, W. (1995). Smoking without nicotine delivery decreases withdrawal in 12-hour abstinent smokers. *Pharmacology Biochemistry and Behavior, 50*, 91–96.

Caggiula, A., Donny, E., White, A., Chaudhri, N., Booth, S., Gharib, M.A., Hoffman, A., Perkins, K., & Sved, A.F. (2001). Cue dependency of nicotine self-administration and smoking. *Pharmacology Biochemistry and Behavior, 70*, 515–530.

Curtin, J., McCarthy, D., Piper, M., & Baker, T. (2006). Implicit and explicit drug motivational processes: A model of boundary conditions. In R. Wiers & A. Stacy (Eds.), *Handbook of implicit cognition and addiction*. Thousand Oaks, CA: Sage Publications.

Frenois, F., Cador, M., Caille, S., Stinus, L., & Le Moine, C. (2002). Neural correlates of the motivational and somatic components of naloxone-precipitated morphine withdrawal. *European Journal of Neuroscience, 16*, 1377–1389.

Hogle, J., & Curtin, J. (in press). Sex differences in the affective consequences of smoking withdrawal. *Psychophysiology*.

McCarthy, D., Bolt, D., & Baker, T. (in press). The importance of how: A call for mechanistic research in tobacco dependence. In T. Treat, R. Bootzin, & T. Baker (Eds.), *Recent advances in theory and practice: Integrative perspectives in honor of Richard M. McFall*. New York: Erlbaum.

McCarthy, D., Piasecki, T., Fiore, M., & Baker, T. (in press). Life before and after quitting smoking: An electronic diary study. *Journal of Abnormal Psychology*.

Mucha, R. (1987). Is the motivational effect of opiate withdrawal reflected by common somatic indices of precipitated withdrawal? A place conditioning study in the rat. *Brain Research, 418*, 214–220.

Panksepp, J., Herman, B., Connor, R., Bishop, P., & Scott, J. (1978). The biology of social attachments: Opiates alleviate separation distress. *Biological Psychiatry, 13*, 607–618.

Piasecki, T., Niaura, R., Shadel, W., Abrams, D., Goldstein, M., Fiore, M., & Baker, T.B. (2000). Smoking withdrawal dynamics in unaided quitters. *Journal of Abnormal Psychology, 109*, 74–86.

Robinson, T., & Berridge, K. (1993). The neural basis of drug craving: An incentive-sensitization theory of addiction. *Brain Research Reviews, 18*, 247–291.

Sayette, M., West, J., Martin, C.S., Cohn, J., Perrott, M., & Hoebel, J. (2003). Effects of smoking opportunity on cue-elicited urge: A facial coding analysis. *Journal of Experimental and Clinical Psychopharmacology, 11*, 218–227.

Stress, Motivation, and Drug Addiction

Nick E. Goeders[1]

Departments of Pharmacology & Therapeutics and Psychiatry,
Louisiana State University Health Sciences Center

Abstract

A growing clinical literature indicates that there is a link between substance abuse and stress. One explanation for the high co-occurrence of stress-related disorders and drug addiction is the self-medication hypothesis, which suggests that a dually diagnosed person often uses the abused substance to cope with tension associated with life stressors or to relieve symptoms of anxiety and depression resulting from a traumatic event. However, another characteristic of self-administration is that drug delivery and its subsequent effects on the hypothalamic-pituitary-adrenal (HPA) axis are under the direct control of the individual. This controlled activation of the HPA axis may produce an internal state of arousal or stimulation that is actually sought by the individual. During abstinence, exposure to stressors or drug-associated cues can stimulate the HPA axis and thereby remind the individual about the effects of the abused substance, thus producing craving and promoting relapse. Stress reduction, either alone or in combination with pharmacotherapies targeting the HPA axis, may prove beneficial in reducing cravings and promoting abstinence in individuals seeking treatment for addiction.

Keywords

HPA axis; reward; vulnerability; stress; relapse

The mere mention of the word *stress* often conjures up images of heart disease, ulcers, and serious psychiatric disorders triggered through negative interactions with the environment. In reality, however, stress is not always associated with negative events. Selye (1975), who is generally accepted as the father of modern stress-related research, defined stress as the nonspecific response of the body to any demand placed upon it to adapt, whether that demand produces pleasure or pain. Accordingly, stress can result from a job promotion or the loss of a job, the birth of a child or the loss of a loved one, or any number of events, both positive and negative, that affect the daily life of an individual.

The two primary biological systems that are typically activated during and immediately after exposure to a stressor are the sympathetic nervous system and the hypothalamic-pituitary-adrenal (HPA) axis (Stratakis & Chrousos, 1995). The activation of these systems produces a stress response, or *stress cascade,* that is responsible for allowing the body to make the changes required to cope with the demands of a challenge. Sympathetic nervous system responses often include the release of the neurotransmitter norepinephrine, an increase in heart rate, a shift in blood flow to skeletal muscles, an increase in blood glucose, and a dilation of the pupils (for better vision), all in preparation for fight or flight (i.e., facing the stressor or attempting to escape from it). The HPA axis is initially activated by the secretion of corticotropin-releasing hormone (CRH) from the hypothalamus in response to a stressor (Goeders, 2002). CRH binds to receptors located in the anterior pituitary, causing the production of several substances, including adrenocorticotropin hormone (ACTH). When ACTH reaches the adrenal glands, it stimulates the biosynthesis and secretion of adrenocorticosteroids (i.e., cortisol in humans or corticosterone in rats). Cortisol travels through the bloodstream to produce a variety of effects throughout the body.

STRESS AND VULNERABILITY TO ADDICTION IN HUMANS

It is not ethical to conduct clinical studies on the effects of stress on the vulnerability for addiction in people without a history of drug abuse because no one should be intentionally put at risk for developing an addiction by being exposed to a substance with the potential for abuse. Therefore, scientists must rely on retrospective studies, and there is a growing body of clinical studies suggesting a link between stress and addiction. Combat veterans, especially those with post-traumatic stress disorder (PTSD), appear to have an elevated risk for substance abuse. Veterans with PTSD typically report more use of alcohol, cocaine, and heroin than veterans who do not meet the criteria for diagnosis of PTSD (Zaslav, 1994). However, people exposed to stressors other than combat, such as an unhappy marriage, dissatisfaction with employment, or harassment, also report higher-than-average rates of addiction. Sexual abuse, trauma, and sexual harassment are more likely to produce symptoms of PTSD and alcoholism or other addictions in women than in men (Newton-Taylor, DeWit, & Gliksman, 1998).

Despite these findings, however, it is difficult to determine if stressors, sexual trauma, or PTSD actually lead to subsequent substance use or if substance use contributes to the traumatic events or the development of PTSD in the first place. Obviously, not everyone who experiences trauma and PTSD is a substance abuser, and not every drug addict can trace his or her addiction to some specific stressor or traumatic event. Nevertheless, prevalence estimates suggest that the rate of substance abuse among individuals with PTSD may be as high as 60 to 80%, and the rate of PTSD among substance abusers is between 40 and 60% (Donovan, Padin-Rivera, & Kowaliw, 2001). These numbers show a clear relationship between PTSD and substance abuse. One explanation for the high co-occurrence of PTSD and drug addiction (i.e., dual diagnosis) is the self-medication hypothesis. According to this hypothesis, a dually diagnosed person often uses the abused substance to cope with tension associated with life stressors or to relieve or suppress symptoms of anxiety, irritability, and depression resulting from a traumatic event (Khantzian, 1985).

VULNERABILITY TO ADDICTION: ANIMAL STUDIES

It is much easier to conduct prospective studies on the effects of stress on the vulnerability for addiction in animals than in humans. These animal studies typically investigate the effects of stress on the propensity to learn drug-taking behavior (which is often referred to as the "acquisition" of drug taking). In a typical experiment, the animals come into contact with a drug and its potentially rewarding effects for the first time (Goeders, 2002), and the researcher investigates what dose or how much time is necessary for them to learn to make the response (e.g., a lever press) that leads to drug delivery, thereby producing reinforcement. Environmental events (e.g., stressors) that decrease the lowest dose that is recognized by an animal as a reinforcer (i.e., that leads to acquisition of the response) are considered to increase vulnerability to acquire drug-taking behavior. Another measure of acquisition is the time required for the animal to reach a specified behavioral criterion (e.g., a specified frequency of the response that leads to drug delivery).

The ability of stressors to alter the acquisition of drug taking in rats has received considerable attention (Goeders, 2002; Piazza & Le Moal, 1998). For example, studies have shown that sensitivity to amphetamine and cocaine is enhanced in rats exposed to stressors such as tail pinch and neonatal isolation. Electric shock to the feet is another stressor used in rat experiments. In a study on the effects of controllable versus uncontrollable stress, my colleagues and I modeled controllable stress by administering shocks whenever the rats made a particular response, and uncontrollable stress by administering shocks that were not contingent on the rats' behavior (Goeders, 2002). Rats that were exposed to uncontrollable stress were more sensitive to low doses of cocaine than rats that were exposed to controllable stress or that were not shocked at all; this finding demonstrates that control over a stressor can change the effects of that stressor on the vulnerability for drug taking (Goeders, 2002).

Given that uncontrollable stress made animals more sensitive to cocaine, my colleagues and I hypothesized that this process may have resulted from the stress-induced activation of the HPA axis. Because corticosterone (cortisol) is secreted as the final step of HPA-axis activation, we next studied the effects of daily injections of corticosterone on the acquisition of cocaine taking. These injections produced an increase in sensitivity to cocaine that was almost identical to what we saw with uncontrollable stress. In a related experiment, rats' adrenal glands were surgically removed (i.e., adrenalectomy) to effectively eliminate the final step in HPA-axis activation. These rats did not self-administer cocaine at any dose tested, even though they quickly learned to respond to obtain food pellets. Thus, the rats could still learn and perform the necessary lever-pressing response, but cocaine was apparently no longer rewarding. In another series of experiments, the synthesis of corticosterone was blocked with daily injections of ketoconazole, and this reduced both the rate of acquisition of cocaine self-administration and the number of rats that eventually reached the criterion for acquisition of this behavior. Taken together, these data suggest an important role for stress and the subsequent activation of the HPA axis in the vulnerability for drug taking.

How does exposure to a stressor increase the vulnerability for drug taking? This biological phenomenon likely occurs via a process analogous to sensitization, whereby repeated but intermittent injections of cocaine increase the behavioral and neurochemical responses to subsequent exposure to the drug (Piazza & Le Moal, 1998). Exposure to stressors or injections of corticosterone can also result in a sensitization to cocaine, and these effects are attenuated in rats that have had their adrenal glands removed or corticosterone synthesis inhibited. Although exposure to the stressor itself may be aversive in many cases, the net result is reflected as an increased sensitivity to the drug. This suggests that if individuals are particularly sensitive to stress or find themselves in an environment where they do not feel that they have adequate control over their stress, they may be especially likely to engage in substance abuse.

STRESS AND RELAPSE TO ADDICTION

Clinical studies of drug addicts have demonstrated that reexposure to the abused substance, exposure to stressors, or simply the presentation of stress-related imagery is a potent event for provoking relapse. However, simply exposing an addict to environmental stimuli or cues previously associated with drug taking can also produce intense drug craving (Robbins, Ehrman, Childress, & O'Brien, 1999). Such environmental stimuli include locations where the drug was purchased or used, the individuals the drug was purchased from or used with, and associated drug paraphernalia. In fact, the cycling, relapsing nature of addiction has been proposed to result, at least in part, from exposure to environmental cues that have been previously paired with drug use. Presumably, the repeated pairing of these cues with the chronic use of the drug can lead to a classical conditioning of the drug's effects, so that exposure to these stimuli following abstinence produces responses reminiscent of responses to the drug itself. These conditioned responses elicit increased desire or craving, thus leading to relapse.

Reinstatement is generally accepted as an animal model of the propensity to relapse to drug taking (Stewart, 2000). With this model, animals are taught to self-administer a drug until they reach a stable level of drug intake; they are then subjected to prolonged periods during which the response that previously resulted in drug delivery no longer does so (i.e., extinction). Once drug-taking behavior has extinguished, or following a specified period of abstinence, the rats are tested to see if specific stimuli will reinstate the response previously associated with drug taking (Goeders, 2002). Such reinstatement of drug-seeking behavior can be elicited by injections of the drug itself or by exposure to brief periods of intermittent electric shock to the feet (i.e., stress). In her review of reinstatement, Stewart (2000) described how norepinephrine and CRH are important for stress-induced reinstatement, which should be no surprise because norepinephrine and CRH are produced during the activation of the sympathetic nervous system and HPA axis, respectively.

Stimuli that were paired with the drug during self-administration can become environmental cues that can be presented following extinction to reinstate responding (See, 2002). Reinstatement that occurs under these conditions is referred to as cue-induced reinstatement. The fact that cue-induced reinstatement occurs suggests that exposure to a physical stressor or a "taste" of cocaine itself is not a necessary prerequisite for relapse. My colleagues and I have reported that the corticosterone synthesis inhibitor ketoconazole reverses the cue-induced reinstatement of cocaine seeking and also decreases the increases in corticosterone observed in the blood during reinstatement (Goeders, 2002). The CRH receptor blocker CP-154,526 also attenuates cue-induced reinstatement. Taken together, these data suggest an important role for the HPA axis in the ability of environmental cues to stimulate cocaine-seeking behavior in rats and relapse in humans. Treatment for relapse may therefore be improved by developing behavioral or pharmacological therapies that reduce HPA-axis responses induced by environmental cues previously associated with drug use.

IMPLICATIONS

Data obtained from both human and animal investigations indicate that exposure to stress increases the vulnerability for addiction. The animal literature suggests that stress increases reward associated with drugs such as cocaine and amphetamine through a process similar to sensitization. The growing literature on drug addiction indicates that there is a similar link between substance abuse and stress, as reflected in the high co-occurrence of PTSD and drug addiction. One explanation for this link is the self-medication hypothesis (Khantzian, 1985), according to which a dually diagnosed person often uses the abused substance to cope with tension associated with life stressors or to relieve or suppress symptoms of anxiety and depression resulting from a traumatic event. On the surface, however, this hypothesis may appear somewhat counterintuitive. Many abused substances (especially cocaine) can induce anxiety and panic in humans and anxiety-like responses in animals through direct effects on CRH release (Goeders, 1997, 2002). One might expect that this augmented HPA-axis activity would increase the aversive effects of the drug and reduce the motivation for it. During the acquisition of drug-taking behavior, however, exposure to aversive, stressful stimuli may actually sensitize individuals, making them more sensitive to the rewarding properties of the drug. Once drug taking has been acquired, the positive aspects of drug reward likely mitigate the drug's potential anxiety-like effects (Goeders, 2002).

However, another characteristic of self-administration is that drug delivery and its subsequent effects on the HPA axis are under the direct control of the individual. This is an important consideration because controllability and predictability of a stressor significantly decrease its aversive effects (Levine, 2000). If the individual controls when the drug is administered, he or she also controls when the activation of the HPA axis occurs. This controlled activation of the HPA axis may result in an internal state of arousal or stimulation that is rewarding to the individual (Goeders, 2002). This internal state may be analogous to the one produced during novelty or sensation seeking (e.g., in thrill seekers or sensation seekers), which may also be involved in drug reward (Wagner, 2001). Drug taking by some substance abusers may therefore be an attempt to seek out specific sensations, and the internal state produced may be very similar to that perceived by individuals who engage in risky, thrill-seeking behavior. Such sensation seekers have been reported to be at elevated risk for abusing a variety of substances, including cocaine, opioids, alcohol, cannabis, and nicotine.

Once an individual has stopped using a drug, exposure to stressors or drug-associated cues can stimulate the sympathetic nervous system and the HPA axis and thereby remind the individual about the effects of the abused substance, thus producing craving and promoting relapse (Goeders, 2002). Therefore, continued investigations into how stress and the subsequent activation of the HPA axis play a role in addiction will result in more effective and efficient treatments for substance abuse in humans. Stress-reduction and coping strategies, either alone or in combination with pharmacotherapies targeting the HPA axis, may prove beneficial in reducing cravings and promoting abstinence in individuals seeking treatment for addiction.

Recommended Reading

Goeders, N.E. (2002). (See References)
Piazza, P.V., & Le Moal, M. (1998). (See References)
Sarnyai, Z., Shaham, Y., & Heinrichs, S.C. (2001). The role of corticotropin-releasing factor in drug addiction. *Pharmacological Reviews, 53*, 209–243.
See, R.E. (2002). (See References)
Shalev, U., Grimm, J.W., & Shaham, Y. (2002). Neurobiology of relapse to heroin and cocaine seeking: A review. *Pharmacological Reviews, 54*, 1–42.

Acknowledgments—This work was supported by U.S. Public Health Service Grants DA06013 and DA13463 from the National Institute on Drug Abuse.

Note

1. Address correspondence to Nick E. Goeders, Department of Pharmacology & Therapeutics, LSU Health Sciences Center, P.O. Box 33932, 1501 Kings Highway, Shreveport, LA 71130-3932; e-mail: ngoede@lsuhsc.edu.

References

Donovan, B., Padin-Rivera, E., & Kowaliw, S. (2001). "Transcend": Initial outcomes from a posttraumatic stress disorder/substance abuse treatment program. *Journal of Trauma Stress, 14*, 757–772.
Goeders, N.E. (1997). A neuroendocrine role in cocaine reinforcement. *Psychoneuroendocrinology, 22*, 237–259.
Goeders, N.E. (2002). Stress and cocaine addiction. *Journal of Pharmacology and Experimental Therapeutics, 301*, 785–789.
Khantzian, E.J. (1985). The self-medication hypothesis of addictive disorders: Focus on heroin and cocaine dependence. *American Journal of Psychiatry, 142*, 1259–1264.
Levine, S. (2000). Influence of psychological variables on the activity of the hypothalamic-pituitary adrenal axis. *European Journal of Pharmacology, 405*, 149–160.
Newton-Taylor, B., DeWit, D., & Gliksman, L. (1998). Prevalence and factors associated with physical and sexual assault of female university students in Ontario. *Health Care for Women International, 19*, 155–164.
Piazza, P.V., & Le Moal, M. (1998). The role of stress in drug self-administration. *Trends in Pharmacological Science, 19*, 67–74.
Robbins, S.J., Ehrman, R.N., Childress, A.R., & O'Brien, C.P. (1999). Comparing levels of cocaine cue reactivity in male and female outpatients. *Drug and Alcohol Dependence, 53*, 223–230.
See, R.E. (2002). Neural substrates of conditioned-cued relapse to drug-seeking behavior. *Pharmacology Biochemistry and Behavior, 71*, 517–529.
Selye, H. (1975). Confusion and controversy in the stress field. *Journal of Human Stress, 1*, 37–44.
Stewart, J. (2000). Pathways to relapse: The neurobiology of drug- and stress-induced relapse to drug-taking. *Journal of Psychiatry and Neuroscience, 25*, 125–136.
Stratakis, C.A., & Chrousos, G.P. (1995). Neuroendocrinology and pathophysiology of the stress system. *Annals of the New York Academy of Sciences, 771*, 1–18.
Wagner, M.K. (2001). Behavioral characteristics related to substance abuse and risk-taking, sensation-seeking, anxiety sensitivity, and self-reinforcement. *Addictive Behaviors, 26*, 115–120.
Zaslav, M.R. (1994). Psychology of comorbid posttraumatic stress disorder and substance abuse: Lessons from combat veterans. *Journal of Psychoactive Drugs, 26*, 393–400.

Section 5: Critical Thinking Questions

1. Moffit (1993) proposed an influential model of antisocial behavior that argued a subset of individuals who exhibit antisocial behavior do so only during adolescence. How does Steinberg's model account for why this might occur?

2. Baker's paper suggests withdrawal-linked relapse emerges from the role of substance use of affect regulation; can negative affect serve as a cue for drug self-administration?

3. What are the treatment implications of the models of withdrawal and relapse presented in this section? How might interventions address implicit cognitions sensitive to drug use effects, the loss of coping responses for negative affect, or the stimulus-driven nature of substance use?

This article has been reprinted as it originally appeared in Current Directions in Psychological Science. *Citation information for this article as originally published appears above.*